Checklists for Searches and Seizures in Public Schools

2005 Edition

by Jon M. Van Dyke
and Melvin M. Sakurai

THOMSON
™
WEST

For Customer Assistance Call 1-800-328-4880

Mat #40206590

ISBN: 0-8366-1405-4

Acknowledgments

The idea for preparing this volume began with a project Melvin M. Sakurai undertook in 1987 for the State of Hawaii Department of Education to provide guidelines for school administrators on how to conduct searches and seizures in a manner that was consistent with the U.S. Constitution and the laws of Hawaii. Dr. Sakurai asked Professor Jon M. Van Dyke to act as a consultant to that effort, and subsequently they decided to work together to prepare this volume to assist administrators and lawyers across the nation.

The authors would like to express their thanks to Janice Weir, who graduated in 1991 from the William S. Richardson School of Law, University of Hawaii, for her assistance in the research and writing for this volume; to Douglas Kaanapu of the Class of 1993 for his assistance in checking the citations; to Douglas Codiga of the Class of 1994 for his assistance in preparing the 1993 edition; to Alicia Leonhard of the Class of 1993 and Kurt Takushi of the Class of 1994 for their assistance in preparing the 1994 edition; to Karl Espaldon of the Class of 1996 for his assistance in preparing the 1995, 1996 and 1997 editions; to Steven Howard of the Class of 1998 for his assistance in preparing the 1998 and 1999 editions; to Sat Khalsa of the Class of 2001 for his assistance in preparing the 2000 and 2001 editions; to Vanessa Jann-Jordan of the Class of 2002 for her assistance in preparing the 2002 edition; and to Helen Shikina for her assistance in preparing the manuscript. Finally, the authors would like to thank Thomas Yamashita, Director of the Management Analysis and Compliance Branch, State of Hawaii Department of Education, for his help and cooperation.

The Authors

JON M. VAN DYKE has been Professor of Law at the William S. Richardson School of Law, University of Hawaii at Manoa, since 1976, teaching Constitutional Law and International Law. Previously he taught at the Hastings College of Law, University of California, in San Francisco from 1971 to 1976 and at the Catholic University School of Law in Washington, D.C. from 1967 to 1969. Professor Van Dyke served as Director of the University of Hawaii Institute for Peace from 1988 to 1990. He earned his J.D. from Harvard in 1967 and his B.A. from Yale in 1964, both cum laude.

Professor Van Dyke's other books are *International Law and Litigation in the U.S.* (co-author 2000), *Sharing the Resources of the South China Sea* (co-author 1997), *Freedom for the Seas in the 21st Century: Ocean Governance and Environmental Harmony* (co-editor 1993), *International Navigation: Rocks and Shoals Ahead?* (co-editor 1988), *Consensus and Confrontation: The United States and the Law of the Sea Convention* (editor 1985), *Jury Selection Procedures: Our Uncertain Commitment to Representative Panels* (author 1977), and *North Vietnam's Strategy for Survival* (author 1972).

MELVIN M. SAKURAI is the owner of Research Information Services, a management consulting firm emphasizing policy analysis and administrative systems design. Dr. Sakurai earned his B.A. (1971), his M.A. (Sociology, 1974), and his Ph.D (Experimental Social Psychology, 1977) from the University of Hawaii at Manoa, and was a Social Science Research Council post-doctoral fellow at the University of Wisconsin in 1977-78 investigating mathematical conflict decision models. Among the many policy and administrative projects directed by Dr. Sakurai during his more than fifteen years of consulting experience in business and government are the development of civil rights complaint administrative guidelines, Family Court procedures, and health care facility regulation procedures.

RELATED PRODUCTS FROM WEST

Checklists for Searches and Seizures in Public Schools
by Jon M. Van Dyke and Melvin M. Sakurai

Civil and Criminal Forfeiture: Federal and State Practice
by Steven L. Kessler

Criminal Defense Checklists
by Nancy Cook and Michele G. Hermann

Criminal Defense Ethics 2d
by John M. Burkoff

Criminal Procedure Handbook
by James G. Carr

Drinking/Driving Litigation Criminal and Civil
by Donald H. Nichols

Drinking/Driving Law Letter
edited by Donald H. Nichols

Drinking/Driving Litigation Trial Notebook
by Donald H. Nichols

Drug Abuse and the Law Sourcebook
by Gerald F. Uelmen and Victor G. Haddox

Drug Testing Legal Manual and Practice Aids
by Kevin B. Zeese

Everytrial Criminal Defense Resource Book
by Nancy Hollander and Barbara E. Bergman

Federal Criminal Appeals
by Lissa Griffin

Federal Rules of Criminal Procedure
with Practice Comments by Michele G. Hermann

Firearms Law Deskbook: Federal and State Criminal Practice
by Stephen P. Halbrook

Grand Jury Law and Practice
by Sara Sun Beale and William C. Bryson

Habeas Corpus Checklists
by Ira P. Robbins
Ineffective Assistance of Counsel
by John M. Burkoff and Nancy M. Burkoff

The Law of Electronic Surveillance
by James G. Carr

Police Misconduct: Law and Litigation
by the National Lawyers Guild

Post-Conviction Remedies
by Larry W. Yackle

Psychological and Scientific Evidence in Criminal Trials
by Jane Campbell Moriarty

Prisoners and the Law
by Ira P. Robbins

Prosecutorial Misconduct
by Bennett L. Gershman

Representation of Witnesses Before Federal Grand Juries
by the National Lawyers Guild

Rights of Juveniles: The Juvenile Justice System
by Samuel M. Davis

Searches & Seizures, Arrests and Confessions
by William E. Ringel

Search and Seizure Checklists
by Michele G. Hermann

Search and Seizure Law Report

Search Warrant Law Deskbook
by John M. Burkoff

Sentencing Defense Manual: Advocacy/Practice/Procedure
by Marcia G. Shein

Vehicle Search Law Deskbook
by Christian A. Fisanick

Warrantless Search Law Deskbook
by Paul R Joseph

If you would like to inquire about these West publications or place an order, please call 1–800–344–5009.

THOMSON ™
WEST

West
610 Opperman Drive
Eagan, MN 55123

> **Visit West on the Internet:**
> http://west.thomson.com

Table of Contents

Volume 1

Chapter 1
Fourth Amendment Overview

Chapter 2
Student Searches Under the Fourth Amendment

Chapter 3

Reasonable Suspicion

Chapter 4

Conducting the Search

Chapter 5

Investigative Stops

Chapter 6

Seizure

Chapter 7

Exclusion of Illegally Obtained Evidence

Chapter 8

Special Procedures for Very Serious Infractions

Chapter 9

Civil Liability for Illegal Searches or Seizures

Chapter 10

Standards Developed by the States

Chapter 11

Sample Forms

Table of Contents

Chapter 1

Fourth Amendment Overview

Research References

West's Key Number Digest
Schools ☞169.5; Searches and Seizures ☞13, 23

KeyCite®: Cases and other legal materials listed in KeyCite Scope can be researched through West's KeyCite service on Westlaw®. Use KeyCite to check citations for form, parallel references, prior and later history, and comprehensive citator information, including citations to other decisions and secondary materials.

---

§ 1:1   The Fourth Amendment

The Fourth Amendment of the Constitution of the United States guarantees that:

> The right of the people to be secure in their persons, houses, papers, and effects, against unreasonable searches and seizures, shall not be violated, and no Warrants shall issue, but upon probable cause, supported by Oath or affirmation, and particularly describing the place to be searched and the persons or things to be seized.

Searches may be defined as a government official's unreasonable physical touching of a person or physical entry into a private area or physical handling of papers and effects. Physical intrusion into private areas includes surveillance devices such as electronic listening or telescopic observation. For a more complete discussion, *see* Chapter 2.

Seizures may be defined as governmental interference with an individual's liberty or possessory interest, including physically taking tangible property, as well as taking intangibles such as private conversations. Silverman v. United States, 365 U.S. 505, 509–10 (1961). Seizing a person occurs when an official, using physical force or a show of authority, has in some way restrained a person's liberty. Terry v. Ohio, 392 U.S. 1, 19 n.16 (1968). The test for whether a person has been seized asks if a reasonable person would have felt free to decline to cooperate with the requests and to terminate the encounter. Florida v. Royer, 460 U.S. 491, 501–2 (1983); Florida v. Bostick, 501 U.S. 429, 433–37 (1991). For a more complete discussion, *see* Chapter 6.

§ 1:2   Interests protected by the Fourth Amendment

The Fourth Amendment protects an individual's justified expectations of privacy against unreasonable government intrusions. Terry v. Ohio, 392 U.S. 1, 9 (1967). This view of the Fourth Amendment is considerably expanded from earlier interpretations. Previous Supreme Court holdings focused mainly on the physical penetration of property-related boundary lines as a measure of Fourth Amendment coverage. This perspective was broadened in Katz v. United States, 389 U.S. 347 (1967). Katz was overheard placing bets from a public telephone booth to which the FBI had attached electronic listening devices. The Court rejected earlier precedents holding that only "constitutionally protected areas" were covered by the Fourth Amendment, and announced the modern approach that: "The Fourth Amendment protects people, not places." *Id.* at 351. After Katz, the Supreme Court began to express a more general concern about the expectations of privacy a person may have for the person's activities and possessions. At the same time, a wider spectrum of government activities that could intrude on those expectations in any way came under scrutiny. The Supreme Court has ruled, for instance, that using a thermal imaging device to obtain facts about heat sources inside a home by detecting gradations in heat patterns on the exterior of a home is a Fourth Amendment search and is presumptively unreasonable without a warrant. Kyllo v. U.S., 533 U.S. 27, 121 S. Ct. 2038, 150 L. Ed. 2d 94 (2001).

The Fourth Amendment does not, however, prohibit all forms of government intrusion. Reasonable intrusions are allowed when legitimate governmental interests are served.

This chapter briefly discusses the relationship between individual privacy expectations and the reasonableness of government intrusions. The objective is to provide a basis for understanding how student searches and seizures are affected by the protective principles of the Fourth Amendment.

§ 1:3 Justified expectation of privacy

The Fourth Amendment does not protect every expectation of privacy. In order to be extended Fourth Amendment coverage, a student's expectations of privacy must satisfy two conditions:

(1) The student must actually exhibit or somehow indicate an expectation of privacy for something; and

(2) The expectation of privacy indicated by the student must also be one that society is prepared to recognize as being reasonable.

See Katz v. United States, 389 U.S. 347, 361 (1967) (Harlan, J., concurring), and New Jersey v. T.L.O., 469 U.S. 325, 339 (1985).

Students can justifiably rely on the Fourth Amendment to protect their expectations of privacy only when both conditions are satisfied, although the first condition is sometimes given insufficient attention. See 1 W. LaFave, Search and Seizure: A Treatise on the Fourth Amendment, § 2.1(c), at 309 (2d ed. 1987).

§ 1:4 Justified expectation of privacy—Actual (subjective) expectation of privacy

A student must exhibit an expectation of privacy in some tangible way. This requirement is satisfied if the student acts in a manner that demonstrates an intention to keep the activity or possession from being exposed to public scrutiny. The student need not take extraordinary precautions against every specific and conceivable risk of exposure or detection. Normally, it is sufficient simply to shield the activity or possession from public view. United States v. Chadwick, 433 U.S. 1, 11 (1976). For example, a student is usually considered to exhibit an expectation of privacy for something placed in a nondescript closed opaque container. United States v. Mehra, 824 F.2d 297, 298 (4th Cir. 1987); *see also* New Jersey v. T.L.O., 469 U.S. at 337. Also, the expectation must be personal to the student. It cannot be asserted vicariously. Rakas v. Illinois, 439 U.S. 128, 133–34 (1978).

Sometimes an activity or possession normally protected by the Fourth Amendment can be removed from coverage by the actions of a student or because of particular circumstances. Examples in relation to student searches and seizures are:

(1) Consent—when the student exposes the student's personal affairs to another person or lets someone have common authority in a private area or possession.

(2) Common or public places—when the student engages in an activity or places a possession in common or public areas that are lawfully accessible to others.

(3) Open view—when the student does not take adequate precautions to shield the student's activities or possessions from public view.

(4) Plain view—when the student leaves something where others may see it even if in an area otherwise protected by the Fourth Amendment.

(5) Voluntary abandonment—when the student intentionally relinquishes expectations of privacy in something.

Each of these situations is discussed in separate sections of this volume.

§ 1:5 Justified expectation of privacy—An expectation recognized by society as reasonable

Just because a student exhibits an actual (subjective) expectation of privacy in something does not necessarily mean that government intrusions on those expectations are prohibited by the Fourth Amendment. Some privacy expectations are not protected because they are not recognized by society as being reasonable and constitutionally enforceable. In O'Connor v. Ortega, 480 U.S. 709 (1987), the Court listed some factors used to determine whether privacy expectations are reasonable: the "intention of the Framers of the Fourth Amendment, the uses to which the individual has put a location, and our societal understanding that certain areas deserve the most scrupulous protection from government invasion." *Id.* at 715, *quoting* Oliver v. United States, 466 U.S. 170, 178 (1984).

To determine whether a privacy expectation is reasonable, the U.S. Supreme Court weighs the likely impacts of a government intrusion on individual privacy and freedom against the interests served by such intrusion. United States v. White, 401 U.S. 745, 786 (1971) (Harlan, J., dissenting); *see also* Terry v. Ohio, 392 U.S. 1, 21 (1968), *quoting* Camara v. Municipal Court, 387 U.S. 523, 534–35 (1967). The critical question in this balancing analysis is whether a particular government intrusion would be so intolerable if left unchecked because it either:

(1) Encroaches so far on the privacy and freedom of people as to be blatantly inconsistent with a free and open society; or

(2) Imposes an unreasonable burden on those who wish to maintain their individual privacy and freedom against the possibility of such an intrusion. *See* Amsterdam, "Perspectives on the Fourth Amendment," 58 Minn. L. Rev. 349, 403 (1974).

This question clearly involves issues of value, philosophy, and policy. It cannot be precisely captured or specified by any formula or simple standard.

§ 1:6 "Reasonableness" of government intrusions

Any government conduct that intrudes on a justified

expectation of privacy is considered to be a search or seizure and must be reasonable according to Fourth Amendment standards. Deciding what specific government conduct amounts to a search does not depend so much on what is done as how intrusive the conduct may be. For example, the mere fact that an official rummages through someone's belongings does not always mean that a search has occurred for Fourth Amendment purposes. Similarly, a seizure is not always indicated when officials take possession of something.

The Supreme Court has applied an increasingly complex standard to test the reasonableness of government intrusions. Whether a search is "reasonable" depends on its context. O'Connor v. Ortega, 480 U.S. at 719, *quoting* T.L.O., 469 U.S. at 337. Previously, the primary measure of reasonableness was a search warrant supported by "probable cause." Individual privacy was protected by a neutral detached figure (a magistrate) who evaluated the sufficiency of factual reasons for an intrusion. The requirement for a warrant has been waived only under exceptional and carefully limited circumstances. Usually, these were situations that required immediate attention and could not await the warrant process. Even in these situations, probable cause is normally needed to justify an intrusion.

In a limited number of restricted contexts, such as administrative searches, the "probable cause" requirement has been replaced by a "reasonable suspicion" standard. These two standards are compared below and discussed more extensively in subsequent chapters.

§ 1:7 "Reasonableness" of government intrusions— "Probable cause" and "reasonable suspicion" compared

Both "probable cause" and "reasonable suspicion" require information sufficient to support a belief that evidence of illegal conduct will be found in a particular place. This requirement is met if it is possible to relate what specific facts and observations are known and to explain how rational inferences from that information provide an objective basis for the belief when combined with any special training and experience school officials might have.

Both standards also require clear logical relationships between

(1) The particular object sought;
(2) A specific illegal activity; and
(3) The place to be searched.

See Dalia v. United States, 441 U.S. 240, 255 (1978); Berger v. New York, 388 U.S. 41, 55–56 (1967).

The object sought must thus be connected in some way with a specific (suspected) illegal activity. In addition, there must be a presently known logical link between the object and the particular place that is searched. Finally, the place to be searched must be plausibly related by nature to the suspected illegal activity. An offense committed in class does not automatically, for example, raise a valid suspicion that evidence will be found in a student's car.

The "probable cause" and "reasonable suspicion" standards share these fundamental requirements, but differ on the degree of certainty required. For "probable cause" the belief that evidence of illegal conduct will be found in a particular place must be unequivocally "more-probable-than-not." Although this level of certainty is less than absolute, it does mean that when the facts are considered as a whole, they do not support the belief that no evidence will be found.

A "reasonable suspicion," on the other hand, requires only a "sufficient probability" that evidence of illegal conduct will be found in a particular place. T.L.O., 469 U.S. at 346. To meet this criterion, it is not necessary to rule out every possible contradictory or innocent belief. It is possible to "reasonably suspect" something even if one also wonders if there might be an innocent explanation for the observed behavior. Despite this lower level of required certainty, "reasonable suspicions" are not ad hoc speculations or mere hunches. They must be based on more than trivial or isolated facts.

§ 1:8 Reduced Fourth Amendment protection for students: *New Jersey v. T.L.O.* (1985)

Certain categories or classes of individuals are afforded less than full protection under the Fourth Amendment; one such group is public school students. The Supreme Court held in New Jersey v. T.L.O., 469 U.S. 325 (1985), that public school officials do not need search warrants or probable cause before searching students under their authority. The Court observed that such legal requirements would unduly hamper teachers and officials in their efforts to maintain order and discipline and ultimately interfere with their effectiveness as educators. *Id.* at 340. The Court concluded that a reduced standard was justified for searches and seizures in school settings because of the substantial government interest in maintaining a proper learning environment for educating children. *Id.* at 340. The Court also stated, however, that student searches must still be "reasonable" within their contexts in order to be lawful. *Id.* at 341.

The T.L.O. case arose when a teacher discovered two female high school students (one of whom was T.L.O.) smoking in a lavatory. Because this behavior violated a school rule, both students were taken to the principal's office and questioned by an assistant vice principal. T.L.O.'s companion admitted to the rule violation, but T.L.O. denied the charge and claimed she did not smoke at all. New Jersey v. T.L.O., 469 U.S. 325, 328 (1985).

The assistant vice principal then asked T.L.O. to come into his private office and demanded to see her purse. Upon opening the purse, he discovered a pack of cigarettes on top. As the cigarettes were being removed, the assistant vice principal also noticed cigarette rolling papers. Because of his prior experience, he suspected that other evidence of drug use might be found. A thorough search of the purse revealed some marijuana, a pipe, several empty plastic bags, a substantial quantity of one dollar bills, an index card listing students who apparently owed T.L.O. money, and two letters implicating T.L.O. in marijuana dealing. New Jersey v. T.L.O., 469 U.S. 325, 328 (1985).

T.L.O.'s mother was then notified and evidence of the drug dealing was turned over to police. Subsequently, T.L.O. confessed to selling marijuana. Based on that confession and the evidence seized during the search of T.L.O.'s purse, delinquency charges were brought against T.L.O. by the State of New Jersey. New Jersey v. T.L.O., 469 U.S. 325, 329 (1985). During that proceeding, T.L.O. alleged that the search of her purse violated provisions of the Fourth Amendment and she sought to suppress both the evidence seized and her confession. New Jersey v. T.L.O., 469 U.S. 325, 329 (1985).

§ 1:9 Reduced Fourth Amendment protection for students: *New Jersey v. T.L.O.* (1985)—*T.L.O.* holdings

The U.S. Supreme Court ruled that both the evidence and T.L.O.'s confession were properly admitted at T.L.O.'s trial. The Court's main holdings can be summarized as follows:

(1) Children in school do have legitimate expectations of privacy which are protected by the Fourth Amendment. New Jersey v. T.L.O., 469 U.S. 325, 334 (1985).

(2) Public school officials act as representatives of the government. Consequently, they must comply with Fourth Amendment restrictions when conducting student searches or seizures. New Jersey v. T.L.O., 469 U.S. 325, 334 (1985). The Court specifically rejected arguments that public school officials are exempt from these restrictions because they act as surrogates for the parents of students rather than as government agents. New Jersey v. T.L.O., 469 U.S. 325, 336 (1985).

(3) Public school officials do not need search warrants *or* probable cause to search or seize evidence from students under their authority. New Jersey v. T.L.O., 469 U.S. 325, 340 (1985).

(4) In the absence of warrants and probable cause, the legitimate privacy interests of public schoolchildren are protected by requiring that searches and seizures must be "reasonable" under all circumstances. New Jersey v. T.L.O., 469 U.S. 325, 341 (1985). To satisfy this requirement a student search must be:

  • *Justified at its inception.* Officials must "reasonably" suspect that evidence indicating that a student has violated or is violating the law or a school rule will be found in a particular place. New Jersey v. T.L.O., 469 U.S. 325, 342 (1985). Such a "reasonable" suspicion requires only sufficient probability, not absolute certainty. New Jersey v. T.L.O., 469 U.S. 325, 346 (1985). The requirement for at least a reasonable suspicion applies to any student search no matter how serious or relatively minor the suspected infraction may be. New Jersey v. T.L.O., 469 U.S. 325, 342 n.9 (1985).

• *Reasonable in scope.* Student searches are gauged in relation to the circumstances that originally justified them. Thus, the scope, intensity, and methods of a search as it is actually conducted must be consistent with its original objective and not excessively intrusive in relation to the nature of a suspected infraction or the student's age and sex. New Jersey v. T.L.O., 469 U.S. 325, 342 (1985).

§ 1:10 Reduced Fourth Amendment protection for students: *New Jersey v. T.L.O.* (1985)— Reduced protection based on class membership

It is important to understand that students are accorded reduced Fourth Amendment protection mainly because of their membership in a class—public school children—and not because of their age, although it is also true that minors have different constitutional protections than adults (*see* Section 1:12). Moreover, the reduced standards specified in T.L.O. generally apply only to searches and seizures conducted by public school officials under whose authority the student falls. *Id.* at 884–85. (*But see* Edwards v. Rees, 883 F.2d 882 (10th Cir. 1989), holding that a vice-principal from one school can seize a student from another school.)

The Supreme Court employs a classification scheme in T.L.O. that singles out public school students and not children per se for reduced Fourth Amendment protection. Consequently, this holding extends to all persons enrolled in the public schools as students, regardless of whether they are juvenile or have just attained the age of majority. Different standards apply, however, to adult education students, university students, and other persons of similar status.

As violence in public schools has increased, courts have been more explicit and detailed in explaining the special legal regime that governs the rights of students in relation to school officials. A New York judge provided the following overview of this subject:

Schools have a very different relationship to their students than police officers have to the private citizens they encounter on the street. Attendance is mandatory, and those required to attend must attend "regularly as prescribed where [the student] resides or is employed, for the entire time the appropriate public schools are in session and . . . be subordinate and orderly while attending" (Education Law sec. 3210(1)(a)). In assuming physical custody and control over its students, a school stands in loco parentis; it has the duty "to exercise such care of them as a parent of ordinary prudence would observe in comparable circumstances." . . . Schools have a duty to adequately supervise the students in their charge and may be held liable for foreseeable injuries proximately related to the absence of adequate supervision . . . . To that end, a school may discipline a student . . . .

People v. Butler, 725 N.Y.S.2d 534, 538 (N.Y.Sup. 2001). Although the "in *loco parentis*" standard remains controversial, and is somewhat inconsistent with language in T.L.O., 469 U.S. at 336, the liability of schools that do not provide safe school environments has become clear (*see* Chapter 14), and that concern requires some closer regulation of potential troublemakers in the school.

§ 1:11 Reduced Fourth Amendment protection for students: *New Jersey v. T.L.O.* (1985)— Applicability: School officials

The T.L.O. holdings apply only to student searches conducted by public school officials. These officials are persons who have primarily an educational function, including administrators (e.g., principals and vice-principals), teachers, and persons with similar duties.

In an opinion letter dated October 29, 1987, the Attorney General of the State of Hawaii concluded that T.L.O. holdings also apply to school security attendants and other noneducational school personnel, but it is unclear whether T.L.O. justifies this decision or if other states will agree with this interpretation. Police officers must conform to the higher "probable cause" standards before commencing a search, even if they are operating on school grounds and with school officials. *See, e.g.,* James v. Unified Sch. Dist. No. 512, 959 F. Supp. 1407 (D. Kan. 1997); State v. Russell, 1997 WL 84661 (Tenn. Crim. App. 1997).

The reasonable-suspicion standard applies to searches

of students conducted by school officials during school functions even if they occur outside the school grounds. Shade v. City of Farmington, Minnesota, 309 F.3d 1054, 1061, 170 Ed. Law Rep. 529 (8th Cir. 2002) ("The nature of administrators' and teachers' responsibilities for the students entrusted to their care, not school boundary lines, renders the Fourth Amendment standard in the public-school context less onerous." For discussion of searches conducted jointly by school officials and school security officers, see section 10:4.

§ 1:12   Constitutional rights of minors

The U.S. Supreme Court recognizes that children are entitled to constitutional protection, but reduces that protection in certain situations to less than would be accorded an adult. In Bellotti v. Baird, 443 U.S. 622 (1979), the Justices recognized three reasons justifying reduced constitutional rights for children: "the peculiar vulnerability of children; their inability to make critical decisions in an informed, mature manner; and the importance of the parental role in child-rearing." *Id.* at 634.

Within the school setting, students have a limited constitutional right to freedom of speech or expression. Tinker v. Des Moines Sch. Dist., 393 U.S. 503, 506 (1969). The test from Tinker, which involved student speech in the form of wearing arm bands to protest U.S. involvement in the Vietnam war, balanced the student's right of free speech against both the school's need to maintain discipline in the operation of the school and the need to protect the rights of others. *Id.* at 513. The Court decided that wearing arm bands did not interfere with these countervailing interests and was therefore permissible speech.

Additional cases limiting children's rights include: Hazelwood Sch. Dist. v. Kulmeier, 484 U.S. 260, 270–71 (1988) (distinguishing First Amendment speech personal to a student from student speech affirmatively promoted by the school—e.g., a school newspaper—and allowing more control over the latter); Bethel Sch. Dist. No. 403 v. Fraser, 478 U.S. 675, 676 (1986) (holding that students do not have the same latitude as adults to use offensive speech in a student election campaign); Ingraham v.

Wright, 430 U.S. 651 (1977) (Eighth Amendment prohibition of cruel and unusual punishment does not apply to the punishment of school children by school officials); and Ginsberg v. New York, 390 U.S. 629, 634 (1968) (holding that merchants cannot sell sexually oriented magazines to a minor although the same material can be sold to adults).

Courts tend to uphold dress codes and even requirements that students wear uniforms, but in 2003, the U.S. Court of Appeals for the Fourth Circuit struck down a middle school dress code prohibiting the wearing of messages on clothing that related to weapons. Newsom ex rel. Newsom v. Albemarle County School Bd., 354 F.3d 249, 184 Ed. Law Rep. 24 (4th Cir. 2003). The policy was challenged by a student seeking to wear a T-shirt depicting three silhouettes of men holding firearms superimposed on the letters "NRA." The court emphasized that the record contained no evidence that such clothing had ever substantially disrupted school operations or infringed other students' rights, and explained that the school's prohibition had the effect of barring "entirely legitimate and even laudatory" political messages.

Goss v. Lopez, 419 U.S. 565 (1975), involved student demonstrators who were temporarily suspended from high school without a hearing prior to their suspension or within a reasonable time following the disciplinary action. The Court held that students have a Fourteenth Amendment property right to public education and then considered how much process is due a student before suspension, concluding that a student should be given "*some* kind of notice and afforded *some* kind of hearing" (emphasis in original at 579). This requirement can be met without too much difficulty, however, because an informal discussion with the student minutes after an incident occurred, and preceding disciplinary action, would be enough to meet this standard, if the student was informed of the accusation and the basis for it, and was allowed an opportunity to explain his or her version of the incident. If the student's presence posed a danger or threat to the school, the student could be removed without even this minimal due process. *Id.* at 582.

Minors involved in juvenile proceedings facing a loss of liberty are entitled to timely written notice of the charges against them, the advice of counsel, the privilege against self-incrimination, and the right to cross-examine witnesses. In re Gault, 387 U.S. 1, 33, 41, 55, 57 (1967). The standard of proof required is "beyond a reasonable doubt" (In re Winship, 397 U.S. 358, 368 (1970)), but a jury trial is not required. McKeiver v. Pennsylvania, 403 U.S. 528, 545 (1971).

Minors have limited but nonetheless important rights of privacy. *See* Hodgson v. Minnesota, 492 U.S. 917 (1990) (a two-parent notice requirement prior to an abortion—with the alternative of a judicial bypass—is constitutional); Ohio v. Akron Ctr. for Reproductive Health, 492 U.S. 916 (1990) (Ohio statute that makes an abortion performed upon an unmarried, unemancipated minor a crime unless one parent is notified by the physician or unless the minor obtains judicial permission is constitutional); Bellotti v. Baird, 443 U.S. 622, 643 (1979) (Massachusetts statute prohibiting minors from obtaining abortions without parental notification is unconstitutional unless the state offers an alternative method of obtaining consent); Carey v. Population Servs. Int'l, 431 U.S. 678, 691–99 (1977) (plurality opinion) (the Constitution will not permit a blanket prohibition on the right to sell or distribute contraceptives to a minor); and Planned Parenthood v. Danforth, 428 U.S. 52, 72–75 (1976) (the state cannot authorize an absolute parental veto over a minor's decision to obtain an abortion).

In the public school setting, Fourth Amendment privacy rights of minor students are circumscribed because of the school's "custodial and tutelary" responsibility for its children. *See* Vernonia Sch. Dist. v. Acton, 515 U.S. 646, 655–56 (1995) ("the nature of those rights is what is appropriate for children in school"). In Vernonia School District, the Supreme Court analyzed a student's privacy rights in the context of a urinalysis testing program aimed at student-athletes. The Supreme Court found it "central" to the case that the subjects of the testing policy were "(1) children, who (2) had been committed to the temporary custody of the State as schoolmaster." *Id.* at 654. The Court held that a student-athlete's privacy expectations were reduced because of (1) the "element of 'communal undress' inherent in athletic participation," *id.* at 657 (*quoting* Schaill by Kross v. Tippecanoe County Sch. Corp., 864 F.2d 1309, 1318 (7th Cir. 1988)), and (2) the relatively high degree of regulation imposed on student-athletes. Vernonia School District, 515 U.S. at 657. This view was confirmed and expanded in Board of Education of Independent School District No. 92 of Pottawatomie County v. Earls, 536 U.S. 822, 122 S. Ct. 2559, 153 L. Ed. 2d 735, 166 Ed. Law Rep. 79 (2002), which, by a 5-4 vote, upheld the policy of the Tecumseh, Oklahoma School District to require all middle and high school students who engage in any extracurricular activity whatsoever to consent to have their urine analyzed for evidence of drug use. (See Chapter 12 for detailed discussion of this issue.)

In conclusion, minors have constitutional rights, but they are somewhat limited in scope when compared to adult rights. Minors are afforded the most protection when their liberty is at stake, differing from adults' rights only in that minors do not have a right to jury trial. Their other constitutional rights are limited by the surrounding circumstances, such as location (e.g., a school setting requires greater control by school authorities) or government interest (e.g., the government has an interest in restricting children's access to obscenity).

An unresolved issue that is likely to be raised in many different contexts is the extent to which constitutional rights apply to private schools whose students receive their tuition from public sources. In the case of Logiodice v. Trustees of Maine Cent. Institute, 296 F.3d 22, 167 Ed. Law Rep. 85 (1st Cir. 2002), the court ruled (2-1), in a case involving a community in Maine that did not operate its own public high school but instead paid a private organization to operate a high school in the district, that the private high school did not have to operate according to constitutional standards.

§ 1:13 Related actions

Users of this volume must keep in mind that other official actions will sometimes occur prior to, in conjunction with, or as a consequence of valid student searches or seizures, including:

(1) Detention or apprehension;

(2) Interrogation or questioning;

(3) Securing confessions;

(4) Reporting offenses to police; and,

    (5)   Disciplinary or restitution proceedings.

These activities have legal and procedural requirements that are separate and distinct from those described here for student searches and seizures. Consult other appropriate administrative or procedural guides for those requirements.

Chapter 2

Student Searches Under the Fourth Amendment

Research References

West's Key Number Digest
Searches and Seizures ⌐13, 13.1, 15, 16, 25, 29

KeyCite®: Cases and other legal materials listed in KeyCite Scope can be researched through West's KeyCite service on Westlaw®. Use KeyCite to check citations for form, parallel references, prior and later history, and comprehensive citator information, including citations to other decisions and secondary materials.

Whenever it appears that searching a student may be necessary, school officials must examine their anticipated conduct carefully to determine:

(1) Whether their plan of action actually amounts to a search because it will intrude on a justified privacy expectation, and, if so,

(2) What standards must be satisfied to make the search reasonable and lawful under the Fourth Amendment.

The first part of this inquiry is analyzed in this chapter. The question of reasonableness is then discussed in Chapter 3.

Although many concrete examples and illustrations are included here, it is not possible to describe every possible situation. The main objective of Chapters 2 and 3 is to provide an understanding of the general principles that become relevant whenever a search is contemplated.

§ 2:1 What conduct amounts to a search under the Fourth Amendment

Section overview. A student search is any attempt to gain access to any item that is shielded from open public view and located in a protected place or thing. Such searches can only be conducted if the school official has a "reasonable suspicion" that the search will produce evidence related to criminal activity, unless the situation is an emergency (Section 2:9) or falls within some other specific exceptions (Sections 2:9, 2:14, and 2:23).

In general:

(1) The more difficult it is to gain access to something that is inaccessible, the more likely the effort to obtain it amounts to a search. Examples of student searches are:

- physically examining the student's person.
- looking through personal possessions.
- handling or feeling any closed opaque item to determine its contents.

- opening any closed opaque container.
- prying open locked containers or possessions.
- enlarging the view into closed or locked areas.
- taking extraordinary steps to penetrate natural or other barriers that screen activities or possessions from open public view.

(2) In the school setting, protected places or things include:

- the student's person and any immediately connected item.
- enclosed stalls within public rest rooms, dressing areas, and similar spaces when occupied by a student.
- any closed opaque container.
- papers, notes, ledgers, calendars, appointment books, literature, and the like.
- any school property assigned for a student's individual use.
- student automobiles or other vehicles.

Virtually any attempt to find or discover something hidden from public view will be considered a search in the school setting.

Breathalyzer tests and urinalysis examinations constitute searches for Fourth Amendment purposes, Juran v. Independence Or. Central Sch. Dist. 13J, 898 F. Supp. 728 (D. Or. 1995), and a search of a student's person would also of course implicate Fourth Amendment issues. Oliver v. McClung, 919 F. Supp. 1206 (D. Ind. 1995). State v. B.A.S., 13 P.3d 244, 246 n.3 (Wash.App. 2000) ("A school official's demand that a student empty his or her pockets constitutes a search."). The Tenth Circuit has ruled that nonconsensual medical examinations of pre-school students constitute a "search" under the Fourth Amendment. Dubbs v. Head Start, Inc., 336 F.3d 1194, 179 Ed. Law Rep. 92 (10th Cir. 2003).

§ 2:2 What conduct amounts to a search under the Fourth Amendment—The judicial inquiry

The judicial determination that a search occurs for Fourth Amendment purposes hinges on whether the government conduct in question intrudes on a justified privacy expectation. That determination is generally made after examining:

(1)   The adequacy of precautions taken to maintain privacy in relation to the foreseeability of government scrutiny;

(2)   Whether the privacy expectation is recognized as reasonable by society;

(3)   How the particular privacy interest in question is affected by the government's conduct; and

(4)   The general implications for personal privacy and freedom that might result from condoning such government conduct.

This inquiry is deliberately constructed so that it cannot be reduced to any rote formula. Thus, it is not possible to decide that a search occurs simply by looking at the conduct involved (no matter how seemingly intrusive or benign) or at the place or thing scrutinized. Something as apparently innocent as looking into an enclosed area can be considered a search that is subject to Fourth Amendment standards. At the same time, such conspicuously intrusive conduct as obtaining voice or handwriting samples may not be viewed as searches under proper conditions. The Massachusetts Supreme Judicial Court has ruled, for instance, that examining a student's homework assignments to determine whether the student was guilty of writing offensive graffiti on school property was reasonable under the T.L.O. standards, if it constituted a search, because individuals do not have a reasonable expectation of privacy in their handwriting and the review of a suspected student's homework, papers, tests, and quizzes is a "minimal intrusion" into the student's privacy. Commonwealth v. Buccella, 751 N.E.2d 373 (Mass. 2001).

The common sense understanding that a search involves a rummaging examination of someone's possessions is only the beginning of the matter. Many other factors are implicated in a judicial inquiry and these will not always be self-evident or intuitive. Although school officials may not be able to undertake a full-scale constitutional analysis regarding each possible violation of justified privacy interests prior to every search, the practical guidelines that follow assist the actual conduct of student searches and alert officials to the appropriate way to handle ambiguous situations.

§ 2:3 What conduct amounts to a search under the Fourth Amendment—General guidelines for school officials

A *student search* is any action taken by a school official to gain access to any item possessed by a student that is shielded from open public view and located in a place or contained within a thing that is reasonably assumed to have a degree of privacy by nature. School officials can search students from other schools under the T.L.O. "reasonable suspicion" standard when they are on the grounds of the school official's school. In re D.D., 146 N.C. App. 309, 554 S.E.2d 346, 351, 158 Ed. Law Rep. 855 (2001), appeal dismissed, review denied, 354 N.C. 572, 558 S.E.2d 867 (2001). In general:

    (1) The more difficulty school officials have in gaining access to something that is otherwise inaccessible, the more likely it is that their conduct amounts to a search. For example, excluding emergencies (Section 2:9) and other specific exceptions (Sections 2:4, 2:14, and 2:23), student searches involve:

- physically examining a student's person, including outer clothing and other closely connected possessions such as handbags and knapsacks.
- looking through personal possessions such as bags, books, and closed containers.
- handling or feeling any closed opaque item to determine its contents when they cannot be inferred by the item's shape or other publicly exposed physical properties.
- opening any closed opaque container.
- forcibly prying open locked containers or possessions such as lockers or automobiles to gain access.
- using extraordinary means to enlarge the view into closed or locked areas, containers, or possessions (e.g., spreading the crack between locker doors with a pry bar to obtain a better view).

- taking extraordinary steps to penetrate natural or other barriers that screen activities or possessions from open public view (e.g., using a ladder to gain a better vantage point for observation).
- requiring students to take a breathalyser test or submit to a urinalysis exam.

(2)   In the school setting, protected places or things reasonably assumed to have a degree of privacy by nature include:

- the student's person and any immediately connected item such as articles of clothing and bags of any sort.
- enclosed stalls within public rest rooms, dressing areas, and similar places when occupied by a student.
- any closed opaque container that might generally be a repository of personal effects, including boxes of any kind, folders, note books, bags and packages of any kind.
- papers, notes, ledgers, calendars, appointment books, literature, and the like.
- any school property assigned for individual use by a student, such as lockers, desks, and work areas not accessible by the public.
- student automobiles or other vehicles.

Almost any attempt to find or discover something hidden from open public view will therefore be considered a search in the school setting.

Under certain highly limited conditions, conduct that is normally regarded as a search can be exempted from Fourth Amendment standards. In the school setting these exceptions occur when otherwise justified privacy expectations are diminished (1) if an activity or possession is in open public view, (2) if an emergency occurs, (3) if consent is given to a search, or (4) if an item is abandoned. Persons or possessions that come under one of these exceptions have reduced Fourth Amendment protection against government intrusions. The next five sections examine each of these exceptions in turn.

§2:4 Observing activity or items in open public view

School officials may observe and detect anything openly exposed to the senses of sight, smell, and hearing so long as: (1) they are and continue to be located in a place where they have a right to be; and (2) they have not used any extraordinary means to gain their vantage point.

In general, they cannot physically handle and examine any openly exposed items by using tactile or taste senses unless all standards and guidelines for a reasonable student search (Chapter 3) or an open public view seizure (Section 6:9) are satisfied first.

As long as the officials remain lawfully located, their senses of sight, smell, or hearing may be focused by:

(1) Craning their neck,
(2) Squatting, bending, or stooping,
(3) Standing on tip-toes,
(4) Leaning around partitions or corners,
(5) Looking, smelling, or listening through preexisting cracks, spaces, or holes, or
(6) Using a tape recorder, if its microphone is no more sensitive than the human ear.

It is also possible to enhance normal sense perceptions artificially by using commonly available devices such as:

• flashlights and other lighting devices, or
• binoculars, simple telescopes, and other magnifying devices.

§2:5 Observing activity or items in open public view—Activity and items openly exposed to public detection (open public view)

There are many occasions when something suspicious is exposed openly to public detection by sight, smell, and hearing. Contacts of this sort are referred to as "open public views" because it is most common to make an initial visual sighting of the suspicious conduct or item. Often referred to as "plain view," open public view does not involve a search because the observation is made without any physical intrusion into a constitutionally protected area. "Plain view" involves a situation where an official has legal justification for making a seizure without a warrant. Three criteria must be met for a seizure to be lawful under the plain view doctrine: the prior intrusion must be valid; the discovery of the items must be inadvertent; and the items found in plain view must be immediately recognizable as evidence. *See* Coolidge v. New Hampshire, 403 U.S. 443, 465 (1970); *see also* 1 LaFave, Search and Seizure, § 2.2(a), at 320–23 (1987).

Situations where something is visually exposed to open public view might involve: (1) student conduct that occurs in public (e.g., when students are observed "pitching pennies" against a hallway wall); (2) contraband observed on the student's person (e.g., a weapon sticking partially out of a shirt's front pocket); (3) an item located somewhere that is not adequately shielded from public view, even if the location is a protected place (e.g., a suspicious object placed at the front of a secured locker that has a wire mesh door, or some incriminating items left uncovered on the front seat of an automobile).

It is also possible for activities or possessions to be exposed openly to the unaided senses of smell or hearing, if, for instance, a student is carrying an open bottle of lighter fluid in a loosely closed paper bag or is loudly extorting another student behind a screening partition during recess. An object, therefore, need not actually be seen to be considered publicly exposed. *See* United States v. Fisch, 474 F.2d 1071, 1076 (9th Cir. 1973) (plain hearing); In re Gregory M., 585 N.Y.S.2d 193 (N.Y. App. Div. 1992) (hearing unusual thud when book bag was tossed by student justified feeling outside of bag to search for gun); United States v. Johnson, 497 F.2d 397, 398 (9th Cir. 1974) (plain smell); Burnham v. West, 681 F. Supp. 1160, 1164 (E.D. Va. 1987) ("The sniffing of plaintiff's . . . hands . . . was not a 'search.' School children do not have a reasonable expectation of privacy in the air surrounding their persons and school officials may sample this air for the purpose of maintaining a proper learning environment to the same extent that they would be justified in conducting a purely visual inspection."); Jennings v. Joshua Ind. Sch. Dist., 877 F.2d 313, 316 (5th Cir. 1989) ("The use of trained dogs to sniff automobiles parked on public parking lots does not constitute a search within the meaning of the fourth amendment.").

If something is in open public view, school officials may

observe and note anything that is evident to the natural senses of sight, smell, or hearing, and may do so without any prior reasonable suspicion. Should either the sensory data or surrounding circumstances give an indication of an infraction, they may wish to investigate further by conducting a search or open public view seizure. At that juncture, they must determine carefully whether the evidence available to them justifies such a step. If it does, they must then comply with all standards and guidelines for a reasonable student search (Chapter 3) or open public view seizure (Section 6:9). If the observations and surrounding circumstances do not give a clear indication of an infraction, then the officials would not be permitted to make any further intrusion.

Open public views are not searches. Open public view observations are not considered searches because they do not involve a physical incursion or intrusion on any justified privacy interest. Consequently, this government conduct is not subject to restrictive Fourth Amendment standards. *See* Illinois v. Andreas, 463 U.S. 765, 771 (1983).

There is no physical incursion because the object is observed while the official is positioned in a place where the official has a right to be. Illinois v. Andreas, 463 U.S. 765, 771 (1983); *see also* Harris v. United States, 390 U.S. 234, 236 (1968). Examples include public locations like corridors, classrooms, or the public areas of rest rooms. See Section 2:6 for further discussion.

There is no intrusion on any privacy interest because students do not have a justified expectation of privacy for anything knowingly left exposed to sensory detection by the public. It does not matter that the conduct or item may be located in a protected place (e.g., a closed locker). If adequate steps have not been taken to shield an item from public detection, its owner has no justified privacy interest. Students are not, however, expected to anticipate and protect against every conceivable means of surveillance. It generally will be sufficient to place an item in a closed opaque container that gives no hint about its contents.

Once an official observes something exposed to open public view, the student cannot restore a justified expectation of privacy by withdrawing the item from public exposure. *See* Project, "Criminal Procedure," 74 Geo. L.J. 499, 507 (1986).

Keep in mind that this discussion is limited to observing something by sight, smell, or hearing. It does not necessarily follow that those observations automatically give an official the lawful right to handle physically or seize the item.

§ 2:6   Observing activity or items in open public view—The difference between observing, handling, and seizing

It is important to understand that lawful observation and detection are separate and distinct from any physical handling or seizure of items in open public view. The circumstances described above only justify sensory observation of objects and student conduct that are exposed to open view. They do not necessarily permit school officials to handle and examine or seize such objects. Open view seizures are discussed in Section 6:9. The following material is only concerned with physical handling and examination.

Any physical handling, tactile examination, or other manipulation of an object (e.g., shaking or feeling a closed opaque container) is considered a search under the Fourth Amendment, because conduct of this sort is exploratory and invasive by nature and primarily intended as a means of prying into hidden places. *See* Leake v. Commonwealth, 220 Va. 937, 265 S.E.2d 701, 704 (1980); Bond v. U.S., 529 U.S. 334, 120 S. Ct. 1462, 146 L. Ed. 2d 365 (2000) (ruling that it violated the Fourth Amendment for a federal immigration official to squeeze the bag of a bus passenger in the overhead bin of the bus). This rationale applies to any object that happens to be observed in open public view regardless of whether it is located in a protected place. Thus, in the absence of an emergency (Section 2:9), consent (Section 2:14), or abandonment (Section 2:23), an official must comply with the same standards and guidelines for conducting reasonable student searches (Chapter 3) or open view seizures (Section 6:9) before physically handling and examining anything exposed to open view.

This restriction is quite consistent with circumstances

where the official comes upon a situation without having any prior suspicions or intention to search. For example, imagine that while strolling down a school corridor the official encounters a student who is carrying an oddly shaped paper bag that gives no clear inference about its contents. In this situation the official can lawfully view the bag, note its shape and any other physical detail, and also can smell any odor emanating from the bag.

If these sensory data are not particularly informative and there is nothing unusual or suspect about the surrounding circumstances, the official cannot then attempt to determine what the bag contains by feeling it. In the absence of additional facts, the official would have no valid reason to engage in a search other than to satisfy the official's curiosity. The same prohibition holds if an identical oddly shaped bag were seen through the wire mesh door of a student's locker.

The situation would be different, however, if either the sensory data or the surrounding circumstances were more informative. Suppose the odor of some dangerous contraband like gasoline is detected or the bag's unique shape gives a reasonable inference that it may contain a weapon. Now the official has more than mere curiosity as a reason for physically handling and examining the object. Thus, additional facts of this kind might justify a student search when suspicious objects are located in protected places or an open public view seizure when they are not. At minimum, they would almost certainly justify an investigative stop for questioning (Chapter 5).

Any seizure of items openly exposed to public scrutiny must satisfy all requirements for open public view seizures specified in Section 6:9.

§ 2:7   Observing activity or items in open public view—Required conditions for open public view observation

School officials may observe and detect anything openly exposed to the senses of sight, smell, and hearing as long as: (1) they are and continue to be located in a place where they have a right to be, and (2) they have not used any extraordinary means to gain the vantage point.

(1)   *They are and continue to be located in a place*

where they have a right to be. This requirement usually means that the official must be located in a public place—regardless of whether the observation is of a public or private area. Maryland v. Macon, 472 U.S. 463, 469 (1985) (store is a public place because public is invited in); Donovan v. Lone Steer, Inc., 464 U.S. 408, 413 (1984) (motel lobby or restaurant is a public place); Illinois v. Andreas, 463 U.S. at 771 (customs agents discovered drugs in a closed container and then called police, who are in a lawful position to observe the item); United States v. Taborda, 635 F.2d 131, 138 (1980) (a person who places objects within a home in such a way that they can be seen from outside has no privacy expectation); Butler ex rel. Butler v. Rio Rancho Public School Bd. of Educ., 245 F. Supp. 2d 1203, 174 Ed. Law Rep. 988 (D.N.M. 2002) (ruling that a school official had the reasonable suspicion necessary to search a car after the official had looked into the passenger side of a car and seen butt end of a knife sticking up between the passenger seat and the center console). Because of their general supervisory authority, school officials have a right to be in almost every area of the school or where students might be during off-campus supervised activities, including corridors, offices, classrooms, eating areas, rest rooms, playing fields, and any other area accessible to students during after-school programs.

School officials can thus observe the public areas of rest rooms, locker rooms, and similar places. They cannot, however, peer or otherwise intrude into enclosed rest room stalls or partitioned dressing areas when they are occupied by students, unless the officials have proper grounds for a student search (Chapter 3). Students occupying these areas have justified privacy expectations by virtue of the primary functions for which such places are provided and not merely to the extent that these spaces are enclosed or made secure. Thus, it is not normally lawful to peer over stall partitions or through ventilation gratings and holes in the ceiling to make an observation. Conduct of this kind amounts to a search and must fully comply with all Fourth Amendment standards.

(2) *They have not used extraordinary means to gain the vantage point.* School officials cannot use any extraordinary means to penetrate natural or artificial barriers that screen student conduct or items from public detection. This rule prohibits the use of sophisticated devices or unusual implements, but it is not meant to prohibit normal physical maneuvers such as bending or leaning. Katz v. United States, 389 U.S. 347, 353 (1967) (it is a "search" when a nonintrusive electronic listening device is used to eavesdrop on a telephone conversation); United States v. Albarado, 495 F.2d 799, 802–3 (2d Cir. 1974) (the use of a magnetometer at an airport security check constitutes a search).

An official cannot claim a valid open public view after scaling a ladder in a public corridor to observe students through high windows of a closed classroom. If, however, the official remains lawfully located, it is possible to focus sight, smell, or hearing by:

• craning the neck;
• squatting, bending, or stooping (James v. United States, 418 F.2d 1150, 1151 n.1 (D.C. Cir. 1969));
• standing on tip-toes;
• leaning around partitions or corners;
• looking, smelling, or listening through *preexisting* cracks, spaces, or holes (United States v. Ard, 731 F.2d 718, 723 (11th Cir. 1984) (smelling through a two-inch crack); United States v. Fisch, 474 F.2d 1071, 1076 (1973) (listening at crack under door)); or
• using a tape recorder if its microphone is no more sensitive than the human ear (United States v. White, 401 U.S. 745, 751 (1971) (official using tape recorder while holding conversation); United States v. Agapito, 620 F.2d 324,

330 and n.7 (2d Cir. 1980); *but see* Raetigg v. State, 406 So. 2d 1273, 1277 (Fla. App. 1981) (a half-inch wide crack is not an open view, especially if other precautions have been taken to ensure privacy); Barryhill v. State, 372 So. 2d 355, 357 (1979) (shining a flashlight through a crack the width of a penny is not plain view).

While focusing one's senses, steps cannot be taken to enlarge the quantity of sensory data by boring holes where none existed; expanding existing cracks, openings, or spaces; squeezing containers to expel odors; or other similar tactics. *See, e.g.,* Hernandez v. United States, 353 F.2d 624, 626 (9th Cir. 1966) (official cannot squeeze luggage in order to discover aroma of marijuana). No physical handling or examination is permitted unless all requirements for reasonable student searches (Chapter 3) or open view seizures (Section 6:9) are fully satisfied first. Hence, an official is not permitted to use tactile and taste senses in an open view situation. But school officials can open a container whose contents can be inferred from their outward appearance. *See* United States v. Russell, 670 F.2d 323, 325 (D.C. Cir. 1982) (official can infer contents of containers from configuration, feel or smell; officer felt outline of gun hidden in paper sack, warrantless search allowed); Arkansas v. Sanders, 442 U.S. 753, 764–65 n.13 (1979) (gun case); United States v. Eschweiler, 745 F.2d 435, 440 (7th Cir. 1984) (envelope with "safe deposit box key" written on outside can be opened because a "container that proclaims its contents on the outside is not a private place.").

Although an official cannot use extraordinary means to gain a vantage point, the official can take the best lawful view available. This location may be one generally accessible to any passerby (e.g., a second floor balcony) or it may be a more restricted place where only school officials have a right to be (e.g., raised platform desks, observation towers, or elevated offices).

It should be noted that the courts are not in agreement as to whether dog sniff searches are an expansion of the "plain smell" theory, or whether dog sniffs are a search at all. *See, e.g.,* Jones v. Latexo Indep. Sch. Dist., 499 F. Supp. 223, 232–33 (1980) (the use of a dog to detect smells is a search, and the dog's nose replaces rather than enhances a human's) and United States v. Place, 462 U.S. 696, 707 (1983) (the decreased intrusiveness of a dog sniff of luggage in a public place such as an airport does not amount to a search).

§ 2:8 Observing activity or items in open public view—Enhancing natural senses

Normal sense perceptions can be artificially enhanced by using ordinary commonly available devices. They cannot, however, be multiplied into new senses through the use of sophisticated devices or instruments. Flashlights and binoculars are appropriate enhancement devices in the school setting.

> (1) *Flashlights and other lighting devices.* Flashlights and other similar devices are permitted when the observation would not be considered a search in the light of day and the flashlight is used merely to penetrate darkness. Marshall v. United States, 422 F.2d 185, 189 (5th Cir. 1970) (the use of a flashlight at night to illuminate what would be visible in daylight is not a search). Officials may shine a flashlight upon a student's person or into darkened recesses so long as they are properly located and do not attempt to pry open or otherwise enlarge the viewing perspective for better observation. Thus, it is not permissible to pry open the space between locker doors or spread apart a student's pockets so that interior contents may be illuminated for inspection.

> (2) *Binoculars, simple telescopes, and other magnifying devices.* Although the use of binoculars and simple telescopes is generally permitted, this practice may be questionable in some circumstances—when very sophisticated or powerful instruments are used, for instance, or when something is not in the normal line of sight for passersby. United States v. Taborda, 635 F.2d 131, 139 (2d Cir. 1980) (forbidding use of telescope); United States v. Kim, 415 F. Supp. 1252, 1256 (D. Haw. 1976) (cannot use telescope to view if official could not see objects without its use).

The most common application of a magnifying device in school settings will be to observe student conduct or items that are out in the open and unobstructed by any screening barriers. In that case, binoculars and simple telescopes may be used: (a) to examine more carefully and clearly something that could have been observed by the naked eye from the same vantage point; or (b) to avoid revealing a surveillance by observing at a distance something that could have been observed from a closer but more conspicuous vantage point. 1 LaFave, Search and Seizure, § 2.2(c), at 339 (2d ed., 1987).

§ 2:9   Emergency intrusions

Section overview. In an emergency, a school official may immediately provide necessary aid to a student to protect or preserve life or avoid injury. Under this exception, it does not matter that the conduct might otherwise be considered a search.

The officials may act on the basis of an emergency after directly observing or receiving any report of:

(1) An unconscious, incapacitated, or injured student;

(2) Smoke, flames, flammable or toxic fumes, or other indications of severe hazard;

(3) Gunfire, explosions, and the like;

(4) Cries for help;

(5) An assault;

(6) Screams of terror; or

(7) Any other true, existing, and acute emergency.

If it is necessary to render aid and assistance, the official may:

(1) Break and enter into closed or locked areas believed to be the site of an emergency, and

(2) Search the person and immediate possessions of an unconscious, severely impaired, gravely injured, or incoherent student to discover:

- the student's identity,
- special medical information which might explain or alleviate the condition, and

- the nature of an injury by examining wounds or other physical conditions such as heart rate or breathing.

§ 2:10   Emergency intrusions—In general

School officials will occasionally encounter emergency situations requiring that immediate assistance be provided to a student to protect life or avoid serious injury. In these circumstances, officials may immediately render necessary aid without regard to whether the conduct might otherwise be prohibited by the Fourth Amendment. Such assistance can take the form of searching a student's person for medical information (see below).

Emergency intrusions are permitted to alleviate acute problems or investigate grave potential harm. Consequently, an official does not need to have a "reasonable suspicion" of an infraction before rendering aid even if the emergency might be connected with an underlying infraction (e.g., a student found severely injured because of an assault).

This exception applies only to *true* and *existing* emergencies. People v. Smith, 7 Cal. 3d 845, 101 Cal. Rptr. 893, 496 P.2d 1261, 1263 (1972). Delaying too long before rendering aid or before commencing a search will weaken any claim that a true emergency required immediate attention. State v. Bridewell, 306 Or. 231, 759 P.2d 1054, 1058 (1988) (a twelve-hour delay is too long); State v. Beaumier, 480 A.2d 1367, 1373 (R.I. 1984) (a police delay of three hours to answer a call regarding a possible gunshot wound indicates that they did not regard the call as emergency).

Similarly, the urgent circumstances justifying an emergency intrusion must be evident when the intrusion takes place. People v. Mitchell, 39 N.Y.2d 173, 347 N.E.2d 607, 610, 383 N.Y.S.2d 246 (1976) (there must be a direct relationship between the area searched and the emergency). If the emergency conditions end (e.g., an unconscious student suddenly regains full consciousness) justification for an emergency intrusion also disappears. United States v. Goldenstein, 456 F.2d 1006, 1010 (8th Cir. 1972) (once the police determined the injured person was no longer in the hotel room, they must stop their search); State v.

Beaumeir, 480 A.2d at 1373 (no need to search once the emergency is over).

§ 2:11 Emergency intrusions—Indications of an emergency and permitted conduct

School officials may act on the basis of an emergency after directly observing or receiving any report of:

(1) An unconscious, incapacitated, or injured student;

(2) Smoke, flames, flammable or toxic fumes, or other indications of severe hazard (Wayne v. United States, 318 F.2d 205, 212 (D.C. Cir. 1963));

(3) Gunfire, explosions, and the like (Wayne v. United States, 318 F.2d 205, 212 (D.C. Cir. 1963));

(4) Cries for help (MacDonald v. United States, 335 U.S. 451, 454 (1948));

(5) Violence (United States v. Jeffers, 342 U.S. 48, 52 (1951));

(6) Screams of terror (United States v. Barone, 330 F.2d 543, 544 (2d Cir. 1964)); or

(7) Any other true, existing, and acute emergency.

Officials are not expected to deliberate about the need for proper cause or to weigh the reliability of a report when confronted with these circumstances. An immediate response to the emergency at hand is clearly justified. Wayne v. United States, 318 F.2d at 212.

During the course of rendering aid, school officials may:

(1) Break and enter into closed or locked areas believed to be the site of an emergency, regardless of whether the area is public or private (Davis v. State, 236 Md. 389, 204 A.2d 76, 81 (1964), cert. denied, 380 U.S. 966 (1965); Wayne v. State, 318 F.2d at 212); and

(2) Search the person and immediate possessions of an unconscious, severely impaired, gravely injured, or incoherent student to discover:
   • the student's identity,
   • special medical information that might explain or alleviate the condition, and

- the nature of an injury by examining wounds or other physical conditions such as heart rate or breathing.

§ 2:12   Emergency intrusions—Scope limits

The authority granted under an emergency intrusion is not unlimited. As a general rule, the purpose of any government intrusion will define and limit its scope. Thus, school officials may intrude only to the extent required for rendering any necessary emergency aid and assistance. Bass v. State, 732 S.W.2d 632, 635 (Tex. App. 1987).

Emergency circumstances never provide justification for roving exploratory searches of protected places or the student's person. United States v. Goldstein, 456 F.2d 1006, 1010 (1972).

§ 2:13   Emergency intrusions—Plain view

School officials may seize any conspicuously incriminating items inadvertently discovered during the course of a lawful emergency intrusion provided that necessary requirements for a plain view seizure are satisfied first (*see* Section 6:5 for a full discussion).

§ 2:14   Consent searches

Section overview. When a student voluntarily consents to a search, school officials do not need any reasonable suspicion to justify the search.

Students can, however, entirely or partially withdraw their consent at any time, and school officials must immediately cease or confine the search accordingly.

It is not advisable to rely heavily on consent searches as a method of investigation. Student consent searches are frequently challenged and invalidated on the basis that they are not truly voluntary. The confusion regarding such searches is illustrated by DesRoches v. Caprio, 974 F. Supp. 542 (E.D. Va. 1997), rev'd 156 F.3d 471 (4th Cir. 1998), which involved a search of 19 students by school officials investigating a missing pair of tennis shoes. One of the students, James DesRoches, Jr., refused to allow the officials to search his backpack. He was suspended from school for ten days, and then brought an action under 42

U.S.C.A. sec. 1983 for damages resulting from the violation of his Fourth Amendment rights. The district court ruled in his favor, stating that students cannot be punished for refusing "to give consent to what would be an unconstitutional search if conducted." 974 F. Supp. at 551. The Fourth Circuit reversed, however, acknowledging that a blanket search of all 19 students was not reasonable, but finding that the search of DesRoches became reasonable "by the process of elimination" after the other 18 had been searched without any discovery of the missing tennis shoes. 156 F.3d at 578.

§ 2:15   Consent searches—In general

In a consent search, a student voluntarily gives a school official permission to search the student's person or property. When consent is given freely and voluntarily, school officials do not need any reasonable suspicion to justify the search. Bumper v. North Carolina, 391 U.S. 543, 548 (1968).

It is important to emphasize that consent searches are entirely different from the voluntary cooperation that may be sought in connection with a valid student search (e.g., asking a student to empty a pocket or to relinquish a particular item voluntarily). The distinction is that for a consent search school officials are seeking access to a person, place, or thing, whereas they already have valid access when asking for cooperation. Consequently, voluntary cooperation does not necessarily involve any form of consent. The importance of this distinction will become clear below.

The most frequent use of consent searches is when school officials want to investigate something based on speculations that are not sufficient for a student search. Because consent searches are vulnerable to challenge on the basis that they are not truly consensual, they should never be motivated by mere curiosity and the school officials should have made a sincere effort to secure facts in sufficient quantity and degree of certainty to support a reasonable suspicion. Consent searches should not be used merely for the sake of convenience.

If school officials reasonably suspect an infraction, they should commence with a student search as described in

Chapter 3 and should not risk a search by consent. Attempts to circumvent Fourth Amendment standards by using consent searches are always highly questionable and frequently ineffective.

§ 2:16 Consent searches—Valid consent

The validity of consent given by a student is evaluated in terms of two factors: (1) whether the consent is given voluntarily and (2) whether the consenting student has proper authority to permit a search.

> (1) *Voluntariness.* Voluntary consent requires that the student make some positive affirming gesture granting school officials permission to search. In addition, the student must make this grant under circumstances that are not coercive when considered as a whole. Schneckloth v. Bustamonte, 412 U.S. 218, 226 (1973) ("voluntary" is to be determined by "careful scrutiny" of the "totality of surrounding circumstances"); Florida v. Bostick, 501 U.S. 429, 111 S. Ct. 2382, 2388 (1991)) ("'Consent' that is the product of official intimidation or harassment is not consent at all.").
>
> If the "affirmation" is ambiguous or if there are clear indications that a student is merely submitting to the authority of the school official, any resulting consent will not be considered voluntary. Words of resignation (e.g., "you'll search anyway") will also suggest that consent is not given voluntarily. Finally, if the student initially attempts to decline, resist, or prevent a search, any subsequent claim of voluntary consent will be highly suspect. Searches conducted under involuntary consent are considered unlawful. Factors the courts consider when determining whether consent is voluntary include the age and amount of education of the student, whether the student has been advised as to constitutional rights, the length of custody, the length and intensity of questioning, and the use of physical punishment. Schneckloth v. Bustamonte, 412 U.S. at 226. Children generally have limited experience and are accustomed to obeying authority, so the question of free will is

important in school situations. Jones v. Latexo Indep. Sch. Dist., 499 F. Supp. 223, 237 (E.D. Tex. 1980). Consent is not voluntary if the student is acquiescing to a show of authority. Donovan v. A.A. Beiro Constr. Co., 746 F.2d 894, 901 (D.C. Cir. 1984).

Normally, when the student is sufficiently mature, intelligent, or sophisticated, voluntary consent can be indicated by:

- simple positive gestures (e.g., nodding the head or moving aside to permit access) and responses (e.g., "yeah," "go ahead," "ok," etc.) (United States v. Griffin, 530 F.2d 739, 743 (7th Cir. 1976) (consent indicated by the accused's moving aside); People v. James, 19 Cal. 3d 99, 137 Cal. Rptr. 447, 561 P.2d 1135, 1143 (1977) (consent indicated by response of "yeah"); *but see* Cipres v. United States, 343 F.2d 95, 97 (9th Cir. 1965) (no consent when the verbal agreement is contradicted by conduct); State v. LaFlamm, 170 Mont. 202, 551 P.2d 1011, 1013 (1976) (no consent without a verbal agreement even though conduct seemed helpful));

- active assistance or participation in the search (United States v. Culp, 472 F.2d 459, 461 (8th Cir. 1973); United States v. Bryant, 370 F. Supp. 452, 455 (W.D. Pa. 1974));

- affirmative statements restricting the scope of any given consent (suggesting an awareness of rights);

- self-incriminating statements made freely prior to giving consent (United States v. Boukater, 409 F.2d 537, 538–39 (5th Cir. 1969); United States v. Bryant, 370 F. Supp. 452, 454 (W.D. Pa. 1974));

- any expressed belief that nothing incriminating will be found (Frink v. State, 597 P.2d 154, 169 (Alaska 1979); In re Corey L., 250 Cal. Rptr. 359 (Cal. App. 1988));

- circumstances suggesting that the student is not in fact a party to any suspected infraction and simply desires to clear his or her name (i.e., a valid motivation to cooperate is evident)

(United States v. Potamitis, 564 F. Supp. 1484, 1487–88 (D.C.N.Y. 1983));

- advising the student that the student has a right to refuse the request for consent and receiving confirmation from the student indicating an understanding of the right; or
- a statement or request by student for school official to retrieve contents from specific location (In re Ronnie H., 603 N.Y.S.2d (App. Div. 1993)).

In State ex rel Juvenile Dept. v. Stephens, 27 P.3d 170 (Ore.App. 2001), the Oregon Court of Appeals found a voluntary consent in a situation where a student and his parent agreed to regular searches of all his possessions as a condition of enrolling in Portland's "Turnaround School," an alternative public school designed for students who had been expelled from other schools for violence, weapons, drugs, or alcohol offenses.

§ 2:17   Consent searches—Coercive factors that may invalidate consent

If undue coercive pressures are brought to bear on a student, any resulting "consent" will tend to be invalidated because it is not viewed as an act of free will.

Coercive pressures can result from committing or omitting some overt act or from more subtle circumstantial cues. In general, no one factor is by itself determinative of coercion. Normally, a court will consider the factual context and how relatively vulnerable a particular student may be to official pressures. All of the circumstances surrounding a student's consent must thus be examined when evaluating voluntariness. Jones v. Latexo Indep. Sch. Dist., 499 F. Supp. 223, 237 (E.D. Tex. 1980) (children have limited experience and are accustomed to obeying authorities, and are therefore in a situation where they are incapable of exercising free will); United States v. Hall, 565 F.2d 917, 921 (5th Cir. 1978) (factors used to evaluate conduct include intimidation, physical or psychological abuse, and threats); Florida v. Bostick, 501 U.S. 429, 111 S. Ct. 2382, 2387 (1991) (quoting from Michigan v. Chesternut, 486 U.S. 567, 569 (1988)) (the "crucial test" is whether, in light of all the surrounding circumstances, the official conduct "would 'have communicated to a reasonable person that he was not at liberty to ignore the police presence and go about his business' ").

Coercive factors include the following:

(1) *Show, use, or threat of force.* Any actual or threatened use of force is highly coercive in school settings. Force can be manifested in many different ways. For example, overt force can be expressed by exhibiting instruments of corporal punishment, physically restraining a student, vigorously intruding upon a student's person or possessions, and any similar act.

Other more subtle forms of conduct can be equally coercive. For example, coercion might be suspected if several school officials surround a student, badger the student repeatedly and extensively, or display a menacing, threatening, or belligerent presence.

The use of force will usually be a decisive factor in determining that consent is not voluntary and therefore invalid. In some rare cases, exercising a measure of force does not necessarily invalidate the consent. This will depend on the particular student's sophistication and prior history. For example, the menacing presence of several school officials may be considered highly coercive in relation to consent given by a cloistered high school student having no previous disciplinary encounters. The same circumstance might not be viewed as even slightly coercive for an intermediate student with several prior arrests and encounters with juvenile court proceedings.

(2) *Threatening serious consequences for refusing consent.* A claim that a student had voluntarily consented to a search would be significantly undermined if the school official implied that certain specified or unspecified consequences may follow for students who withhold consent. School officials may inform the student that they will attempt to conduct a regular student search sometime in the future if consent is refused. School officials cannot, however, imply that such a search

is virtually certain or that it would automatically follow from the refusal. United States v. White, 617 F.2d 1131, 1134 (5th Cir. 1980) (when an FBI agent asked for consent, he explained that obtaining a warrant would not be automatic and that defendant had a right to refuse; the resulting consent was voluntary); Dotson v. Somers, 175 Conn. 614, 402 A.2d 790, 794 (1978) (when police asked for consent to search and said they could obtain a warrant anyway, the situation was inherently coercive).

(3) *Temporary detention.* Valid consent can be given by students who are temporarily detained or removed to a more private place (e.g., a school official's office) if the surrounding circumstances are not coercive when considered as a whole. State v. Stein, 203 Kan. 638, 456 P.2d 1, 2 (1969); *but see* Fewless ex rel. Fewless v. Board of Educ. of Wayland Union Schools, 208 F. Supp. 2d 806, 815, 167 Ed. Law Rep. 153 (W.D. Mich. 2002), where the court described a strip search of a 14-year-old special education student in a school office measuring eight feet by eight feet as "a situation akin to police custody."

(4) *Prior illegal conduct by school officials.* Any consent obtained by exploiting prior illegal conduct will generally be held invalid. Wong Sun v. United States, 371 U.S. 471, 485 (1963) ("knowledge gained by the government's own wrong cannot be used by it"). For example, if a school official were to obtain consent from a student by using information gathered through illegal surveillance, the consent would be considered invalid because it is improper to gain an advantage from a prior illegality (*see* Chapter 7). Consequently, taints of this sort can invalidate even a consent that might otherwise be judged voluntary. The usual remedy in a criminal setting for tainted consent would be to exclude the evidence at trial, but the Supreme Court declined to address the question whether use of the exclusionary rule was the proper remedy for Fourth Amendment violations committed by pub-

lic school officials. New Jersey v. T.L.O., 469 U.S. 325, 327–28 (1985).

It is sometimes possible to purge the consent of any taint and restore its validity if the connection with a prior illegality is attenuated. One example would be if a long interval containing a significant intervening event separated the illegal conduct from the granted consent. Brown v. Illinois, 422 U.S. 590, 604 n.11 (1975). Another attenuating factor might be the presence of intervening circumstances such as if a student is allowed to confer with parents or an attorney or is notified of the right to refuse consent. Carnejo-Molina v. INS, 649 F.2d 1145, 1149 (5th Cir. 1981) (attorney); People v. Williams, 62 Ill. App. 3d 824, 20 Ill. Dec. 154, 379 N.E.2d 1222, 1226 (1979) (mother). *But see* State v. Badger, 141 Vt. 430, 450 A.2d 336, 344 (1982) (father's presence was not an attenuating factor because he was unfamiliar with the criminal justice system). A third attenuating factor occurs when officials obtain the information gained through a "consent" from an independent source. Commonwealth v. Frodyma, 393 Mass. 438, 471 N.E.2d 1298, 1300 (1984); State v. O'Bremski, 70 Wash. 2d 425, 423 P.2d 530, 532–33 (1967). Finally, less flagrant or less conspiratorial illegalities may sometimes be excused. United States v. Leon, 468 U.S. 897, 907–8 (1984). *See* Section 7:4 for further discussion.

(5) *Fraudulent or mistaken claim of lawful authority.* Any knowing or erroneous misstatement implying that school officials have absolute legal authority to conduct a search or to obtain consent will almost certainly invalidate any resulting consent. Bumper v. North Carolina, 391 U.S. at 550. This tactic is considered extremely coercive because students confronted with a claim of legal authority would be under the impression that they cannot refuse without violating the law.

(6) *Deception.* Consent gained by deception, subterfuge, or pretext will usually be held invalid. Thus, school officials cannot obtain consent to

search for some innocuous item (which a student is presumably unconcerned about protecting) while actually intending to search for other incriminating evidence that is otherwise inaccessible.

(7) *Failure to grant students their right to refuse consent or confer with counsel.* The Constitution as presently interpreted does not require that students must be informed of their right to refuse consent or their right to confer with legal or other counsel, because the student is merely being asked to allow access to some place or thing. That grant of permission is not viewed as an overt act of self-incrimination even if its purpose is to discover something incriminating. Thus, no coercion will be found if school officials simply fail to announce these rights. Schneckloth v. Bustamonte, 412 U.S. at 234; Commonwealth v. Snyder, 597 N.E.2d 1363, 1369 (Mass. 1992) (there is no authority requiring a school administrator not acting on behalf of law enforcement officials to furnish Miranda warnings); Com. v. Ira I., 439 Mass. 805, 791 N.E.2d 894, 178 Ed. Law Rep. 491 (2003) (affirming this conclusion); In re Corey L., 250 Cal.Rptr. 359, 360–61 (Cal.App.1988) ("Questioning of a student by a principal, whose duties include the obligations to maintain order, protect the health and safety of pupils and maintain conditions conducive to learning, cannot be equated with custodial interrogation by law enforcement officers"); In the Matter of L.A., 21 P.3d 952 (Kan. 2001) ("During an investigation of a violation of school policy, a school security officer is not required to give a student Miranda warnings."); In the Matter of V.P., 55 S.W.3d 25 (Tex.App. 2001) (ruling that the continued questioning of a 14-year-old student by an assistant principal after the student had requested to see his attorney was not a "custodial interrogation" requiring that questioning stop when an attorney is requested); *but see* State v. Johnson, 68 N.J. 349, 346 A.2d 66, 68 (1975) (state constitution requires waiver of

Fourth Amendment rights, so voluntary consent must include knowledge of the right to refuse); In re R.H., 568 Pa. 1, 791 A.2d 331, 334, 162 Ed. Law Rep. 453 (2002) (ruling, by a 4-2 vote, that school police officers were obliged to advise students being questioned of their constitutional rights to remain silent and to the assistance of a lawyer under Miranda v. Arizona, 384 U.S. 436, 86 S. Ct. 1602, 16 L. Ed. 2d 694, 10 A.L.R.3d 974 (1966), because these school police officers, although "employees of the school district," were "judicially appointed and explicitly authorized to exercise the same powers as municipal police on school property").

However, it will be deemed highly coercive if a school official does not honor a student's refusal of consent or a request to confer with legal or other counsel. People v. Johnson, 48 N.Y.2d 565, 399 N.E.2d 936, 937, 423 N.Y.S.2d 905 (1979).

Finally, any consent given after conferring with legal counsel is very likely to be considered valid. Commonwealth v. Harris, 387 Mass. 758, 443 N.E.2d 1287, 1292 (1982); Frink v. State, 597 P.2d 154, 169 (Alaska 1979).

(8)   *Personal factors that affect a student's vulnerability to coercion.* Personal factors such as a student's maturity, intelligence, and sophistication are important to a determination that surrounding circumstance may be coercive when considered as a whole. State v. Badger, 141 Vt. 430, 450 A.2d 336, 344 (1982). A Florida court ruled that a freshman during the second week of school had not consented to a search of his wallet (which discovered marijuana and a razor blade) by the assistant principal and resource officer in an empty office, after the student testified that "he did not feel that he could refuse the request to be searched." A.H. v. State, 846 So. 2d 1215, 1217, 177 Ed. Law Rep. 1250 (Fla. Dist. Ct. App. 5th Dist. 2003). A Michigan federal judge ruled that a 14-year old student with Attention Deficit Hyperactivity Disorder (ADHD) did not give valid consent to a strip search, even though the school

officials testified that they had stressed three times that the search could only be conducted if it was voluntary, and the student had said "I don't have anything to hide," because the student was not told about the "very intrusive type of strip search of the person" that was to be performed and had not been given the opportunity to talk to a parent, counselor or attorney. Fewless ex rel. Fewless v. Board of Educ. of Wayland Union Schools, 208 F. Supp. 2d 806, 814–15, 167 Ed. Law Rep. 153 (W.D. Mich. 2002) ("The 'consent' was merely acquiescence and was not freely or voluntarily given."). Very young children are considered highly vulnerable to coercion almost by definition because of their immaturity and lack of sophistication about worldly matters. Consequently, even a mildly coercive setting can invalidate consent. Jones v. Latexo Indep. Sch. Dist., 499 F. Supp. 223, 237 (E.D. Tex. 1980). This same reasoning allows a somewhat greater quantity and intensity of coercive factors for older students who have had a wider range of experiences.

Aside from obvious considerations of age, school officials must also be aware that students can be vulnerable to coercion because of personal factors that may not be readily apparent. For example, a student may be intoxicated by drugs or alcohol; affected by grief, anger, or other personal circumstances; or disturbed by the nature of events immediately preceding a request for consent. People v. Helm, 633 P.2d 1071, 1077 (Colo. 1981) (intoxication is one factor to consider, but it does not always invalidate consent); Commonwealth v. Angivoni, 383 Mass. 30, 417 N.E.2d 422, 425 (1981) (must consider factors of emotional trauma from witnessing accident and pain from injuries).

Merely establishing that a student's subjective state of mind is vulnerable to coercion does not itself negate consent. Invalidation results when a weakness is knowingly exploited to gain consent. An example might be if school officials obtained consent knowing that a student was despondent and not particularly attentive at the time. But valid consent has been found in some cases when school officials acted in good faith and did not take advantage of any apparent susceptibility to coercion. For example, suppose a student were impaired by drugs. Valid consent might still be secured if the school official was not aware of the intoxication and did not otherwise exert any coercion.

Questions of subjective vulnerability notwithstanding, it will be difficult to avoid suspicions of coercion unless a school official also takes into account each particular student's level of maturity and sophistication. This standard is not easy to meet (*see* Section 2:22).

§ 2:18   Consent searches—Proper authority to consent

An additional critical question is whether a student who gives access to the person, place, or thing a school official wishes to search has proper authority to make such a grant. As discussed above, although the voluntariness of consent is always questionable, there is no doubt that a student can voluntarily consent to the search of the student's own person or possessions. It is substantially less clear, however, whether one student can consent to a search of another student's property when the nonconsenting student objects or is not present.

As a general rule, third-party consent of this kind is valid as long as a person of "reasonable caution" would believe that the consenting student has some common authority over the place or thing to be searched. *See* Illinois v. Rodriguez, 497 U.S. 177 (1990). The consenting third-party student does not need any ownership rights to grant valid consent. There are several variations of common authority to consider:

(1) *Consent by third parties with no legal interest in the place or thing searched.* An example might involve an enclosed school storage area assigned to several students for their exclusive but undivided joint use. In order to give valid consent, a

third-party student needs only to have common authority over the place or thing searched. This authority would be indicated by having actual use, access, or control. It is not necessary for third parties to have any legal property interests. Thus, one student can validly consent to the search of a jointly assigned storage area even if the other student is not present to object. United States v. Matlock, 415 U.S. 164, 170 (1974) (consent over area of common authority is "valid as against the absent, nonconsenting person" who shares authority over the area); Frazier v. Cupp, 394 U.S. 731, 740 (1969) (joint user has authority to consent).

(2) *Consent by third parties with legal property interests and actual use and control.* Jointly owned property such as automobiles and other possessions falls into this category. Persons having both a possessory (legal) interest and actual use or control of property can give valid consent to search that property. It does not matter what the proportionate share of ownership may be so long as the interests are undivided. J.L. Foti Constr. Co. v. Donovan, 786 F.2d 714 (6th Cir. 1986).

If the interests in jointly owned property are divided so that certain parts are under exclusive control by one party, then the other parties cannot give valid consent to search that exclusive area. *But see* Frazier v. Cupp, 394 U.S. 731, 740 (1969), where the defendant had given the person who consented to a search permission to use only one compartment of defendant's gym bag; the Court refused to make "metaphysical subtleties" and ruled that consent had been given for a search of the entire gym bag.

(3) *Consent by third parties with legal property interests but no actual use or control.* This unusual category encompasses school property assigned for individual student use such as storage lockers. Although this area of the law is still unsettled, most courts hold that valid consent cannot be given by third parties having only a

legal interest in property but no actual use or control, because consent does not rest on property law but instead rests on expectations of privacy. United States v. Matlock, 415 U.S. at 171 n.7. Thus, school officials cannot assume the third-party role and validly give some other authority (e.g., police) permission to search a student's locker. *See* Dotson v. Somers, 175 Conn. 614, 402 A.2d 790, 795 (1978) (the owner of a house could not give consent to search a room occupied by another person because that person had a lock on the door and exercised full control over the contents and occupants of the room).

(4) *Third-party consent when the target of a search is present or available.* Valid third-party consent cannot generally be given when the actual target of a search is present or readily available. Thus, if both occupants of a jointly assigned locker are present and officials want to search the locker because of a suspected infraction by the first, they cannot obtain valid consent from the second. In addition, if under similar circumstances the target student refuses to give consent, the target student's refusal cannot be overridden by the other student's consent. Also, consent by an absent student cannot be used over the objection of a student who is present. Tompkins v. Superior Court, 59 Cal. 2d 65, 27 Cal. Rptr. 889, 378 P.2d 113, 116 (1963).

It is generally held that if the target student is present but remains silent and does not object to consent given by a third party having proper common authority, the consent is valid.

Needless to say, school officials should not deliberately seek opportunities where the target student is absent or unavailable in order to conduct a third-party consent search.

(5) *Lockers and other school property assigned to students for their individual use.* Some states explicitly recognize that students have justified expectations of privacy in school property assigned for their individual use. Accordingly, school officials located in these states cannot

grant themselves permission to conduct a valid third-party consent search of such areas. *See* State v. Engerud, 94 N.J. 331, 348, 463 A.2d 934, 943 (1983); State v. Michael G., 748 P.2d 17, 19 (N.M. App. 1987); In re Dumas, 357 Pa. Super. 294, 515 A.2d 984, 985 (1986); State v. Brooks, 718 P.2d 837, 838–39 (Wash. App. 1986); State v. Joseph T., 336 S.E.2d 728, 737–38 (W. Va. 1985). *See also* "Hawaii Dep't of Education Regulations," Chapter 19, Subchapter 4, subsection 8-19-14.

But see Singleton v. Board of Educ. USD 500, 894 F. Supp. 386, (D. Kan. 1995); In re Isiah B. v. State, 500 N.W.2d 637 (Wis. 1993); Zamora v. Pomeroy, 639 F.2d 662, 670–71 (10th Cir. 1981); State v. Stein, 203 Kan. 638, 456 P.2d 1, 3 (1964); and People v. Overton, 24 N.Y.2d 522, 526, 249 N.E.2d 366, 301 N.Y.S.2d 479, 482 (1969), where the courts explicitly rejected students' expectation of privacy in their school lockers. The Supreme Court did not discuss in New Jersey v. T.L.O. whether school children have privacy expectations in lockers, desks, or other school property provided for their use. 469 U.S. 325, 337 n.5 (1985).

§ 2:19 Consent searches—Scope limits

The scope and intensity of all consent searches must be strictly limited to the terms of the consent given, because the authority to search derives exclusively from the consent itself. It is not unusual for a student to consent to a search but also impose limitations or restrictions (e.g., that the search must be confined to only a certain area). School officials must comply with these limitations or the search will be invalid. People v. Torand, 622 P.2d 565, 565 (Colo. 1981) (searches based on consent must be confined as to scope, area, purpose, and/or time as limited by consentee); Florida v. Jimeno, 500 U.S. 248, 251 (1991) ("The standard for measuring the scope of a suspect's consent under the Fourth Amendment is that of 'objective' reasonableness—what would the typical reasonable person have understood by the exchange between the officer and the suspect?"); State ex rel. Juvenile Dep't of Washington County v. Doty, 906 P.2d 299 (Or. App. 1995) (finding consent for search of backpack but not for pockets).

The scope and intensity of the search must also be consistent with the stated purposes of a school official's request. Voluntary consent will rarely be given without an explanation of purpose and some indication of what is being sought. Any resulting consent search must be conducted consistently with that explanation. This rule means that only places and things that might reasonably contain the designated item may be searched (including closed but not sealed or locked containers). People v. Torand, 622 P.2d at 565–66; Florida v. Jimeno, 500 U.S. at 248. See Section 4:3 for additional discussion of scope and intensity limits.

School officials cannot destroy property or break into locked containers while conducting a consent search. See Florida v. Jimeno, 500 U.S. at 251–52, discussing State v. Wells, 539 So. 2d 464 (Fla. 1989), aff'd on other grounds, 495 U.S. 1 (1990) ("consent to search the trunk of a car did not include authorization to pry open a locked briefcase inside the trunk"). Consent does not give an official authority to conduct a roving exploratory search. United States v. Dichiarinte, 445 F.2d 126, 129–30 (7th Cir. 1971) (official cannot obtain consent to look for specified items and then do a general exploratory search).

Finally, consent is usually viewed as granting permission for an immediate search on one single occasion. School officials must avoid obtaining consent and then delaying for a long period before actually conducting the search. Any attempt to extend consent from one to many different occasions will also generally be invalid. People v. Shelton, 110 Ill. App. 3d 625, 66 Ill. Dec. 367, 442 N.E.2d 928, 932 (1982) (generally consent is for an immediate and single search). But see Gray v. State, 441 A.2d 209, 221–22 (Del. Super. 1981) (search must be conducted within a "reasonable" time of consent; twenty hours deemed reasonable in this case); People v. Nawrocki, 6 Mich. App. 46, 148 N.W.2d 211, 213 (1967) (giving police permission to search vehicle "at any time" allows multiple searches). (See Section 2:10 for discussion regarding delay in the context of emergencies.)

§ 2:20 Consent searches—Withdrawal of consent

Students can withdraw their consent entirely or partially at any time. If they do, the official must immediately cease or confine the search accordingly. Mason v. Pulliam, 557 F.2d 426, 428 (5th Cir. 1977); United States v. Homburg, 546 F.2d 1350, 1350–51 (9th Cir. 1976). *But see* People v. Kennard, 488 P.2d 563, 564 (Colo. 1971) ("after consent has been granted to conduct a search, that consent cannot be withdrawn").

The withdrawal of consent is not retroactive. Anything lawfully discovered prior to the revocation remains valid and seizable. Jones v. Berry, 722 F.2d 443, 448–49 (9th Cir. 1983); State v. Johns, 679 S.W.2d 253, 262 (Mo. 1984) (consent cannot be revoked after incriminating evidence has been found).

§ 2:21 Consent searches—Plain view

A school official may seize any incriminating items inadvertently discovered during the course of a valid consent search provided that necessary requirements for a plain view seizure are satisfied first (Section 6:5).

§ 2:22 Consent searches—Consent by students in particular

Consent obtained from students is inevitably subject to question, because several intrinsically coercive factors are associated with students and these cannot be easily or effectively overcome. They include:

(1) A general lack of maturity and sophistication which make students below college age especially susceptible to even slightly coercive pressures (Jones v. Latexo Ind. School Dist., 499 F. Supp. 223, 237 (E.D. Tex. 1980)); Fewless ex rel. Fewless v. Board of Educ. of Wayland Union Schools, 208 F. Supp. 2d 806, 814–15, 167 Ed. Law Rep. 153 (W.D. Mich. 2002);

(2) The highly authoritative supervisory role assumed by administrators, teachers, and other school personnel, which increases the likelihood that student consent may represent the mere acquiescence to authority and not a voluntary exercise of free will (Jones v. Latexo Ind. School Dist., 499 F. Supp. 223, 237 (E.D. Tex. 1980)); and

(3)   The substantial difficulty of explaining to students what their legal status and Fourth Amendment rights are—especially very young children.

Although the Constitution does not require prior disclosure of Fourth Amendment rights (*see* Section 2:17), some states may require an affirmative waiver of those rights. *See* State v. Johnson, 68 N.J. 349, 346 A.2d 66, 68 (1975) (New Jersey constitution requires waiver of Fourth Amendment rights). In the absence of such disclosures there can be doubts about whether students actually understand that school officials cannot demand or compel a search unless they have lawful justification.

§ 2:23   Abandoned property

Section overview. When there are clear indications that a student has voluntarily relinquished a justified privacy interest in something, the item is considered abandoned.

Abandonment can be reasonably inferred when a student:
(1)   Disclaims ownership,
(2)   Disassociates himself or herself from the item,
(3)   Intentionally leaves or hides the item in a public place, or
(4)   Throws the item away while in flight from or at the approach of school officials who have a lawful purpose for pursuing or approaching the student.

Abandoned property can be searched or seized without any prior reasonable suspicion.

Garbage and trash containers can generally be treated as areas containing abandoned property in the school setting and searched accordingly.

Lost property is distinguished from abandoned property by the absence of any clear indication that justified privacy interests have been relinquished intentionally. Lost property can, therefore, only be searched and examined for purposes of discovering ownership.

§ 2:24   Abandoned property—Abandonment requirements

Abandoned property is not protected by the Fourth Amendment. Consequently, school officials may search and seize abandoned items without having any reasonable suspicion. Moss v. Cox, 311 F. Supp. 1245, 1249 (E.D. Va. 1970) (without probable cause).

The determination that something may be abandoned is concerned with the protection of legitimate privacy interests rather than property or possessory rights. When a student abandons something, any remaining expectation of privacy in the item disappears. Some clear indication is therefore required that the student intends to give up a justified privacy interest voluntarily before something is considered abandoned. California v. Hodari D., 499 U.S. 621, 111 S. Ct. 1547, 1549 (1991) (a "rock" that turned out to be crack cocaine was considered "abandoned" when it was "tossed away" by a youth fleeing from a police officer); City of St. Paul v. Vaughn, 306 Minn. 337, 237 N.W.2d 365, 370–71 (1975) (relevant to determine whether someone has relinquished a reasonable expectation of privacy is whether the discard occurred in a public place where any curious passerby could look at the object); Anderson v. State, 133 Ga. App. 45, 209 S.E.2d 665, 667 (1974) (marijuana was considered abandoned when a person relieved himself of possession by hiding it under a rock on a beach, seventy-five feet from where he stood).

Typically, the intention to relinquish a privacy interest can be reasonably inferred from some observable act of a student (see below). But it is not sufficient to focus on what a student does or does not do without considering all of the relevant circumstances. The mere divestiture of physical possession does not itself support any presumption or conclusion of abandonment. For example, a student who temporarily sets down a closed opaque container while speaking with school officials has not abandoned the container in a constitutional sense.

Similarly, student conduct that might suggest abandonment cannot be prompted by some illegal act of school officials. In that case there would be no voluntary intent to abandon because the circumstances are considered coercive. To illustrate, a student who discards something to avoid detection has not abandoned it if that action is prompted by school officials conducting an unlawful search. State v. Reed, 284 So. 2d 574, 575 (La. 1973); Commonwealth v. Pollard, 450 Pa. 138, 299 A.2d 233, 236 (1973).

The intention to relinquish a justified privacy interest voluntarily may be inferred when a student:

(1)　Disclaims any ownership or possessory interest in the item (State v. Moore, 603 A.2d 513 (N.J. Super. 1992) (when defendant was asked "if this was his bag," he answered in the negative); Miller v. State, 498 N.E.2d 53 (Ind. App. 1986) (the court ruled defendant had abandoned a gym bag when he stated that it belonged to another student); United States v. Hawkins, 681 F.2d 1343, 1345 (11th Cir. 1982));

(2)　Attempts to verbally or otherwise disassociate himself or herself from the item (United States v. Colbert, 474 F.2d 174, 177 (5th Cir. 1973));

(3)　Intentionally leaves or attempts to hide the item in a public place (Section 2:3) (Anderson v. State, 209 S.E.2d at 667); or

(4)　Attempts to avoid detection by throwing something away while in flight from or at the approach of school officials who have a lawful purpose for pursuing or approaching the student (United States v. Jones, 707 F.2d 1169, 1172 (10th Cir. 1983); United States v. Koessel, 706 F.2d 271, 274 (8th Cir. 1983)).

Several of these situations involve the *lawful* conduct of school officials which causes the student to abandon the item; as long as the school official is acting lawfully, the property is truly abandoned, and it is in a public place, then the abandoned property can be seized and examined.

Sometimes, abandoned property will be found in a protected place (Section 2:3), such as enclosed rest room stalls, dressing areas, or school lockers assigned for individual student use. School officials may search and examine such places or the items in them only if it is clear that the area has actually been vacated or that the student's right of individual use has expired. This status can be inferred if a student departs the area and leaves no indication that he or she intends to return (e.g., the student removes other possessions from the locker and leaves it unlocked). Another example might be when a student surrenders the keys, lock, or combination to a locker.

If they do not have sufficient grounds to conclude that

the area has been vacated or that the student's right to individual use has expired, school officials cannot lawfully
search "abandoned" property located in a protected place
without first satisfying all requirements for a student
search (Chapter 3).

§ 2:25 Abandoned property—Garbage and trash

School officials can generally treat garbage and trash as
validly abandoned property in the school setting and
search them accordingly. No justified privacy interest is
generally recognized in garbage and trash, especially in
public trash containers, because it is reasonable to
conclude that a person who knowingly places something
for disposal and possible open public exposure does not
intend to retain any privacy interest in that thing.

Some state courts have recognized privacy interests in
garbage. See People v. Edwards, 71 Cal. 2d 1096, 80 Cal.
Rptr. 633, 458 P.2d 713, 718 (1969) (where a trash can
was located close to a house and trash removers were the
only other people with access to them, the owner had a
valid expectation of privacy in garbage); State v. Tanaka,
67 Haw. 658, 701 P.2d 1274, 1276–77 (1985) (the Hawaii
Constitution recognizes that individuals can have reasonable expectations of privacy for garbage deposited in closed
opaque containers). But garbage and trash is of a different
character in the school setting compared with private
homes and businesses. In public schools, there are no
private trash containers or protected places that might
normally hold such containers. Moreover, discarded items
will be intermingled with the trash and garbage of other
students and thus be exposed to open view. The school
setting can be compared to multioccupancy dwellings
where trash containers are used by several persons, and
garbage deposited in such containers is consequently open
to all the occupants' view. See Smith v. State, 510 P.2d
793, 795 (Alaska 1973); United States v. Harruff, 352 F.
Supp. 224, 226 (E.D. Mich. 1972). But see People v. Smith,
52 Cal. App. 3d 514, 125 Cal. Rptr. 192 (1975).

Of course, small litter bags located in a student's locker
can only be searched by first satisfying all requirements
for a reasonable student search (Chapter 3).

§ 2:26   Abandoned property—Lost property

Lost properties are items found in public places under circumstances where no one immediately claims a possessory interest or can be identified as owners. An item is "lost" rather than "abandoned" if there is no observable or circumstantial basis for inferring that the student has intentionally relinquished the privacy interest in it.

A school official can search lost property only for the purpose and to the extent necessary to determine ownership.

Because there is no clear indication that justified privacy interests have been abandoned for lost property, the plain view seizure doctrine cannot be applied to permit a search of the "found" items (Section 6:5).

§ 2:27   Probation subject to a valid search condition

Section overview. When a student is on court-ordered probation subject to a valid search condition, the student cannot have a reasonable expectation of privacy over his person or property for Fourth Amendment purposes.

Conditions of probation for minors are devised and imposed by juvenile courts for reformative and rehabilitative purposes of the juvenile probationer. They may sometimes permit school officials to search a minor's person or property with or without a warrant. Knowledge of such conditions as they pertain to individual students normally would be helpful to the school official in a search situation. Ignorance of the condition, however, will not invalidate what otherwise would constitute an unreasonable search. People v. Tyrell, 876 P.2d 519 (Cal. 1994).

In Tyrell, a police officer conducted a search of a juvenile at a high school football game and retrieved a bag of marijuana. At the time of the search, the officer was unaware that the minor was on probation and was subject to a condition that required him to submit to warrantless searches by any law enforcement officer, including a school official. The California Supreme Court reversed a lower court ruling that the officer lacked probable cause to search the juvenile, and that the fortuity of the existence of the search condition did not validate an otherwise improper search. The court ruled that a juvenile probationer subject to a valid search condition does not have a reasonable expectation of privacy over his person or property, and that one must first have a reasonable expectation of privacy before there can be a Fourth Amendment violation.

In a school setting, therefore, if a student is subject to probationary conditions requiring him to submit to warrantless searches, a school official need not even show reasonable suspicion to conduct the search, at least in California. Because such conditions are the exception rather than the rule, however, it is obviously still best to follow the reasonable suspicion guidelines in Chapter 3.

Chapter 3

Reasonable Suspicion

Research References

West's Key Number Digest

Constitutional Law ☞278.5; Schools ☞172; Searches and Seizures ☞23

§ 3:1 Defining the term

Section overview. As long as constitutional standards are satisfied, a school official may generally search for any item that:

(1) Has a known logical relationship or nexus (Section 3:3) with a specific student infraction, either a violation of law or a school rule (Warden v. Hayden, 387 U.S. 294, 307 (1967)), if

(2) The item is likely to be found in the place to be searched (Warden v. Hayden, 387 U.S. 294, 307 (1967)).

The "proper objects" of a student search can be divided into the following categories:

(1) *Fruits* of the infraction, such as stolen property.

(2) *Instrumentalities* or the means by which an infraction is committed, such as a can of spray paint used to commit vandalism.

(3) *Contraband* or items that students are prohibited from possessing while in school either by law or local school rules, such as weapons or illicit substances.

(4) *Evidence* or other evidentiary material related to an infraction, such as the blood-stained shirt from a violent assault.

In order to "reasonably suspect" something, school officials must have facts of sufficient quantity and certainty to establish a sufficient probability that the suspicion may be true. To justify acting on a "reasonable suspicion," the school official must be able to:

(1) Identify specific observations or knowledge;

(2) Indicate the rational inferences that were drawn from all available observations and facts considered as a whole; and

(3) Explain how the available facts and rational inferences provided a particular and objective

basis for the suspicion when they were combined with the special background, training, and experiences the school official has.

In other words, in order to justify conducting a student search, a school official's "reasonable suspicion" must establish connections between:

(1)   A particular student and some specific infraction;
(2)   The particular object sought and a specific infraction; and
(3)   The particular object and the place searched.

Persons, places, and things that are the subject of a student search must be described with sufficient particularity and detail to assure that they can be identified with reasonable certainty.

§ 3:2   Defining the term—What is a reasonable suspicion?

In order to demonstrate that they have a valid reasonable suspicion, school officials must be able to:

(1)   Describe their specific observations or knowledge (In re P.E.A., 754 P.2d 382, 388 (Colo. 1988));
(2)   Indicate what rational inferences they drew from all the available observations and facts considered as a whole (In re P.E.A., 754 P.2d 382, 388 (Colo. 1988)); and
(3)   Explain how available facts and rational inferences provide a particular and objective basis for the suspicion when they are combined with the special background, training, and experiences they have as school officials (United States v. Brignoni-Ponce, 422 U.S. 873, 884–85 (1975)).

In addition, their suspicions must be based on facts of sufficient *quantity* and *certainty*. A single isolated noncritical fact that is unconfirmed by any other circumstantial fact or observation will not generally be sufficient to support a valid reasonable suspicion. Factors that can contribute to a reasonable suspicion are discussed in Sections 3:5 and 3:6.

The level of certainty required is a "sufficient probability" that the suspicion may be true. New Jersey v. T.L.O., 469 U.S. 325, 346 (1985). It is not necessary that the facts rule out all other explanations entirely. School officials can "reasonably suspect" an infraction even if it is just as likely (but not more likely) that the facts and observations supporting the suspicion might have an innocent explanation. In re Frederick B., 192 Cal. App. 3d 79, 87, 237 Cal. Rptr. 338, 343 (1987) ("the possibility of an innocent explanation does not deprive the officer of the capacity to entertain a reasonable suspicion of criminal conduct").

The margin of error tolerated for a reasonable suspicion applies only to the facts and observations that form its objective basis. There is no allowance for substantive mistakes about the content of any applicable law. If an official mistakenly believes that some student conduct is a law violation or prohibited conduct when it is not, any related search and seizure of evidence will be invalid. People v. Teresinski, 26 Cal. 3d 457, 463, 162 Cal. Rptr. 44, 47, 605 P.2d 874, 876 (1980), vacated on other grounds, 449 U.S. 914 (1980).

Reasonable suspicions that do not prove to be true. A search that ultimately turns up nothing incriminating will not be considered invalid or illegal as long as it was justified at its inception by a valid reasonable suspicion.

§ 3:3   Defining the term—What officials must suspect: The nexus between infraction, object, and place

This section is concerned with the *nature* of "reasonable suspicions" (i.e., what must be suspected). In order to justify conducting a student search, a school official's suspicions must include all of the following:

(1)   They must lead to a reasonable suspicion that a particular student has committed or is committing an infraction;

(2)   They must establish a nexus or link between the particular item sought and a specific suspected infraction (New Jersey v. T.L.O., 469 U.S. at 345); and

(3)   They must link the sought-after item with the particular place to be searched (United States v. Thomas, 757 F.2d 1359, 1367–68 (2d Cir. 1985)).

These relationships are necessary preconditions. Student searches cannot be conducted simply because a school official reasonably suspects something. For example, an official may reasonably suspect the violation of some school rule upon observing a student who attempts to hide among cars in the student parking lot during class hours. That suspicion by itself, however, would not justify a pat down search for drugs (although it might justify questioning the student). Cales v. Howell Public Schools, 635 F. Supp. 454, 457 (E.D. Mich. 1985). A search would be improper until additional evidence is obtained, because such a suspicion would be ambiguous. The student's conduct might be consistent with any number of rule violations. The student might be a truant, might be stealing hubcaps, or may have left class to meet a friend. But nothing in the situation as described supports any suspicion that the student possesses drugs.

The nexus requirement is designed to protect against roving exploratory searches where government officials arbitrarily probe into places and things until something incriminating is finally discovered.

A brief discussion of each necessary relationship is presented below.

(1) *The nexus between student and infraction.* School officials must have sufficient facts and observations to explain how and why a particular student is suspected of having committed some specific infraction. United States v. Cortez, 449 U.S. 411, 417–18 (1981) (based upon the whole picture, officials must have a particularized and objective basis for suspecting the particular person of a violation). Although the Supreme Court has reserved the question of particularity in student searches (New Jersey v. T.L.O., 469 U.S. at 342 n.8), it is logical to assume that some specificity will be required. *But see* Vernonia Sch. Dist. v. Acton, 515 U.S. 646 (1995), and Board of Education of Independent School District No. 92 of Pottawatomie County v. Earls, 536 U.S. 822, 122 S. Ct. 2559, 153 L. Ed. 2d 735, 166 Ed. Law Rep. 79 (2002), discussed at Ch. 12 (individualized suspicion not required for random urinalysis testing of students engaging in athletics and other extracurricular activities).

School officials cannot indiscriminately search a large group of students merely because of a suspected infraction that cannot be connected with any particular student. Bellnier v. Lund, 438 F. Supp. 47, 54 (N.D.N.Y. 1977); *see generally* Chapter 13 below. For example, suppose an official observes that special tools were used to tamper with the classroom fire sprinkler system but no other facts would lead to a suspicion of any particular student. The official cannot conduct a sweep search of every student in class to find the special tools.

Note that the margin of error implied by a "reasonable suspicion" standard (compared with "probable cause") applies only to the student-infraction nexus itself. Any search based on mistakes about what is or is not a law violation or prohibited conduct is invalid (*see* Section 3:2).

(2) *The nexus between item and infraction.* School officials must be able to explain how and why the particular item sought is linked to a suspected infraction. Observations and known facts must raise a sufficient probability that the item is contraband or the fruits, instruments, or evidence of some specific infraction. Warden v. Hayden, 387 U.S. at 307.

School officials cannot validly search for an item that is not linked to a specific infraction. Even if it is virtually certain that a particular item is to be found, a search for it would be unlawful without the proper link with an infraction. To illustrate, suppose an official observes a student making many trips between a classroom and a locker to deposit various common items such as books and personal effects. Although it is absolutely certain that the items described will be found, officials cannot conduct a valid search unless these items are connected with some infraction like theft.

The mere speculation that items may be related to an infraction is not sufficient to justify a student search. Officials must have a reasonable suspicion.

Finally, suspicion or even certainty that a student has violated one school rule does not justify a general search to determine whether the student might have violated other rules. *See* State v. B.A.S., 13 P.3d 244 (Wash.App. 2000) (ruling that a warrantless search of a student's pockets, discovering packets of marijuana, after the student was discovered in the school parking lot without authorization, was unconstitutional, because the suspicion that the student had violated the school's "closed campus" rule "did not provide reasonable grounds for concluding that a search would reveal evidence of that or additional violations of law or school rules").

(3) *The nexus between item and place.* Even if a proper relationship can be established between the item sought and an infraction, school officials must still explain how and why it is suspected of being presently located in the place to be searched. United States v. Thomas, 757 F.2d 1359, 1367–68 (2d Cir. 1985). Any search conducted without facts sufficient to establish a sufficient probability about where evidence may be found would amount to an illegal roving exploratory search. For example, suppose officials reasonably suspect a particular student of forcibly stealing a readily identifiable purse. They could not lawfully search the student's possessions, locker, and automobile in an effort to find the purse without first having additional facts about its possible location. *But see* In re P.E.A., 754 P.2d 382, 383 (Colo. 1988) (two students and their lockers were searched for evidence of drugs; when school officials failed to find any evidence, they inquired how the two students arrived at school; upon discovering the students had ridden in P.E.A.'s car, the officials searched P.E.A., his locker, and his car, finally finding drugs in a closed container in the trunk; search held valid).

Note that it is not necessary for the suspected location of sought-after items to be controlled or owned by the suspected student. Evidence of a student's misconduct may be hidden in a friend's locker and a search of the friend's locker would be lawful (provided all other applicable standards are satisfied first).

Factors relevant to establishing the proper nexus relationships are discussed in Sections 3:5 and 3:6.

One final point: The nature of the suspicions held by school officials is critically important. The focus, scope, and restrictive limits of any related student search are prescribed by those suspicions, because a student search must be reasonably and logically related (as actually conducted) to the suspected infraction, thing, and place that justified the intrusion to begin with.

§ 3:4   Defining the term—Particularity as to the things sought and places searched

The Fourth Amendment requires that before a search can be lawfully conducted the things sought and the places to be searched must be particularly described so that they can be identified with reasonable certainty. These requirements are generally realized with a warrant in criminal situations, and although the U.S. Supreme Court has reserved the particularity issue in school searches and seizures, school officials who are guided by the general principles that follow will not run afoul of the Fourth Amendment.

The objective of the "particularity" requirement is to remove as much discretion as possible so that searches do not become general and exploratory. This requirement also helps to avert searches that are based on vague or questionable information. If something cannot be described particularly, real questions can be raised about its relation to an infraction or its present location. Go-bart Co. v. United States, 282 U.S. 344, 357 (1931).

Finally, particularity is directly related to the reasonableness of a search. In order for a search to be considered reasonable as actually conducted, it must be no more expansive in scope or intensity than would be justified by the particular thing being sought (Section 4:3). Similarly, the reasonable duration of a search is prescribed in relation to finding the particular object sought (Section 4:5).

Generally, establishing the proper nexus relationships specified in Section 3:3 will also satisfy any requirement for particularity in the school setting.

(1) *Particularity as to the place searched.* In the
school setting it should not be very difficult to describe adequately the place to be searched.
Schools have comparatively few protected places
where students might conceal potential objects of
a search (*see* Section 2:3).

It will normally suffice to describe obvious or
distinctive physical characteristics of personal
possessions that might contain sought-after
items (e.g., a blue handbag with a shoulder
strap). Further, it is not necessary to describe
precisely small receptacles that might contain
very diminutive items. United States v. Dunloy,
584 F.2d 6, 10 (2d Cir. 1978) (when the area to
be searched is extremely confined, such as a safe
deposit box, the description does not need to say
more). School property assigned for individual
use can be described by location or serial number
(e.g., locker number *XXX*). For student automobiles it is sufficient to describe the make, year,
color, and license number.

Even if the particularity requirement is liber-
ally construed it is imperative that school officials
exercise due care in describing the place to be
searched. First, if the place to be searched is
deliberately or inadvertently described more
broadly than indicated by reasonable suspicions,
any related search could be invalidated. For
example, if officials reasonably suspect that
dangerous contraband is hidden in a student's
locker, then they should not describe the place to
be searched in such broad terms that every other
storage area assigned to that student becomes
subject to search. Such a broad description might
be viewed as an unlawful generalized exploratory
search.

A second reason for exercising care is that the search
must be strictly limited to the suspected place or places.
United States v. Hillyard, 677 F.2d 1336, 1339 (9th Cir.
1982) (when objects, such as vehicles, can be moved from
place to place, it is reasonable to issue warrants for both
possible locations) (*see* Section 4:3). Consequently, officials
should also avoid describing the search so narrowly as to

preclude searching anything but one specific small receptacle. For example, suppose the officials described the "place" to be searched as a distinctive closed container located within a student's locker. In that case, they can validly gain access to and search the container but cannot actively search other parts of the locker. Similarly, they cannot lawfully search the purse of a student if a small metal tin hidden there was described as the place to be searched for marijuana. The purse could only be opened to obtain the tin. Some courts are less rigid in requiring a logical link between the object of a search and the manner in which it is conducted. In Thompson v. Carthage Sch. Dist., 87 F.3d 979 (8th Cir. 1996), for instance, the court of appeals allowed school officials to reach in and pull out small soft objects from the jackets of male high school students during a mandatory suspicionless search for knives and other metal weapons. The court justified its conclusion by saying that "in a school setting, Fourth Amendment reasonableness does not turn on 'hairsplitting argumentation.'" *Id.* at 983 (quoting from New Jersey v. T.L.O., 469 U.S. 325 (1985)). "Moreover," the court enigmatically concluded, once the school officials "reasonably decided to quickly search many children's pockets for dangerous weapons, it is not realistic to require them to abort the search of a particular child who does not appear to be in possession of such contraband." *Id. See also* Section 6:5 for a discussion of plain view seizures.

(2) *Particularity as to the things sought.* A multitude of items and objects can be contraband or the fruits, instruments, or evidence of student infractions. This uncertainty makes it impossible to state any concise rules of particularity for the objects of a search. Legal scholars in this area have, however, noted several general principles that can serve as useful guides for school officials.

- *Fruits of an infraction (usually stolen property).* Stolen property must be described in specific and particular terms. Generally, it will not suffice to describe such items as being of a certain type or class. The reason is that stolen property usually consists of items that anyone can legally possess. Namen v. State, 665 P.2d 557, 562–63 (Alaska App. 1983) (stolen jewelry mixed with legally owned jewelry must be particularly described). Simple generic descriptions such as "stolen property," "book," "radio," or "jewelry" provide no assurance that stolen items can be correctly identified by school officials conducting a search. In addition, it is not unreasonable for officials to expect a student reporting a theft to provide more than a generic description of the stolen property.

Usually, it will be sufficient to note some unique or distinguishing characteristic of the property such as its condition or appearance. Henry v. United States, 361 U.S. 98, 104 (1959) (look at the nature of the property and the manner and circumstances in which it is possessed). Sometimes a general description is permitted if the officials are accompanied by an expert or victim who can identify the stolen property. Commonwealth v. Farrar, 271 Pa. Super. 434, 413 A.2d 1094, 1099 (1979) (the sister of a victim of theft was able to identify the stolen property).

- *Instruments and evidence of an infraction.* Considerations similar to those for stolen property also apply when describing the instruments and evidence of student infractions. Sometimes these items may be very common and legally possessed by anyone.

  More general descriptions are permitted when the nature of an infraction is such that the item searched for is unusual and unlikely to be possessed by many students. A generalized identification is tolerated because of the preexisting evidentiary or instrumental link with an infraction. United States v. Johnson, 690 F.2d 60, 66 (3d Cir. 1982). For example, suppose school officials suspect a particular student of damaging classroom walls with a ballpeen hammer (because of the distinctive impressions left by each blow). It would be sufficient to describe the object sought as a "ballpeen hammer" or even as a "hammer" without any additional detail. Under the circumstances, there is a "reasonable suspicion" that any hammer discovered during a search of the student's possessions will be correctly identified as the instrument of that infraction. (Note: A separate issue of proof is connected with verifying that the hammer discovered actually was used to commit the property damage.)

Sometimes more particular and specific descriptions are precluded by the nature of an infraction. Again, some ambiguity may be tolerated as long as the item is not described in broadly inclusive terms. For example, suppose a student is suspected of terroristic threatening in connection with loan sharking activities. It would be acceptable to describe the items sought as "books and records of loan sharking." Similarly, descriptions such as "can of gold spray paint" or "handgun" can also be sufficient. Even without more particular descriptions, these instruments could be correctly identified with reasonable certainty because of the nature of the suspected infraction.

Although less particularity is demanded when describing the instruments of an infraction, officials must avoid overly broad and sweeping descriptions. These might invalidate any resulting search because it would be viewed as exploratory in character. For example, it would be objectionable to describe the sought-after items as "tools" or "all papers" in the property damage and loan sharking examples above.

The main requirement for "mere evidence" to be relevant (and therefore the valid object of a search) is that it must contribute to the determination of innocence or guilt. It is not necessary for mere evidence to prove ultimate guilt conclusively. Mere evidence must simply make any fact that is consequential to the determination of guilt more or less likely than it would be without the evidence. Warden v. Hayden, 387 U.S. at 307.

- *Contraband.* Contraband items can be described in very general terms because they are illegal to possess by nature. Thus, generic terms such as "narcotic drugs," "drugs," "flammable substance," or "explosive" will generally suffice. People v. Schmidt, 172 Colo. 285, 473 P.2d 698, 700 (1970).

  The nexus required for *fruits, instruments,* and *contraband* is automatically given by the self-evident relationship these items have with student infractions. Warden v. Hayden, 387 U.S. at 307.

- *The special case of material protected by the First Amendment.* Some local school rules prohibit students from possessing items that are allegedly obscene, pornographic, or indecent. Officials must exercise care in enforcing this prohibition because any attempt to search or seize such items may implicate the First Amendment right to free expression. Roaden v. Kentucky, 413 U.S. 496, 504 (1973). *But see* Ginsberg v. New York, 390 U.S. 629, 634 (1968) (minors do not have the same access to sexually oriented magazines as adults); Bethel School Dist. No. 403 v. Fraser, 478 U.S. 675, 684 (1986) (school officials are acting in loco parentis when they protect school children from sexually explicit, indecent, or lewd speech). *See* Section 1:12 (Constitutional Rights of Minors).

  First Amendment considerations are relevant whenever something is seized because of what it says and not because of what it is, such as a book sought because its contents are thought to be obscene, as opposed to a stolen book sought as the fruit of a crime. The Supreme Court has consistently held that nonobscene books, films, recordings, and other similar material can be searched and seized for evidentiary purposes but not simply because of their contents.

  "Obscene" material is not protected by the First Amendment (Miller v. California, 413

U.S. 15, 23 (1973)), but it is always hard to be sure what is actually obscene. According to the Miller definition, a work is considered obscene if "the average person, applying contemporary community standards finds that the work, taken as a whole, appeals to prurient interests; the work depicts or describes in a patently offensive way, sexual conduct specifically defined by state law; and the work taken as a whole lacks serious literary, artistic, political, or scientific value." *Id.* at 24. Because of the complexity of this definition, it is almost always difficult to be certain whether an item is obscene until a jury has ruled on the question. The seizure of materials thought to be obscene frequently raises problems related to the doctrine of prior restraint.

The Supreme Court looks with extreme disfavor on government conduct that restricts in advance the right of citizens to express freely or have access to ideas protected by the First Amendment. The search or seizure of allegedly obscene material can have this kind of "prior restraining" effect, because the search or seizure will generally occur prior to any final determination of obscenity. If any of the seized material is later found not to be obscene, the right to express ideas actually protected by the First Amendment will have been unjustly restrained by the prior search or seizure. Consequently, there is a presumptive First Amendment protection for all books, films, recordings, and similar material. In general, such items may be searched or seized only if very specific and particular descriptions are given for such items and if Fourth Amendment warrant and probable cause requirements are strictly followed. Roaden v. Kentucky, 413 U.S. at 504 ("prior restraint calls for a higher hurdle in the evaluation of reasonableness").

- Officials must exercise great care in describing anything that is generally lawful and commonly found in the place to be searched. For example, it would not be proper to describe the object of a search as "stolen coins" if one intended to search a student's coin purse, because that is a usual location for coins. Without more particular descriptive information it would not be possible to differentiate between any allegedly stolen coins and coins lawfully belonging to the student. Namen v. State, 665 P.2d at 562.

- Less particularity is required when the nature of an object does not permit a more specific or precise description. Examples are generic items such as "brown paper bags," "dice," or "pencils." United States v. Davis, 589 F.2d 904, 906 (5th Cir. 1979).

- It is not necessary to specify every available descriptive detail as long as any omitted facts are not essential to the reasonable certainty of correct identification. For example, a vehicle search is not invalidated if officials describe a student's car by stating its make, color, and license number but fail to specify the year of manufacture. United States v. Rytman, 475 F.2d 192, 193 (5th Cir. 1973) (wrong identification number does not invalidate search).

- Descriptive errors are also generally forgiven if the item can be correctly identified by other available details. For example, if officials misstate the color of a stolen handbag but correctly specify that it has a distinctive identifying crease, the error is not fatal. United States v. Rytman, 475 F.2d 192, 193 (5th Cir. 1973) (because the item was the only one of its kind at the search location, the error in the identification number was not fatal).

- Sometimes an otherwise acceptable description can be defective by being broader than is consistent with the reasonable suspicion on which it is based. For example, if officials reasonably suspect that the evidence of an infraction is hidden in a student's "appointment calendar," it would be overly broad to describe the object sought as "all personal possessions." People v.

Frank, 38 Cal. 3d 711, 214 Cal. Rptr. 801, 700 P.2d 415, 421 (1985).

§ 3:5   Defining the term—Factors that reasonably connect a particular student with a specific infraction: The student-infraction nexus

An infinite number of factual circumstances might arouse a suspicion that something illicit is afoot. Not all of these situations will provide the lawful basis for searching a student. School officials may conduct a search only when their suspicions link a particular student with some specific infraction based on articulable facts of sufficient quantity and certainty.

Although it is not possible to formulate a general set of rules, officials can reasonably suspect students of past, present, or imminent infractions based on their *conduct, appearance,* or *location.* Various related factors are discussed below.

Three preliminary important points need to be kept in mind. First, a note of caution: one isolated factor is not generally sufficient to support a reasonable suspicion. In most cases a cluster of consistent complementary factors is required. For example, it is doubtful that a reasonable suspicion could be justified if school officials merely observed a furtive gesture and had no other complementary facts.

The second point is that this discussion concerns the nexus between a particular student and some specific illicit conduct. Officials cannot proceed to search a student based only on the reasonable suspicion of an infraction. Proper relationships are required between the infraction, object, and place (*see* Section 3:3). Very often, the factors discussed below will also provide facts relevant to these other necessary relationships.

Finally, keep in mind that even if a search is not permitted based only on the reasonable suspicion of an infraction, it is possible to conduct an investigative stop on that basis alone (Chapter 5). Such a "stop" provides an opportunity to question a suspected student and perhaps establish the necessary basis for a search.

    (1) *Suspicious conduct and furtive gestures.* A school official's suspicions will often be aroused by

observing some unusual conduct or behavior. Sometimes the conduct may have obviously suspicious connotations (e.g., the student is actually observed concealing a weapon). At other times the conduct may be objectively innocent but suspicious because of the context in which it occurs.

Suspicious conduct is anything that might indicate an infraction to the trained and experienced eye. It is accepted that school officials have an acute perspective because of special training and day-to-day experiences in the school setting. Consequently, they might find something highly suspicious even when it appears quite innocent to the lay observer.

Sometimes, objectively innocent behavior can be suspect because it appears out of context with surrounding circumstances. To illustrate:

- The manner and circumstances under which a student is observed to possess something can strongly suggest the commission of an infraction. For example, an observation of a student carrying twenty reams of copy paper late after the end of classes gives some indication of a theft. State v. Bailey, 410 So. 2d 1123, 1125 (La. 1982) (rolling an industrial battery charger down the street at 1:00 a.m. gives indication of a theft).
- The time of day when something is observed might be important (especially late after the end of classes). Commonwealth v. Ellis, 233 Pa. Super. 169, 335 A.2d 512, 514–15 (1975). Occasionally, the combination of time and location might be suspicious, for example, when a student is observed in a place where she or he should not lawfully be at that time of day. State v. Gluck, 83 Wash. 2d 424, 518 P.2d 703, 705–6 (1974).
- Efforts to conceal an item may be suspicious. In re Williams, 36 Ill. App. 3d 917, 344 N.E.2d 745, 747–48 (1976) (youths trying to hide a television behind a bush exhibited suspicious behavior).

- Stealthy movements, attempts to hide, or the quick and abrupt departure from an area all cast suspicion on a student who displays such behavior. 3 W. LaFave, Search and Seizure, § 9.3(c), at 448.

- Refusing to answer lawfully addressed questions about an object or giving evasive, implausible, or blatantly false explanations about how it came to be possessed and for what purpose can also be suspicious. State v. Bailey, 410 So. 2d at 1125 (when two people were rolling a battery charger down the street at 1:00 a.m., denied owning a car, and claimed to be without identification, the police officer was correct in being suspicious about the story). Silence is one of many factors to consider when evaluating suspicion. People v. Simon, 45 Cal. 2d 645, 290 P.2d 531, 534 (1955); In re Armand, 454 A.2d 1216, 1219 (R.I. 1983); *but see* Terry v. Ohio, 392 U.S. 1, 34 (1968) (White, J., concurring) ("refusal to answer furnishes no basis for arrest").

Generally, one isolated suspicious act or furtive gesture will not be sufficient to justify a reasonable suspicion. For example, if a student merely hesitates when responding to questions or casually attempts to avoid such encounters, the student cannot immediately be suspected of an infraction. Those observations could only support a reasonable suspicion in combination with other complementary facts or because of the extent to which they are manifested by a student. For example, an official might reasonably suspect a student who engages in many different furtive gestures or who makes an extreme effort at avoidance. *See* In re S.K., 647 A.2d 952 (Pa. Super. 1994) (student's "furtive activity" (e.g., turning away from school officer, walking toward a bathroom stall, and touching pockets in random fashion) enhanced reasonable suspicion already present (smell of cigarette smoke and student's admission of smoking)).

(2) *Demeanor.* The mere fact that a student appears nervous, agitated, or excited in an official's presence does not by itself convey a reasonable suspicion that she or he has committed an

infraction. Likewise, showing an awareness of the official's presence or acting startled upon seeing the official is not a sufficient basis to "reasonably suspect" an infraction.

Typically, the demeanor of students can only give added weight to other known facts which themselves bear some indication of a reasonably suspected infraction. Coffman v. State, 782 S.W.2d 249, 250 (Tex. App. 1989) (a student, out of class without an excuse, first ignored an assistant principal and then became excited and aggressive, clutching his book bag behind him; such behavior is enough for reasonable suspicion).

(3) *Unusual physical state.* The observation that a student's physical state appears out of the ordinary may give a sufficient basis to "reasonably suspect" an infraction. For example, if a student is obviously under the influence of drugs or alcohol, officials may be justified in suspecting the possession or use of illicit substances. Shamberg v. State, 762 P.2d 488, 492 (Alaska App. 1988); Widener v. State, 809 F. Supp. 35, 38 (E.D. Pa. 1992) (student was observed "acting 'sluggish' and 'lethargic' or in a manner otherwise consistent with marijuana use"). Observations of this kind are often sufficient by themselves to justify a reasonable suspicion. However, the better practice is to have other corroborating facts before initiating any search. For example, it is not inconceivable that a student suffering an epileptic seizure may appear intoxicated. Consequently, a search of the student's person for drugs may violate the student's justified privacy expectations.

School officials are prohibited from using race or ethnic background to establish this type of suspicion.

(4) *Resemblance to a suspect's description.* In large schools, officials do not know everyone by name or even by sight. School officials may therefore sometimes have to act on the basis of valid reports or descriptions of a suspect.

School officials may use such descriptions as

the basis for suspecting a particular student provided: (a) the report or description is from a reliable source (*see* Section 3:7); (b) the description is more specific and detailed than a list of general characteristics that could fit many students; and (c) the suspected student fits the description in more than a vague or general way.

A valid suspect description must contain sufficient distinguishing points of comparison to eliminate most of the student population from suspicion. School officials should avoid relying on ethnic identifications alone because of the dangers of over-generalizations and of reinforcing stereotypes. Although the resemblance to a description must be more than general, it is not necessary that the suspect precisely match every one of several comparison points. Officials are permitted to assume that one or a very few descriptive elements might be in error.

(5)   *Attempts to flee from school officials.* Attempts to flee are highly suggestive of an infraction. Such behavior can be determinative when combined with other factors that already arouse suspicions. Thus, if there is already some indication that a particular student has committed an infraction, the student's flight at an official's approach might (in combination with other facts) provide the necessary basis for a reasonable suspicion. Peters v. New York, 392 U.S. 40, 66 (1968); In re Raul G., 2003 WL 1909376 (Cal. App. 2d Dist. 2003).

(6)   *Nature of the area: "Suspect" locations.* Sometimes officials can reasonably suspect a student of being involved with an infraction based on the nature of the area in which the student is observed. Schools have many "suspect" areas where certain infractions occur regularly. For example, students often gamble or smoke in rest rooms and under hidden stairwells. Other areas might be the "turf" where student gangs commit extortion and assault. *See, e.g.,* In re Frederick B., 237 Cal. Rptr. 338, 342–43 (Cal. App. 1987).

In most cases, simply being in the vicinity of a suspected area is not sufficient to justify the reasonable suspicion of an infraction. *See, e.g.*, M.S. v. State, 808 So. 2d 1263 (Fla. Dist. Ct. App. 4th Dist. 2002) (ruling that reasonable suspicion did not exist to search a student based on the fact that another student he was with had run into the administration building after which marijuana had been found in the administration building bathroom). It is probably best to use the illicit nature of suspected areas as a means of interpreting or giving meaning to other suspicious observations and circumstances.

(7) *Nearness to the scene of an infraction.* Sometimes officials can reasonably suspect a student because of spatial or temporal proximity to the scene of an infraction. Obviously, a student who is actually present at the scene of an infraction becomes highly suspect.

Spatial and temporal proximity can also be a factor when all officials have is a suspect's description. To assess the possibility that bona fide suspects can be identified on the basis of proximity, one must consider: (a) whether the suspect's description is sufficiently particular (see above); (b) the range of possible flight (i.e., how much physical distance can be attained from the time of an incident to observation of the suspect); (c) whether there are many students in the vicinity who might match the suspect's description; (d) if there is a known or probable direction of flight that might focus attention to a more restricted area; (e) whether a particular suspicion based on proximity is further corroborated by other suspicious conduct or furtive gestures (see above); and (f) whether there are linkages with other related infractions for which more detailed suspect descriptions are available. People v. Mascarenas, 666 P.2d 101, 108 (Colo. 1983).

A student may be suspected of a nearby infraction to the extent that the student more than generally matches a suspect's description, is found within the possible range and probable direction of flight, and manifests other suspicious conduct.

(8) *Student's prior history.* School officials may
sometimes use the student's prior record of
infractions to corroborate a presently held reasonable suspicion. This might occur when they
observe suspicious conduct that is consistent with
or plausibly related to prior infractions. For
example, a student previously disciplined for
vandalizing school property with spray paint
might be suspected of repeating that offense if
observed hiding a can of spray paint. State v.
Drake, 662 A.2d 265 (N.H. 1995) (an anonymous
informant's tip that a student would be carrying
drugs with him to school that day taken in light
of existing suspicions and reports about his drug
involvement was "more than enough" to justify a
search); In re S.F., 607 A.2d 793 (Pa. Super.
1992) (rumors of student's prior involvement with
narcotics, plus observation of his nervously carrying a clear plastic bag and a wad of bills, were
found to be sufficient to establish reasonable
suspicion to justify a search); Coffman v. State,
782 S.W.2d 249, 250 (Tex. App. 1989) (when a
student had been disciplined on three or four
prior occasions, a school official can use that
knowledge to corroborate the need for a search
when the student behaves suspiciously and is
out of class without permission); State v. Brooks,
718 P.2d 837, 839 (Wash. App. 1986) (when an
informant provides information that the student
is selling drugs from his locker, knowledge of
three prior reports of that student using drugs
can be used to justify a search).

Although a student's prior record can have cor-
roborative value, that record alone does not
justify the harassing, opportunistic, or arbitrary
suspicion of any student.

Note that school officials can only consider the
student's official record of infractions or other
demonstrable facts. They cannot rely on some
vague or unsubstantiated assertion that the
student may be a bad character. In re Pima
County Juvenile Action, 733 P.2d 316, 317 (Ariz.
App. 1987) (although a student's name had been

mentioned in a staff meeting in connection with drugs, no specific information justified a search).

§ 3:6 Defining the term—Factors related to the nexus between infraction, object, and place

To search a student lawfully, officials must not only suspect an infraction but also must link the item sought to that infraction and a particular place.

Each required relationship stands alone. Even if they are absolutely certain of finding something in a particular location, no search is permitted if the item cannot be connected with a specific infraction. Similarly, if they only know that something is the fruit of an infraction but not where it may be presently located, no search is permissible.

(1) *The item-infraction link.* Items sought as fruits, instruments, and contraband will generally have a self-evident connection with specific infractions (*see* Section 3:4). Warden v. Hayden, 387 U.S. 294, 307 (1967). Other evidence can be linked by establishing that it contributes to the determination of innocence or guilt.

Thus, the item-infraction link should follow directly from the reasonable suspicion that connects a particular student with some specific infraction. For example, if officials suspect a particular student of vandalizing the control valve of a fire sprinkler system, their search may reasonably be directed at instruments of the crime such as a wrench. A victim reporting a robbery of a distinctively marked purse at knife point reasonably links those items to the crime as fruit and instrument respectively.

Note that the item-infraction link must be based on at least a reasonable suspicion. No search is permitted if officials have only an unsupported hunch that something may be connected with an infraction.

(2) *The item-place link.* The most vexing problem here is to establish a reasonable suspicion about the present location of sought-after items. To develop this link, school officials must explain how and why the item is believed to be presently located in the particular place to be searched.

Sometimes, officials will have direct observations or information from other valid sources that create a sufficient item-place link. In other cases, the link will be given by reasonable inferences relating to the location or nature of the infraction, or surrounding circumstances. Because schools have relatively few protected places where students can conceal items, this requirement may sometimes be easy to meet. *See* Section 2:3.

Under some circumstances it may be reasonable to assume that items related to a past infraction are still to be found in a particular place where the infraction is known to have occurred. If a student is known to have regularly sold drugs from her or his car, for example, it might be reasonable to suspect that drugs are still to be found there.

Occasionally, the location of related items can be reasonably inferred from the nature of an infraction. For example, it is reasonable to assume that large or bulky stolen property will be hidden in large containers such as a student's locker rather than in her small purse. Similarly, some very valuable contraband is not likely to be hidden in a knapsack that the student casually leaves out of his direct control for long periods.

Sometimes, the circumstances under which an infraction is detected may give a reasonable inference about the location of related items. For example, an official might happen upon a student vandalizing food on the cafeteria loading dock. In this situation, it is reasonable to suspect that instruments of that offense may be found on the student's person. *See also* In re Doe, 887 P.2d 645 (Haw. 1994) (search of a student's purse based on suspicion of smoking marijuana was reasonable because a purse is the "most probable place for concealing a plastic bag of marijuana and related paraphernalia").

In many cases, the inferences school officials reach may not give an exclusive suspicion, but will only narrow the range of possible suspected locations. If the reasonably suspected location of an item can be narrowed to only a few places, then they may search all of the suspected places. Wynn v. Board of Educ., 508 So. 2d 1170, 1171–72 (Ala. 1987) (a search for missing money involving a student's books, desk, purse, and shoes is reasonable when the student was one of two suspects). Note that this guideline does not provide authority to conduct roving exploratory searches. In re Dumas, 515 A.2d 984, 986 (Pa. Super. 1986) (when a student's infraction was possessing cigarettes and an assistant principal seized them, no grounds existed to search the student's locker and jacket). Officials must have at least a level of reasonable suspicion that focuses on only a few places. This rule allows them to search when the true location of an item is about as likely to be at one of a few places as another. No search is permitted if the level of suspicion is not sufficient or the item "could be anywhere."

§ 3:7 Defining the term—Valid sources of information for a reasonable suspicion

This section looks at valid sources of information that officials can rely on to support a reasonable suspicion. In the school setting these sources of information include: (1) personal observations and knowledge; (2) the reliable reports of other school officials; (3) reports of eyewitnesses and victims; and (4) informant tips.

Various standards of reliability have evolved in the law for each informational source. School officials must confirm that applicable standards are generally satisfied before relying on any source.

    (1) *The official's personal observations and knowledge.* Perhaps the most reliable basis for a reasonable suspicion is something the official observes directly and interprets in light of knowledge and experience. This direct observation assures an accurate recounting of what facts were known and how they were interpreted to arrive at any suspicions motivating a search.

School officials have special background, training, expertise, skills, experiences, and other specific knowledge (of their own schools) that give them an acute perspective for interpreting any observations in the school setting. It is generally accepted therefore that school officials may see something suspicious in student conduct that might not be recognized by the casual or untrained observer.

Because of these special skills and experiences, school officials are not limited to the objective facts at hand when justifying a reasonable suspicion. They can draw relevant inferences (even from fragmented or disparate facts) by relying on personal skills, experiences, insight, and expertise. For example, they might reasonably suspect a student of committing some offense because of direct observations and knowledge of that student's disciplinary record. Similarly, they might reasonably suspect the possession of a dangerous flammable compound or prohibited substance like marijuana because of their familiarity with its distinctive odor. *Compare* In re Johnny F., 2002 WL 397046 (Cal. App. 2d Dist. 2002), unpublished/noncitable, (Mar. 14, 2002) and review denied, (June 12, 2002) (explaining that the security aide "was familiar with the odor of marijuana from having confiscated it from students"), Rinker v. Sipler, 264 F. Supp. 2d 181, 178 Ed. Law Rep. 730 (M.D. Pa. 2003) (ruling that a school official had the individualized reasonable suspicion necessary to conduct a search for drugs based on the official's determination that the student *"looked stoned, smelled of marijuana and was somewhat incoherent"*), Com. v. Lawrence L., 439 Mass. 817, 792 N.E.2d 109, 178 Ed. Law Rep. 919 (2003) (ruling that probable cause for a search existed after a vice-principal confronted a student who was "reeking" with the odor of marijuana, when the vice-principal knew that the student had been found with marijuana in his pocket a month earlier and after the student gave an ambiguous answer to the question whether he had been smoking marijuana), and Com. v. Lawrence L., 439 Mass. 817, 792 N.E.2d 109, 178 Ed. Law Rep. 919 (2003) (ruling that a school official had probable cause to search a student who "reeked" of marijuana), with A.H. v. State, 846 So. 2d 1215, 177 Ed. Law Rep. 1250 (Fla. Dist. Ct. App. 5th Dist. 2003) (ruling that the suspicion of a physical education teacher with no special training on drugs that because a student's speech was slurred, he was "on something," was not sufficient to constitute reasonable suspicion). A suspect's action in walking away from school officials can serve to amplify suspicion, In re Raul G., 2003 WL 1909376 (Cal. App. 2d Dist. 2003), but such actions are also subject to being misinterpreted.

The observations of the school officials must actually support the suspicion that school rules are being violated. A Florida court ruled, for instance, that a teacher's observation that a student was not "acting himself" and had bloodshot eyes was not sufficient to establish the "reasonable suspicion" necessary for a search. A.N.H. v. State, 832 So. 2d 170 (Fla. Dist. Ct. App. 3d Dist. 2002). The court explained that these observations

can result from a variety of non-criminal circumstances, including the appearance and behavior associated with a common cold. The Supreme Court has unequivocally stated that a seizure is not justified when factual circumstances can describe a large category of presumably innocent people. Reid v. Georgia, 448 U.S. 438, 100 S. Ct. 2752, 65 L. Ed. 2d 890 (1980). A.N.H.'s physical state was consistent with innocence, and thus could not give rise to reasonable grounds to suspect that he was involved in some criminal activity.

A.N.H. v. State, 832 So. 2d 170 at 172 (Fla. Dist. Ct. App. 3d Dist. 2002).

Caution: Suspicions cannot be based only on a general unsubstantiated claim of expertise. Sullivan v. State, 626 S.W.2d 58, 60 (Tex. Crim. App. 1982) (a statement such as "in my personal and professional opinion" is not a showing of specialized knowledge). Officials must be able to explain the nature and extent of any special skills, experience, or expertise that contributed to their suspicion. For example, they might cite the completion of a special police training program teaching marijuana recognition as the basis for suspecting that a student possessed that contraband when a distinctive odor emanated from the student's knapsack. People v. Poole, 48 Cal. App. 3d 881, 886, 122 Cal. Rptr. 87, 89 (1975).

See also State ex rel Juvenile Dep't of Lincoln County v. Finch, 925 P.2d 913 (Or. App. 1996) (holding that the decision of an assistant principal to search a jacket for a weapon because the jacket "seemed heavier than . . . what a jacket should have been" was not justified by a reasonable suspicion because the additional weight could have been caused by a benign item such as a 35 mm camera lens).

(2) *Reliable reports of other school officials.* School officials can reliably base a reasonable suspicion on the reports of another official. Such action is valid even if they are ignorant of the reporting official's basis of suspicion. Any related search conducted will be valid as long as the other official's suspicions are supported by articulable and sufficient facts. State v. Hill, 3 Ohio App. 3d 10, 443 N.E.2d 198, 200 (1981). Thus, even without knowing all of the facts, officials can lawfully suspect a student of possessing dangerous contraband based on the reported suspicions of a teacher. United States v. Hensley, 469 U.S. 221, 232 (1985) (information contained in one police district's wanted flyer can be used by another district as a basis for a search).

Courts also recognize a general presumption of reliability for any observations related to one official by another official. This provision is not, however, a panacea for faulty suspicions. A defective suspicion (e.g., *see* Section 3:8) is not magically transformed into valid grounds for a search simply because another official reports it. The best practice is to confirm the reporting official's basis of suspicion before proceeding with any action. If the other official could have conducted a lawful search based on that official's suspicions, then the searching official may also do so based on the report. Sometimes another official will pass on information or clues about an infraction, but not any specific suspicions. The searching official may use this information as long as it is reasonably selective and factual.

(3) *Reports of eyewitnesses and victims.* School officials will often receive reports from eyewitnesses or victims of an infraction. A distinction is usually made between eyewitnesses or victims and informants (*see* (4) below). Jaben v. United States, 381 U.S. 214, 224 (1965). Unlike informants, eyewitnesses and victims do not generally have much involvement with illicit undercurrents in school and they are not privileged to know much about illegal activities. United States v. Lewis, 738 F.2d 916, 922 (8th Cir. 1984). Eyewitnesses and victims are also viewed as having a "public-spirited" desire to assist in the enforcement of rules. They are motivated by a concern for the general well-being of their school. Consequently, there is less skepticism about the information they provide. In fact, eyewitness and victim reports are often considered presumptively reliable and officials will have less trouble justifying a reasonable suspicion based on such reports as compared with informant tips. Chambers v. Maroney, 399 U.S. 42, 46–47 (1970).

Despite the presumption of reliability, it is still proper to evaluate the basis of knowledge and veracity of any eyewitness or victim report. The determination that such reports are reliable requires a showing of:

- the facts that underlie the eyewitness' or victim's report, and
- the factors that caused the official to believe the report was credible.

Basis of knowledge. Establishing a proper basis of knowledge should not be difficult in proper cases. Normally, it will suffice to demonstrate that the student was in a position to observe what she or he reported. In most cases, eyewitnesses will be reporting their firsthand experience as a victim or the direct observation of some infraction. United States v. Ross, 713 F.2d 389, 393 (8th Cir. 1983).

School officials should be cautious about any reported facts that cannot be properly interpreted without some expertise. Facts of that sort cannot be used without a demonstration of the eyewitness or victim's expertise. For example, suppose an eyewitness reports smelling marijuana among the possessions of another student. That report would call for some explanation about how the eyewitness is qualified to identify marijuana by smell. Patty v. Commonwealth, 218 Va. 150, 235 S.E.2d 437, 439 (1977).

Veracity/credibility. Again it should not normally be difficult to establish the credibility of eyewitness or victim reports. Eyewitnesses and victims are regarded as presumptively reliable reporters of fact because of their altruistic motivations and firsthand exposure. Chambers v. Maroney, 399 U.S. 42, 46–47 (1970). Usually, it will be sufficient if some details of the report can be corroborated. United States v. Wilson, 479 F.2d 936, 940–41 (7th Cir. 1973). But even here the degree of verification required is comparatively modest.

Caution is advised when officials receive an "eyewitness" or "victim" report so detailed and intimate that it suggests more than an innocent knowledge about illicit activities in school. In that case it may be more correct to treat the report as an informant tip which is subject to much closer scrutiny.

Sufficiency. A major concern officials should have about eyewitness and victim reports is whether they provide proper justification for a search. Because eyewitnesses and victims are not "insiders," they will not always have the full story about an infraction. Their reports will frequently provide sufficient basis to reasonably suspect the commission of an infraction, and perhaps even the particular student who committed it, but these suspicions are not by themselves sufficient to permit a search. There must in addition be proper relationships between the infraction, the item, and the place (Section 3:3). School officials must examine all the relevant circumstances carefully to determine whether these requirements are satisfied.

A report involving a student's possession of a weapon or firearm on campus, however, may add weight to a school official's decision to investigate the allegation, possibly with a search. In re Joseph G., 38 Cal. Rptr. 2d 902 (Cal. App. 1995) (fact that a citizen-informant identified herself and named a particular student are "factors which weigh in favor of investigating the truth of her accusation . . . particularly when weighed against 'the gravity of the danger posed by possession of a firearm or weapon on campus'") (citations omitted).

Even if eyewitness and victim reports may not themselves justify a search, they can provide sufficient reason for an investigative stop (Chapter 5). Results of that investigation may subsequently furnish justification for a search.

(4)   *Informant tips.* School officials can validly base a reasonable suspicion on tips and information provided by student informants. These students are distinguishable from innocent eyewitnesses or victims by being so much a part of the illicit undercurrent in schools that they come to know about many illegal activities. Because of their connection to illicit activity, the veracity of informant tips cannot be assumed.

To justify a reasonable suspicion based on informant tips officials must be able to:

● show the basis of the informant's knowledge, and

● explain what underlying factors or circumstances caused the official to believe the tip was credible.

Officials cannot simply recount the informant's unsupported opinions or make conclusory assertions about the informant's reliability. An explicit demonstration is required.

Basis of knowledge. To explain the basis of an informant's knowledge, officials must be concerned with the nature of the informant's perceptions and reasoning. The first part of that inquiry is addressed by showing either (a) that the informant made a direct firsthand observation, or, if no source is explicitly mentioned (b) that the tip contains sufficient incriminating detail about the infraction to suggest strongly that it is not merely a casual rumor. State v. Dixon, 337 So. 2d 1165, 1167 (La. 1976). The second part of thisinquiry requires a showing that the informant did not relate any conclusions based on faulty or illogical reasoning.

In sum, officials should be skeptical about any tip containing secondhand rumors or faulty reasoning. They should also be wary of any tip based on facts that require some expertise for proper interpretation. For example, tips that a student possesses drugs or counterfeit currency or sold "something illegal" may require that an official show how the informant is qualified to identify drugs or counterfeit money. Patty v. Commonwealth, 235 S.E.2d at 439.

Veracity/credibility. Reliance on the credibility of a tip can be justified by showing: (a) that the informant had some motive for speaking truthfully (other than for compensation or immunity) (United States v. Ross, 713 F.2d 389, 393 (8th Cir. 1983) (informant had no reason to falsify the information)); (b) that some significant incriminating detail is verified by a credible source (e.g., the school official's direct observations) (Carter v. United States, 729 F.2d 935, 939 (8th Cir. 1984)); (c) that the informant admitted to a similar infraction (on the premise that no rational person would risk being sanctioned simply to provide a false tip) (United States v. Harris, 403 U.S. 573, 583 (1971)); or (d) that other students can corroborate the tip (Jones v. United States, 362 U.S. 257, 271 (1960)).

Sometimes the fact that an informant has previously furnished reliable information can contribute to the credibility of the tip. Jones v. United States, 362 U.S. 257, 271 (1960). This factor is seldom determinative, however. The only real concern is whether the tip at hand is truthful. An informant's past reliability provides little factual indication about the present truthfulness of the tip.

Anonymous informants. Occasionally, school officials will receive anonymous tips. Although extreme caution is advised, anonymous tips can provide the basis for a valid reasonable suspicion. Anonymous tips are generally upheld when: (a) the anonymous informant stands to gain nothing by providing the tip; (b) the information is inherently plausible because it relates to a well known or ongoing problem; (c) there are indications of prior reliability (e.g., the informant's voice sounds like the same tipster who previously furnished accurate information); or (d) the tip is detailed, specific, and timely and not a vague blanket accusation having no reference to time, location, or quantity. Martens v. District No. 220, Bd. of Educ., 620 F. Supp. 29, 32 (D.C. Ill. 1985). *But see* Florida v. J.L., 529 U.S. 266, 120 S. Ct. 1375, 146 L. Ed. 2d 254 (2000) (ruling that an anonymous tip was not sufficient to justify a frisk); In re A.T.H., 106 S.W.3d 338, 344 (Tex. App. Austin 2003) (explaining that a tip from an unidentified caller was insufficient to establish the reasonable suspicion necessary to justify a search for marijuana); In re K.C.B., 141 S.W.3d 303 (Tex. App. Austin 2004) (holding that a tip from an anonymous student without any supporting details was not sufficient to justify a search for marijuana, but also adding that it might be sufficient to justify a search for a weapon because of the greater governmental interest in ensuring safe schools); In re Doe, 104 Haw. 403, 91 P.3d 485, 188 Ed. Law Rep. 979 (2004), as amended, (June 2, 2004) concluding that an anonymous tip stating only that a certain student had marijuana and was selling it on campus, without any other details, did not provide the reasonable suspicion needed to justify a search of the student).

Officials should be especially leery of tips that are no more detailed than might be reported by any casual passerby or if the informant demonstrates no special familiarity with the affairs of the accused student. Commonwealth v. Cruse, 236 Pa. Super. 85, 344 A.2d 532, 535 (1975) (when information passed to authorities anonymously is of a type available to anyone, authorities must investigate further in order to corroborate the tip).

§ 3:8 Defining the term—Examples of reasonable suspicion based on the report of an eyewitness or informant

(1) A search of the accused student's locker conducted after a witness implicated him in a theft was held to be reasonable. R.D.L. v. State, 499 So. 2d 31 (Fla. App. 1986).

(2) A student informant whose school locker was in the same bay as that of the defendant told the

vice principal that the defendant kept a blue metal box in his locker from which he was selling marijuana. The reasonableness of the vice principal's search was buttressed by her own observations and three prior reports by teachers of defendant's suspected drug use. Hallucinogenic mushrooms were subsequently found in the box. State v. Brooks, 718 P.2d 837 (Wash. App. 1986).

(3)   An unnamed student told the school principal that the accused student sold drugs at school. This information was held to have provided grounds for a search. The search was found to be reasonably related to the school's objective of keeping drugs off school premises. In re M.H., 401 N.W.2d 28 (Wis. App. 1986).

(4)   The swimming coach informed two assistant principals that a student had told him that the defendant had tried to sell marijuana to the student. The court held that the student-informant's statement to the coach constituted an eyewitness account of a breach of school rules and the law, which "may be presumed reliable, although police and other government officials must remain alert to the existence of particular circumstances that would indicate unreliability." State v. Michael G., 748 P.2d 17, 20 (N.M. App. 1987) (citing 1 W. LaFave, Search and Seizure, § 3.4(a)(2d ed. 1987)).

(5)   A police officer was told by a minor that two other minors, M.M. and F.M., possessed marijuana with intent to sell. Subsequent searches of M.M. and F.M. uncovered no contraband. When they were asked how they came to school that day, they said they had come in P.E.A.'s car. The subsequent search of P.E.A.'s car was deemed to be reasonable. In re P.E.A., 754 P.2d 382, 389 (Colo. 1988).

(6)   A teacher in the school library informed the assistant principal that a student appeared to be under the influence of alcohol. The assistant principal sent the school's security officer to the library, where the teacher pointed out the

student in question. The security officer, upon seeing that the student's eyes were glassy, his face was flushed, and his speech was slurred, questioned the student. The security officer and the assistant principal then conducted a search of the student's car, which turned up vials of cocaine kept in the car's ashtray. The search was held to be reasonable. Shamberg v. State, 762 P.2d 488 (Alaska App. 1988).

(7)   One student reported that the accused student possessed cocaine. The subsequent search was held to be based on reasonable suspicion. In re Corey L., 250 Cal. Rptr. 359 (Cal. App. 1988).

(8)   Two students implicated the plaintiff in a bomb threat that had been made to the school by telephone. The seizure and interrogation of the plaintiff by the school principal was held to be justified at its inception, and because of the serious nature of the suspected offense, the scope of the interrogation was held to be reasonable. Edwards v. Rees, 883 F.2d 882, 884 (10th Cir. 1989).

(9)   Upon separating two gangs who were about to clash, a school dean was told by one of the gang members that a member of a third group of students, observing the confrontation, had a gun. The dean instructed a police officer to search the implicated student, and a machete knife and scabbard were subsequently found inside the student's trouser leg. The uncorroborated information provided by an unidentified informant was held to justify the reasonableness of the search. In re Alexander B., 270 Cal. Rptr. 342 (Cal. App. 1990).

(10)   Two students decided to arrange to buy marijuana from defendant and then report defendant to the school principal. The defendant agreed to sell marijuana to one student, then later told the other student that he sold only tobacco products. This denial provoked an altercation which delivered the second student and the defendant to the principal's office, where the second student accused the defen-

dant of possessing marijuana. The principal's subsequent search of the defendant's jacket was held to be reasonable. Berry v. State, 561 N.E.2d 832 (Ind. App. 1990).

(11) A school administrator's preexisting knowledge of an earlier fight, plus the eyewitness report of two students that a gun linked to the fight was seen in the defendant's possession, together with the administrator's failure to find the gun on the defendant's person or at the places he had been most recently, justified the search of defendant's locker. Commonwealth v. Carey, 554 N.E.2d 1199 (Mass. 1990).

(12) After a student found with drugs implicated the accused student, school officials had abundant "articulable suspicion" to search the accused student. In re Devon T., 584 A.2d 1287, 1300 (Md. Spec. App. 1991).

(13) A student reported to the assistant principal that the accused student had tried to sell a gun to him at school. This information was held to be sufficient to provide reasonable grounds for a subsequent search of the accused student's locker. In re S.C. v. State, 583 So. 2d 188, 190 (Miss. 1991).

(14) A campus supervisor overheard two students, whom she believed to be "good" students, speaking to each other concerning a rumor that there was a gun on campus. She questioned the students, and one of them told her the student in question had been in possession of a gun the day before. A subsequent search of the student conducted in the vice principal's office—which discovered a gun and marijuana—was held to be justified. In re Dubois, 821 P.2d 1124 (Or. App. 1991).

(15) The behavior and appearance of a high school student attending a dance led a school monitor to believe the student was under the influence of alcohol. Subsequently, the monitor required two other students—who had been with the first student at a prior party—to blow in his face so he could smell their breath. The court held that

the monitor "had reasonable suspicion that the two [other students] had also consumed alcohol, and he was warranted in attempting to verify that fact." Martinez v. School Dist. No. 60, 852 P.2d 1275, 1278 (Colo. App. 1992).

(16)   A strip search conducted by a dean and a teacher was found reasonable because it was motivated by a series of tips associating the plaintiff with drug use, accompanied by apparent admissions made by plaintiff, an unusual bulge in his crotch area, and his furtive behavior. The tips, from a police officer, a teacher, a teacher's aide, students, and a school bus driver, were held to be reliable and cumulative. Although the search did not find any contraband, plaintiff's 28 U.S.C.A. Section 1983 claim for damages was dismissed. Cornfield v. Consolidated High Sch. Dist. 230, 991 F.2d 1316 (7th Cir. 1993).

(17)   An assistant principal was informed by a guidance counselor that she thought one of her students had a bag of marijuana, based on information from another student and on a prior incident where the defendant had been found with a burned marijuana cigarette. The subsequent search—which uncovered seventy-five vials of cocaine—was held to be justified at its inception. State v. Moore, 603 A.2d 513 (N.J. Super. App. Div. 1992).

(18)   A plainclothes police officer corroborated his observation of what appeared to be a drug sale with information he received prior to the event from six or seven people, both students and teachers, who had said that the accused student had been flashing large sums of money around and had narcotics. The subsequent search of the student conducted in the vice principal's office—which discovered numerous vials of cocaine—was held to be reasonable. In re S.F., 607 A.2d 793 (Pa. Super. 1992).

(19)   A high school principal's warrantless search of student's locker was reasonable where another student had told a reliable faculty member, who

in turn told the principal that the student had placed marijuana in a book bag. The principal could reasonably decide to search the locker for the book bag before confronting that student. Commonwealth v. Snyder, 597 N.E.2d 1363, 1368 (Mass. 1992).

(20)   A teacher overheard two students talking about drug activity on school grounds. A subsequent search of one of these students' lockers turned up marijuana. Marijuana was also retrieved from a cigarette package that the second student attempted to discard upon being called to the office. Finally, this second student directly implicated other students when asked by the assistant principal who else in school possessed marijuana. The court found that the totality of the circumstances was clearly sufficient to constitute reasonable suspicion to authorize the subsequent searches of the lockers and bookbags of the other identified students. People v. Taylor, 625 N.E.2d 785 (Ill. App. 1993).

(21)   A search of a student's pants pockets, uncovering drugs, was reasonable at its inception, when school officials brought the student into the office one day after receiving a credible report that the student was carrying a .25 automatic pistol. Wilcher v. State, 876 S.W.2d 466 (Tex. App. 1994).

(22)   The questioning of a student suspected of abusing a child was justified at its inception when the victim identified the student as her abuser. Doe v. Bagan, 41 F.3d 571, 573 n.3 (10th Cir. 1994).

(23)   Information provided by an informant that a student would be carrying a substantial amount of LSD with him to school that day taken together with existing suspicions of the student's involvement with drugs provided more than enough reasonable suspicion to justify a search of the student's pockets. An expanded search of the student's knapsack which uncovered a weapon was reasonable because of the discovery of a pipe, rolling papers, and a trace

amount of marijuana in the first search. State v. Drake, 662 A.2d 265 (N.H. 1995).

(24)   A woman's accusation that a student had stolen $150 from her and information that the student was in trouble with the police provided school officials with reasonable suspicion to conduct a search of the student's person and locker. Singleton v. Board of Educ. USD 500, 894 F. Supp. 386 (D. Kan. 1995).

(25)   A student informant's statement that another student had been drinking at a party the previous night coupled with the odor of alcohol detected by the vice principal and physical evidence indicating that the student had been at the party justified requiring the student to take a breathalyser test to measure his alcohol level prior to an early-morning field trip. Juran v. Independence Or. Central Sch. Dist. 13J, 898 F. Supp. 728 (D. Or. 1995).

(26)   Information from confidential informant that student was distributing drugs was sufficient to justify search of student's pen for drugs. State v. Biancamano, 666 A.2d 199 (N.J. App. 1995), cert. denied, 673 A.2d 275 (N.J. 1996).

(27)   Information from a confidential student informant that a shotgun would be found in the trunk of another student's car was sufficient to provide reasonable suspicion that the shotgun would be found in that car. Farias v. State, 1995 WL 737473 (Tex. App. 1995).

(28)   Information from a student informant of students believed to have stolen the school's locker combination book, coupled with a rash of locker break-ins, justified searching the book bag of one of the targeted students. S.A. v. State, 654 N.E.2d 791 (Ind. App. 1995).

(29)   Information from two teachers that defendant's friend was selling drugs coupled with defendant's suspicious behavior and defendant's possession of a "very unusual item"—a flashlight—provided reasonable suspicion to search the flashlight for contraband. People v. Dilworth, 169 Ill. 2d 195, 661 N.E.2d 310 (1996), cert. denied, 517 U.S. 1197 (1996).

(30)   Tip from student informant that another stu-
        dent was carrying drugs provided reasonable
        grounds to justify search. C.B. v. Driscoll, 82
        F.3d 383 (11th Cir. 1996), reh. & en banc hear-
        ing denied, 99 F.3d 1157 (11th Cir. 1996).

(31)   A tip from a previously reliable student that
        another student possessed LSD was sufficient
        to justify a search of the second student's
        wallet. Holland v. State, 1997 WL 7025 (Tex.
        App. 1997).

(32)   Information from an anonymous source that a
        male high school student had passed cigarettes
        to another student at the school cafeteria justi-
        fied a search of the student's pockets, which re-
        vealed 17 individually-wrapped foil packages of
        LSD. King v. State, 1997 WL 235475 (Tex. App.
        1997).

(33)   It was reasonable to search a student's book
        bag, pockets, shoes, and socks, based on the
        statement of another student that she had
        purchased marijuana from him. State v.
        Tinkham, 719 A.2d 580 (N.H. 1998).

(34)   A tip from an anonymous informant that a
        named Hispanic female eighth-grader was car-
        rying marijuana in her backpack was sufficient
        to justify a search of the backpack after the
        school official corroborated that a Hispanic
        eighth-grader with that name was carrying a
        backpack, and after the student admitted she
        was carrying a cigarette lighter, in violation of
        school rules. In the Matter of C.S., 1998 Tex.
        App. LEXIS 7436 (Tex. App. 1998).

(35)   A tip from a trustworthy student informant
        that a eighth-graders had been drinking beer in
        the girls' locker room was sufficient to seek the
        consent of the students to search their back-
        packs, lockers, pockets, shoes and socks. Green-
        leaf v. Cote, 77 F. Supp. 2d 168 (D. Me. 1999).

(36)   An unsolicited tip from a student that another
        student had something in his bag that he
        should not have, combined with an initial denial
        of the second student that the bag was his, was
        sufficient to constitute reasonable suspicion to

search the bag. In the Matter of Murray, 525
S.E.2d 496 (N.C.App. 2000).

(37) A tip from a student to the school's Crime Stop-
per organizer, who was also the school librar-
ian, that another student had marijuana concealed in the headband of his baseball hat was
sufficient to establish reasonable suspicion to
search the student's hat. In the Matter of L.A.,
21 P.3d 952 (Kan. 2001).

(38) Information from a substitute teacher, plus
suspicions based on student behavior and false
answers to reasonable questions, were sufficient
to justify a search of students. In re D.D., 146
N.C. App. 309, 554 S.E.2d 346, 158 Ed. Law
Rep. 855 (2001), appeal dismissed, review
denied, 354 N.C. 572, 558 S.E.2d 867 (2001).

(39) Statements by unnamed informants that a
student had a knife was sufficient to require
him to empty his pockets, which revealed a
lipstick tube, and the security supervisor was
justified in opening the tube because it was
something "a male would not ordinarily carry."
In re Aldo G., 2002 WL 86873 (Cal. App. 4th
Dist. 2002).

(40) Observation by a teacher of a knife being used
to open an orange juice container on a school
bus was sufficient to justify a pat-down search
of all eight students who were going to an auto
body shop for vocational training. Shade v. City
of Farmington, Minnesota, 309 F.3d 1054, 170
Ed. Law Rep. 529 (8th Cir. 2002).

(41) An Ohio court ruled that a search for drugs was
justified on the basis of a tip from a student
corroborated by what a teacher had overheard.
State v. Adams, 2002-Ohio-94, 2002 WL 27739
(Ohio Ct. App. 5th Dist. Licking County 2002).

(42) An Illinois court that a tip from one student
was sufficient to justify the search of a student's
car for a handgun, particularly in light of the
danger presented by such a weapon on campus.
People v. Williams, 339 Ill. App. 3d 956, 274 Ill.
Dec. 516, 791 N.E.2d 608, 178 Ed. Law Rep.
453 (2d Dist. 2003).

(43)   Another case where the court may have relaxed
        the reasonable suspicion standard somewhat in
        light of the danger presented is In re Ana E.,
        2002 WL 264325 (N.Y. Fam. Ct. 2002), where
        the court upheld a search of the bag of a female
        student who was fighting with another female
        student, noting the "hysterical state of the
        student," "her threat to make the other student
        bleed," and the reluctance of the student's
        classmates to give the school official the book-
        bag. When searched, a knife was found in the
        bag.

(44)   A California federal court ruled that sufficient
        reasonable suspicion was provided by unidenti-
        fied parent calling from a car near the school
        who provided a contemporaneous, real-time de-
        scription of a nonstudent who was bringing a
        20-gauge shotgun tucked into his shorts onto
        the school grounds. U.S. v. Aguilera, 287 F.
        Supp. 2d 1204, 183 Ed. Law Rep. 137 (E.D. Cal.
        2003). The court also explained that extending
        "the *T.L.O.* standard to non-student visitors
        who present a credible threat of physical harm
        to students on campus would seem a small and
        logical step."

§ 3:9 Defining the term—Other examples of reasonable suspicion

(1)   A class had accumulated nine dollars for a class
        project, which was placed in an envelope and
        given to one student for safekeeping. All stu-
        dents except for the accused student and an-
        other student left the room. When the others
        returned, the envelope and money were missing.
        The teacher told the other students to search
        the accused student's books and person, which
        they did. The court held "that the very limited
        search that occurred was not excessively intru-
        sive and was reasonably related to the objective
        of the search." Wynn v. Board of Educ., 508 So.
        2d 1170, 1172 (Ala. 1987).

(2)   A school police officer observed two students
        exchanging paper currency in an area where

the officer had earlier made narcotics-related detainments. One of the students refused to accompany the officer to the dean's office, and then attempted to flee. The student was wrestled to the ground, handcuffed, and searched. The court ruled that reasonable suspicion for the search existed, based on the observance of money exchanging hands in an area known for drug-related transactions. In re Frederick B., 237 Cal. Rptr. 338, 342–43 (Cal. App. 1987).

(3) The assistant principal, who had disciplined the accused student on three or four prior occasions, asked for the student's hall pass upon seeing him in the hall during class hours. The principal testified that the student appeared nervous, excited, and aggressive. When the principal asked the student to open his bag, the student refused and then tried to flee. The court found the assistant principal's suspicion to be reasonable in light of (a) the student's prior propensity to get in trouble and (b) his being in the hall without a hall pass. Coffman v. State, 782 S.W.2d 249, 250 (Tex. App. 1989).

(4) A student told the school's vice principal that the defendant was selling marijuana in the parking lot. The vice principal believed the information to be reliable because of his past experience with the informant, and because he had received other reports that the defendant was involved with drugs. When the vice principal searched the accused student, he found a slip of paper with a telephone pager number on it. He knew pagers were often used by drug dealers. A security officer searched the student's locker but found nothing. The officials found a pager and a notebook inside the student's car; the notebook had names with dollar amounts next to the names. When officials found a locked briefcase in the car's trunk, the accused student said he did not know who owned it, then said it was a friend's and that he did not know the combination. When the officials pried open the

briefcase they found 80.2 grams of marijuana. The searches were held to be reasonable. State v. Slattery, 787 P.2d 932 (Wash. App. 1990).

(5)   A student complained that a portable radio he had brought to school was missing. A school official went to the coat rack to pat down the students' jackets. When he felt something very heavy in one jacket, he asked the jacket's owner what it was, and was told that it was a gun. The pat-down of the jackets was held to be reasonable. In re L.J., 468 N.W.2d 211 (Wis. App. 1991).

(6)   A student informed a security guard that he needed to obtain a new security card. In accordance with school policy, he had to leave his bookbag with the guard. When the student tossed the bag onto a metal cabinet, an unusual thud alerted the guard, who rubbed his hand along the bottom of the bag and felt the outline of a gun. A school dean subsequently searched the bag. The unusual metal thud, while itself insufficient to furnish a reasonable suspicion that the bag contained a weapon, was sufficient to justify the investigative touching of the outside of the bag. When the touching disclosed the presence of a gun-like object, only then was there reasonable suspicion to justify the search of the inside of the bag. In re Gregory M., 627 N.E.2d 500 (N.Y. 1993).

(7)   After being alerted of a fight allegedly involving students and weapons, school security personnel observed a student in the vicinity of the fight scene, coming out of some nearby bushes. During the course of an investigatory stop, a security guard noticed a plastic baggie in the student's pocket, which was later determined to contain cocaine. The court ruled that the guard had reasonable suspicion to suspect that a search would uncover evidence of a violation of the law. State v. Serna, 860 P.2d 1320 (Ariz. App. 1993).

(8)   A school security officer entered a restroom and smelled cigarette smoke. He saw a student who,

upon seeing the officer, turned and walked in the direction of a stall. Upon being questioned, the student admitted that he was smoking. The officer also observed the student fidgeting with his pockets. He then searched the student's pocket and retrieved a pack of cigarettes. He then searched further and found in another of the student's pockets what later proved to be crack cocaine. The court found that the student's admission of smoking and the smell of cigarette smoke created enough reasonable suspicion to conduct the search for cigarettes. The other observed "furtive" behavior merely enhanced this reasonable suspicion. The court also ruled the second search reasonable because finding the pack of cigarettes in the first search justified the second. In re S.K., 647 A.2d 952 (Pa. Super. 1994).

(9) During school hours, two school officials found four students at an area across the street from the high school. The area was known as a place where students congregated and smoked cigarettes and marijuana. The officials smelled the odor of burning marijuana. Other than the four, no other persons were in the area. A search of one of the student's purse revealed a small bag of marijuana. The court held that the search was justified at its inception based on the odor of marijuana detected and the students' presence at the suspect area. The search was also reasonable in scope because it was limited to the student's purse, the "most probable place" a teenage girl would conceal marijuana, and because it ceased once the contraband was found. In re Doe, 887 P.2d 645 (Haw. 1994).

(10) Reasonable suspicion to seize and search a student's jacket was based on a teacher's "direct knowledge of defendant's increasingly disruptive behavior, his previous comments regarding weapons and damage to staff, his physical aggression toward [the teacher] and defendant's intent to continue the confrontation with the other student despite [the teacher's] efforts to

diffuse the situation." People v. McKinney, 655 N.E.2d 40, 44 (Ill. App. 1995).

(11)   A certified drug addiction counselor was conducting a smoking cessation class at New Trier High School in Illinois, when she began to suspect that a ninth-grader behaving erratically might be under the influence of drugs. She took the student into an adjacent room and instructed a nurse to give him a limited physical examination, including taking his blood pressure. He also told the student to remove his outer shirt and empty his pockets. The U.S. Court of Appeals for the Seventh Circuit ruled that the symptoms identified by the counselor—dilated pupils, bloodshot eyes, and unruly behavior—"were sufficient to ground [her] suspicion." The search was thus deemed to be reasonable and not unduly intrusive, even though it uncovered no marijuana or other drugs and even though a drug test taken the next day revealed definitively that he had not been using marijuana. Bridgman v. New Trier Township High Sch. Dist. 203, 128 F.3d 1146 (7th Cir. 1997). The Bridgman decision was followed in Hedges v. Musco, 204 F.3d 109 (3d Cir. 2000), where the court rejected the claim brought by parents of a high school student who was forced to submit to a urinalysis and forced blood extraction after she was suspected of being high on marijuana or alcohol. The court ruled that the search was reasonable because her uncharacteristic gregariousness, her flushed face, her glassy eyes, her dilated pupils, and her abnormal behavior all provided "particularized and objective basis" for a medical examination. Id. at 117 (quoting from United States v. Cortez, 449 U.S. 411, 417–18 (1981)).

(12)   A student who had violated the school's no-smoking policy on five occasions during the previous seven weeks was found by a teacher in the boys' bathroom when he should have been in class. The teacher escorted the student to the vice-principal's office. The vice-principal

noticed the odor of smoke coming from the student and asked him to empty his pockets. The student voluntarily complied. One of the items he removed was a wallet five inches long and one inch thick. The vice-principal asked the student to open the wallet, and when he did a baggie fell out that appeared to contain marijuana. The vice-principal then called the city police department, and the student was arrested for possession of marijuana within 1000 feet of a school. The Wisconsin Court of Appeals ruled that each step of the search process was reasonable in light of the information available to the school officials. State v. Marola, 1998 WL 237638 (Wis. App. 1998) (unpublished opinion).

(13)   It was reasonable for school officials to search the pockets, shoes, book bag, and locker of a student who had arrived late to school, smelled like marijuana, and admitted he was standing with people who were smoking marijuana that morning. Bartram v. Pennsbury School District, 1999 U.S. Dist. LEXIS 7916 (E.D. Pa. 1999).

(14)   A school police officer had reasonable suspicion to search a student who was staggering in the hallway, with his eyes closed, and who spoke with slurred speech. Commonwealth v. J.B., 719 A.2d 1058 (Pa. Super. 1998).

(15)   After a fire in the boys' restroom burned part of the wall and ceiling tiles, it was reasonable for the assistant principal to search a 14-year-old boy with behaviorial and learning problems who had previously been found smoking in school restrooms and who was in the vicinity of the restroom at the time of the fire. State v. D.K.G., 1999 Wash. App. LEXIS 713 (Wash. App. 1999).

(16)   A New York court found that it was reasonable to search an individual at a high school who did not have an appropriate identification card, could not identify a single teacher or counselor at the school, was wearing indicia of gang affiliation, and had been approached by another individual in a threatening manner. People v. Butler, 725 N.Y.S.2d 534, 540 (N.Y.Sup. 2001).

(17)   A Texas court ruled that a school principal and school police officer had reasonable suspicion to search a student after seeing him smoking in the parking lot, wearing baggy shorts, "messing with" a pocket in these shorts, and refusing to empty his pocket when asked. Russell v. State, 74 S.W.3d 887, 165 Ed. Law Rep. 829 (Tex. App. Waco 2002).

(18)   A Florida court ruled that reasonable suspicion for a search existed after a baggie of marijuana was found close to a student, the student was known to associate with persons who smoked marijuana, and a note was found indicating that a plan existed to smoke marijuana. State v. N.G.B., 806 So. 2d 567, 162 Ed. Law Rep. 633 (Fla. Dist. Ct. App. 2d Dist. 2002).

(19)   A Texas court concluded that a search of a student's locker was reasonable based on an assistant principal's suspicion that the student had stolen credit cards, because the student was the only person who was in the office at the time of the theft. Shoemaker v. State, 971 S.W.2d 178, 127 Ed. Law Rep. 1117 (Tex. App. Beaumont 1998).

(20)   A California court ruled that reasonable suspicion for a search of a student's backpack and locker for stolen goods existed based the report from a campus assistant that the student had been "in the locker room, unsupervised, for an unusual length of time" plus the report of a teacher "that several items were missing from that same locker room." In re Karena B., 2003 WL 658696 (Cal. App. 4th Dist. 2003).

(21)   A Nebraska court ruled that a search of a student's car was justified based on a security officer having overheard the student telling another student he had some "big bags," a slang term for marijuana, and noted also that the student manual says that a student's vehicle (and locker) is subject to search if the school officials suspect that the student is in possession of illegal drugs. In re Michael R., 11 Neb. App. 903, 662 N.W.2d 632 (2003), review overruled, (Aug. 27, 2003).

(22)   A California state court ruled that a school law
        enforcement officer had reasonable suspicion
        take a student to the principal's office for disci-
        pline and conduct a pat-down search of the
        student based on seeing a "neatly folded red
        bandanna hanging from the back pocket of his
        pants" which violated the school's rule against
        gang-related symbols and "indicated that
        something was about to happen or that [the
        student] was getting ready for a confrontation."
        In re William V., 111 Cal. App. 4th 1464, 4 Cal.
        Rptr. 3d 695, 697, 180 Ed. Law Rep. 840 (1st
        Dist. 2003), review denied, (Dec. 23, 2003) and
        cert. denied, 124 S. Ct. 2182, 158 L. Ed. 2d 747
        (U.S. 2004).

(23)   A New York state court ruled that a school
        safety agent had reasonable suspicion to con-
        duct a search for a weapon when, after respond-
        ing to a telephone call about intruders, he
        observed three boys running, one of whom
        dropped and retrieved an object that was
        thought to be a weapon. In re Steven A., 308
        A.D.2d 359, 764 N.Y.S.2d 99 (1st Dep't 2003).

(24)   A Texas state court found that an assistant
        principal had reasonable suspicion to search a
        17-year-old student's backpack after the student
        was discovered away from the class he was sup-
        posed to be attending, was evasive about his
        class obligations, and tried to dispose of the
        backpack. Briseno v. State, 2003 WL 22020800
        (Tex. App. Dallas 2003) (unpublished).

(25)   A Washington state court found that school se-
        curity officers had reasonable suspicion to
        conduct a search of a student based on finding
        a student known to have been involved with
        drugs previously in an area known for drug use.
        State v. Huff, 121 Wash. App. 1069, 2004 WL
        1206998 (Div. 1 2004) (unpublished).

§ 3:10   Defining the term—Reasonable suspicion defects

To justify a student search, officials must reasonably

suspect that a particular student has committed some specific infraction, and that particular objects related to the suspected infraction are presently to be found in a certain identifiable place. The elements necessary to support a valid reasonable suspicion were discussed in preceding sections. This section is concerned with defects that can discredit the claim of a reasonable suspicion and invalidate any related search.

(1) *Stale reasonable suspicion.* Reasonable suspicions justifying a lawful search must rest on facts that accurately reflect circumstances as they are *at the time the search is conducted.* In other words, a lawful search must be based on underlying facts that indicate a reasonable suspicion at the time the search is actually conducted. Hemler v. Superior Court, 44 Cal. App. 3d 430, 118 Cal. Rptr. 564, 566 (1975).

This requirement may not be satisfied if there is a long delay in commencing the search. It is not simply the passage of time that creates a problem. The main concern is whether reasonable suspicions of the past remain reliable because of material changes of circumstance. Extenuating events can occur purely as a matter of change over time.

Although old information can indicate a present reasonable suspicion to search, officials must consider several factors in addition to elapsed time in determining whether facts and information from the distant past may still justify a search.

The problem of stale information is most relevant to the item-place nexus, because the reasonableness of a suspicion that evidence is presently to be found in a particular place can diminish rapidly over time. Hence, the following discussion focuses primarily on the location of sought-after evidence.

- *Nature of the infraction.* A relevant concern is whether the suspected infraction is merely a single isolated incident or a continuous long-term violation. United States v. McCall, 740 F.2d 1331, 1336 (4th Cir. 1984).

If the suspected infraction appears to be a one-shot offense, suspicions about the location of evidence will remain valid for only a few days at best. People v. Siemieniec, 368 Mich. 405, 118 N.W.2d 430, 431–32 (1962). The passage of time reduces the validity of the suspicion, because nothing acts to fix the location of the sought-after items or even necessitates their retention. The evidence could be moved or simply discarded.

If the alleged infraction involves a firearm or other weapon on campus, however, the time period before the implicating information becomes stale may be longer. In re Joseph G., 32 Cal. Rptr. 2d 902 (Cal. App. 1995) (information passed to school official on Friday evening is sufficient to justify Thursday morning search).

The situation is different for a recurring or continuous offense. Here it is reasonable to expect that related items will be preserved and stored or hidden in particular places so they can be conveniently used in further commissions of the offense. Consequently, the passage of time becomes less important and old information may continue to justify a search. The claim that a suspected infraction is recurring or continuous might be justified by its inherent nature, and/or any direct knowledge of its recurring character. United States v. McCall, 740 F.2d at 1336–37; United States v. Tucker, 638 F.2d 1292, 1299 (5th Cir. 1981) (gambling ring).

Some illicit activities are inherently difficult to abandon after only one or a few occasions. Examples might include violations requiring an elaborate or complicated scheme, such as setting up an extensive supply and distribution network to traffic drugs. Another somewhat unlikely case might be if equipment or other immobile resources such as an office were essential to the offense (e.g., students might be involved in converting stolen auto parts using school shop equipment). In either case, it is reasonable to suspect that items related to the infraction must necessarily be retained and stored in particular places. It is this character- istic that can continue to validate even old suspicions about certain infractions.

Occasionally, officials may have direct infor- mation about the recurring nature of an offense. For example, an informant may furnish the tip that illicit substances are always kept by a student for sale in the student's locker.

- *Nature of the thing sought.* Some illicit activi- ties may involve items that are not very in- criminating in themselves, such as pliers used to tamper with a fire alarm system or a pocket knife used to commit extortion. It is reasonable to assume that the owner of such items will keep them in usual and customary places even after committing an infraction with them. In that case, suspicions justifying a search in the past may still be valid even after some time.

Other situations where perpetrators can be reasonably expected to retain possession of suspected items include situations when: (a) the item is an important part of a student's personal affairs (e.g, a diary or record of illegal transactions); (b) the item cannot be easily moved or transported without being detected (e.g., a large quantity of stolen property); (c) the item is difficult to sell or dispose of because it would immediately expose the student's infraction (e.g., trying to sell marked or very distinctive stolen property to other students might lead someone to alert school officials); or (d) the student mistakenly believes that sus- pected items are no longer detectable or retriev- able (e.g., when one student does not realize that stolen goods have not been disposed of as planned by an accomplice but instead have been hidden in their jointly assigned storage area).

It is not necessary to justify any delay in commencing a search if information or suspicions are challenged as being stale. The critical issue is whether the information and facts at hand (even if old) still indicate a present reasonable suspicion.

(2) *Unreliable informant tips.* Factors related to the reliability of informant tips are discussed in Section 3:7. Several U.S. Supreme Court holdings have relaxed standards for evaluating the reliability of informant tips. *See* Illinois v. Gates, 462 U.S. 213, 228–46 (1983). These decisions do not, however, mean that an official can use unreliable informant tips to support a reasonable suspicion.

(3) *Material misstatements.* Important and material facts cannot be misrepresented or selectively omitted to manipulate favorably the factual basis justifying a search.

The claim of a reasonable suspicion will invariably be nullified if (a) officials act in bad faith by knowingly and intentionally misstating what they knew and/or how it came to be known, and (b) the misstatement is essential to show that a reasonable suspicion exists.

(4) *Failing to establish the student-infraction-object-place nexus.* The suspicions officials cite as justification for a search can be defective if they do not establish all the necessary links between student, infraction, and place (*see* Section 3:3), because any resulting search will be so unconstrained that it amounts to an illegal roving exploratory search.

§ 3:11 Defining the term—Examples of cases where the court determined that the evidence did not provide a reasonable suspicion

(1) A 15-year-old student was observed hiding in the school parking lot, and she gave a false name when questioned by a security guard. The court ruled that these actions "created reasonable ground for suspecting that some school rule or law had been violated," but it did "not create a reasonable suspicion that a search would turn up evidence of drug usage." The court ruled that

the search of her purse and her body (she was forced to take off her jeans and lean over so her brassiere could be visually examined) "was not reasonable at its inception." Cales v. Howell Pub. Sch., 635 F. Supp. 454, 457 (E.D. Mich. 1985).

(2)   A 16-year-old student was stopped by the assistant principal who noticed that the student was carrying a vinyl calculator case with "an odd-looking bulge," which he tried to hide. The assistant principal forcibly seized the case and found marijuana-filled baggies inside. The court suppressed this evidence, ruling that the assistant principal was not able to articulate any "facts to support a reasonable suspicion that William was engaged in a proscribed activity justifying a search," and that his "suspicion that William was tardy or truant from class provided no reasonable basis for conducting a search of any kind." In re William G., 709 P.2d 1287, 1289, 1297 (Cal. 1985).

(3)   A teacher observed a student getting a pack of cigarettes from his locker, and notified the assistant principal who conducted a search of the locker. A pack of cigarettes in a jacket in the locker contained marijuana. The assistant principal searched the locker because he suspected the student was involved with drugs. Because the assistant principal was unable to state any basis for this suspicion and because the initial discovery of cigarettes did not justify a suspicion that there would be more cigarettes in the locker, the court refused to allow the marijuana as evidence. In re Dumas, 357 Pa. Super. 294 (1986).

(4)   A school principal discovered defacement of school property and directed the teachers to search each student's bookbags, pockets, and pocketbooks for magic markers. He ordered another search when a teacher informed him that she had seen students with "Walkmans" or radios, which were forbidden by school rules. When a teacher reported that she smelled

marijuana in a hallway area, each student again was searched. The three "sweep searches" were held to have violated the students' Fourth Amendment rights. Burnham v. West, 681 F. Supp. 1160, 1166 (E.D. Va. 1987).

(5)   A search was conducted on a student found outdoors on school grounds near some bleachers, a place students went to "skip classes, smoke cigarettes, or use drugs." The decision to search the student "arose solely because his name had been mentioned in staff conversations during discussions of drug use and sales at the school." The principal had no personal knowledge and had received no specific reports regarding the student's conduct. The court ruled that the cocaine found in one of the student's pockets could not be admitted into evidence. In re Appeal in Pima County Juvenile Action, 152 Ariz. 431, 432 (App. 1987).

(6)   A student who had been threatened by a knife the previous day reported that either T.J. or another student had a knife at school. The court assumed, but did not decide, that the assistant principal's search for the weapon was justified at its inception. The court ruled, however, that when the school official continued the search to examine a zippered side pocket in the accused student's purse, which contained a plastic bag with cocaine, the Fourth Amendment had been violated. The assistant principal had searched the side pocket after taking everything out of the purse and finding no sign of a weapon. The side pocket did not bulge, nor did the assistant principal feel anything in it besides the plastic bag. The court characterized this search as a "scavenger hunt" because the side pocket "clearly contained no weapon." T.J. v. State, 538 So. 2d 1320, 1322 (Fla. App. 1989).

(7)   A school principal, who had previously received information that a student was selling drugs, became suspicious one morning when the student said he was leaving school to attend his grandfather's funeral. The court ruled that this

suspicion justified the principal's investigation of the reasons given by the student for leaving campus, and his "patting down" the student for safety reasons. The court also held, however, that the principal's subsequent searches of the student's "clothing and person [including requiring him to pull down his pants], locker, and vehicle were excessively intrusive in light of the infraction of attempting to skip school." Coronado v. State, 835 S.W.2d 636, 641 (Tex. Crim. App. 1992).

(8) A student was questioned for 45–60 minutes in the administrative office because of his use of an off-limits staircase and his wearing of a jacket in violation of school rules. After a discussion in which he was "cooperative and relaxed," the student was asked to empty out his pockets and was subjected to a pat-down search, which produced a handgun. The court suppressed this evidence, ruling that the school administrator's "inchoate and unparticularized suspicion or hunch" was not sufficient to outweigh the student's "Fourth Amendment expectation of privacy as he sat in that administrative office." People v. Pruitt, 662 N.E.2d 540, 551 (Ill. App. 1996), appeal denied, 667 N.E.2d 1061 (Ill. 1996).

(9) An assistant principal saw three middle school male students huddled together, and noticed that one of the boys had money in his hand and was "fiddling" in his pockets. These observations were held to be insufficient to provide a reasonable suspicion to justify a search, even though the student had a reported "bad attitude" and the drug problem was growing at this school. A.S. v. State, 693 So. 2d 1095 (Fla. App. 1997).

(10) The Massachusetts Supreme Judicial Court determined that it was unreasonable to search a student prior to a hearing regarding his missing classes and his failure to appear for a disciplinary hearing, when the school officials had no evidence that the student had any

contraband and nothing in his physical appearance supported such a suspicion. Commonwealth v. Damian D., 752 N.E.2d 679 (Mass. 2001).

(11) A Michigan federal judge ruled that reasonable suspicion did not exist for a search based on tips provided by students who were known to have had motives to falsely accuse another student and had continually harassed the other student. Fewless ex rel. Fewless v. Board of Educ. of Wayland Union Schools, 208 F. Supp. 2d 806, 167 Ed. Law Rep. 153 (W.D. Mich. 2002).

(12) A Texas court ruled that a police officer patrolling an area near a high school did not have a reasonable suspicion sufficient to justify a patdown search of a high-school-aged individual wearing a Dion Sanders football jersey, based solely on an anonymous tip that a person wearing such a jersey had been smoking marijuana in the area, when the individual was cooperative and did not make "any erratic, suspicious, furtive, or threatening gestures." In re A.T.H., 106 S.W.3d 338, 347 (Tex. App. Austin 2003). "To rise to the level of a reasonable suspicion, an anonymous tip must be corroborated by facts more substantial than those easily observable, such as attire or location." In re A.T.H., 106 S.W.3d 338 at 346 (Tex. App. Austin 2003).

§ 3:12 Student vehicles

Section overview. Student automobiles and other transportation devices are treated as protected places having a reasonably assumed degree of privacy by nature (Section 2:3). It does not matter whether a student has full legal ownership, partial ownership, or only actual use and control of the vehicle. Students have a justified expectation of privacy in vehicles that they park on campus or use to attend school-supervised activities (except government owned vehicles). Accordingly, school officials must comply with all standards and guidelines of reasonableness when searching student vehicles (Sections 3:1) in the absence of an emergency (Section 2:9), consent (Section 2:14), or abandonment (Section 2:23).

Parents and others who merely have some legal interest in the vehicle or who are passengers cannot challenge a lawful search conducted by school officials unless they can clearly establish a justified expectation of privacy in the vehicle.

§ 3:13   Student vehicles—Governing principles

The U.S. Supreme Court has held that persons have reduced expectations of privacy with regard to a vehicle and its contents. Consequently, the Court allows much greater latitude in conducting vehicle searches as compared with searches of personal possessions.

To justify its finding of this reduced privacy interest, the Court has observed (1) that the inherently mobile character of vehicles can easily frustrate law enforcement objectives when a search warrant must be obtained (California v. Carney, 471 U.S. 386, 393 (1985)), (2) that the vehicle's exterior and most of its interior is commonly exposed to open public view (Cardwell v. Lewis, 417 U.S. 583, 590 (1974)), and (3) vehicles are already subject to pervasive regulatory schemes that intrude on ownership and other possessory rights (California v. Carney, 471 U.S. at 393). The Court has ruled that police officers may conduct a warrantless search of an entire vehicle if the officer has probable cause to believe that the evidence of a crime will be discovered. United States v. Ross, 456 U.S. 798 (1982). Such a search can take place eight hours after a car has been impounded, because "the justification to conduct such a warrantless search does not vanish once the car has been immobilized." Florida v. Meyers, 466 U.S. 380, 382 (1984). An appropriate warrantless search can also take place of an unattended automobile parked in a public parking lot. Cardwell, supra; Carney, supra. One court has ruled that once a dog "alerts" to the presence of drugs, the police have probable cause to conduct a warrantless search of an automobile parked in a public school's parking lot (and that the dog sniff can be conducted without particularized suspicion because it is not a "search" (citing United States v. Place, 462 U.S. 696 (1983)). In the Matter of Dengg, 1999 Ohio App. LEXIS 851 (Ohio App. 1999).

Despite reduced expectations of privacy, vehicles are not viewed as moving targets subject to random arbitrary searches. In previous years, the Court has held that before full Fourth Amendment protection can be relaxed, the government must identify an *exigent* circumstance related to the mobile character of a vehicle. Coolidge v. New Hampshire, 403 U.S. 443, 460 (1971). For example, law enforcement efforts could easily be frustrated if police had to obtain a search warrant before examining something incriminating left openly exposed to public view in a locked automobile. Under those circumstances the unknown owner might simply come back and drive away before police returned with a warrant. Several Supreme Court cases have been inconsistent in referring to the "exigent circumstances" requirement. *See* 3 W. LaFave, Search and Seizure, § 7.2(b) at 39 n.65; California v. Acevedo, 500 U.S. 565, 111 S. Ct. 1982, 1986 (1991). Lower courts are currently divided on whether exigent circumstances are required. *See, e.g.,* United States v. Cisneros-Mireles, 739 F.2d 1000, 1002 (5th Cir. 1984) (required exigent circumstances); United States v. Finefrock, 668 F.2d 1168, 1172 (10th Cir. 1982) (did not require exigent circumstances); State v. Ritte, 68 Haw. 253, 710 P.2d 1197, 1201 (1985) (must have exigent circumstances); State v. Ringer, 100 Wash. 2d 686, 674 P.2d 1240, 1248–49 (1983) (same).

Vehicles are fully protected if no such exigency is evident, because there would then be no practical reason not to comply with all Fourth Amendment requirements. For example, suppose the sole owner of a locked vehicle is arrested in his home. No related exigency exists in that situation because there is little chance of the vehicle being moved.

In the school setting, the exigency related to the mobile character of student vehicles is reduced because:

    (1)   Students have only limited access to their vehicles during the school day and most school-supervised activities;

    (2)   Students are under more or less constant supervision during the school day or a school activity, so it is convenient for school officials to inform students of their intention to search and to request voluntary cooperative entry by key; and

    (3)   The exterior and major portions of a vehicle's

interior are commonly exposed to the open public view of any casual passerby.

In addition, because of the T.L.O. holding, school officials do not have the burden of obtaining a search warrant, which might exacerbate any remote exigency. Consequently, it is very difficult to argue that extreme circumstances justify stepping outside the bounds of a normal student search. *But see* State v. Slattery, 56 Wash. App. 820, 825, 787 P.2d 932, 935 (1990) ("School officials were confronted with exigent circumstances that warranted an immediate search because Slattery or a friend could have removed his car from the school grounds.").

Accordingly, school officials must generally comply with all applicable standards and guidelines of reasonableness when searching student vehicles (Section 3:1). Nonetheless, courts have been relatively flexible in allowing searches of student automobiles. An Indiana federal court found reasonable the search of a student's car, after the student had been found in the parking lot without authorization or valid explanation, because it was well known that students utilized that area for smoking. Anders v. Fort Wayne Community Schools, 124 F.Supp.2d 618 (N.D.Ind. 2000). Similarly, the Mississippi Supreme Court ruled that it was constitutional for school officials to search a student's truck after seeing empty beer cans in the back of the truck and receiving reports that a 17-year-old student had been drinking in the school parking lot. Covington County v. G.W., 767 So.2d 187 (Miss. 2000).

As with any other personal property or protected area, *students cannot refuse to allow a lawful and valid search conducted by school officials.* If they have proper grounds for a search and the student refuses to give entry by key, the school officials may break into the vehicle to conduct the search.

§ 3:14　Student vehicles—Standing to challenge vehicle searches

Student drivers do not always have full legal ownership because automobiles and other vehicles are often expensive. Ownership may be shared with parents or other persons, or the student driver might only have actual use and control of the vehicle and no possessory interest.

These situations might cause confusion about who can properly challenge a vehicle search conducted by school officials.

Before an individual can challenge the search of a student's vehicle she or he must show a justified expectation of privacy in the vehicle (Section 1:3). Rakas v. Illinois, 439 U.S. 128, 143 (1978). Because student drivers are recognized as having such privacy interests (see above), they obviously have proper standing to challenge a search conducted by school officials. In re J.R.M., 487 S.W.2d 502, 509 (Mo. 1972) (son has standing to object to a search of a car he frequently uses but is legally owned by his father). This right does not necessarily belong to other persons regardless of what legal or possessory interest they may have in the vehicle.

Legal ownership alone is not sufficient to establish the necessary privacy interest. United States v. Metzger, 778 F.2d 1195, 1200 (6th Cir. 1985) (when a spouse surrenders the use of a vehicle to his wife, he loses standing). As a result, parents cannot automatically challenge a lawful vehicle search conducted by school officials while it is under the control of a student and parked on school property or at school-supervised activities. It does not matter that parents might have full legal ownership; they must still establish a justified privacy interest to have proper standing.

Similarly, passengers and other persons are viewed as having relinquished their expectations of privacy for anything left out of their immediate control in a vehicle. Thus, any incriminating item discovered during the course of a lawful vehicle search can be used as evidence against the owner. The inquiry for passengers is whether they had a justified expectation of privacy as to the vehicle. Factors to consider are whether the passenger has access to the vehicle, the distance the passenger is from the vehicle, and the length of time the passenger leaves the property in the vehicle. People v. Pohlmann, 13 Ill. App. 3d 779, 300 N.E.2d 302, 304 (1973).

§ 3:15 Student vehicles—Open public view

School officials may lawfully observe the exterior and exposed interior of a vehicle using the senses of sight, smell, and hearing according to Section 2:4. These sense data may provide the basis for a student search as described in Section 3:1.

Remember that any physical handling or examination by tactile or taste senses is only permitted if all requirements for a student search are satisfied first.

§ 3:16   Student vehicles—Scope limits

The scope of a vehicle search must be consistent with its initial justification. In most cases, this will be determined by the item being sought. If school officials reasonably suspect that stolen cylinders of flammable welding gas are hidden in a student's car, they may search the interior and trunk but not the glove compartment or under seats because such items could not plausibly be hidden in those places. Conversely, virtually every area of the car can be searched if they suspect a small handgun. *See* Section 4:3 for additional discussion.

§ 3:17   Student vehicles—Plain view

School officials may seize any incriminating item inadvertently discovered during the course of a lawful vehicle search provided all requirements for a plain view seizure are satisfied first (Section 6:5). *See, e.g.,* Bundick v. Bay City Ind. School Dist., 140 F.Supp.2d 735, 738 (S.D.Tex. 2001) (upholding a seizure of a machete from a toolbox in a student's truck after a dog trained to detect narcotics, gunpowder, alcohol and medications had "alerted" on the truck).

Chapter 4

Conducting the Search

Research References

West's Key Number Digest
Searches and Seizures ⊙⇒25, 53, 55

KeyCite®: Cases and other legal materials listed in KeyCite Scope can
be researched through West's KeyCite service on Westlaw®. Use
KeyCite to check citations for form, parallel references, prior and
later history, and comprehensive citator information, including citations to other decisions and secondary materials.

---

§ 4:1 Notice and announcement

Before actually conducting a search, school officials must
give notice and announce their identity and purpose to the
student whose person or possessions are to be searched. It
is not necessary to explain any suspicions in detail nor to
justify or debate them with the student. It will suffice to
say:

> My name is (name) and I am (position). I have a reasonable
> suspicion that evidence of (infraction) will be found at (loca-
> tion) and I will be conducting a search.

Notice and announcement acknowledges the student's
individual right of privacy by providing an opportunity to
surrender that privacy peacefully and cooperatively. It
also can help avert unnecessary violence. More specifically:

  (1) It notifies the student of the official's intention
       and purpose.

  (2) It indicates the authority under which the search

is sanctioned and alerts the student that the student is *not* entitled to resist or deny the search.

(3) It provides a brief opportunity for the student to avoid any unjustified invasion of privacy by pointing out obvious errors of identification.

(4) It gives the student an opportunity to minimize the intrusion by voluntarily surrendering the sought-after item or pointing to its exact location. Kerr v. California, 374 U.S. 23, 57 (1963) (Brennan, J., dissenting); State v. Carufel, 112 R.I. 664, 314 A.2d 144, 147 (1974).

Once the official has given adequate notice, the student must be afforded an opportunity to surrender his or her privacy cooperatively by allowing the search. At this point, the student has no right to deny the lawful search. If the student attempts to resist, the official may take reasonable action to compel the search, including breaking open places like lockers or vehicles. Force may be used against the student to compel a search only if there is an imminent and substantial threat.

Note that no forcible action should be taken against property or person until the student actually denies access for a search. Any conduct that is inconsistent with a willingness to grant access may be interpreted as a denial. Examples include refusing to open a locker, tightly clutching a purse or other container, voicing an intention not to relinquish possession of something, raising pseudo-legal objections, or even maintaining an extended silence. If the student fails to respond in a reasonable time, the official can lawfully infer a refusal. People v. Abdon, 30 Cal. App. 3d 972, 976–77, 106 Cal. Rptr. 879, 882 (1972).

School officials should be very careful about using any forcible action when the student gives an equivocal response that cannot be clearly interpreted as denying access. If they are uncertain that the student is resisting a search, they should clarify the matter before proceeding to use any force. But keep in mind that the officials are not asking for consent (Section 2:14). Once the student refuses, they may act reasonably to compel the search.

Exceptions. The notice and announcement requirement is not absolute. A search will be lawful as long as there is substantial (if not exact technical) compliance with this requirement. In addition, several exceptions to this requirement have been recognized: (a) when it would be a useless gesture to give notice because the officials are absolutely certain a student knows the purpose of the intrusion; (b) when the officials have substantial reason to believe that important evidence may be destroyed as a result; (c) when the officials have substantial reason to believe that someone inside a place may be in danger of bodily harm or when an announcement might lead to violence. Miller v. United States, 357 U.S. 301, 309–10 (1958).

§ 4:2   Search strategy overview

Students must be given an opportunity to relinquish the item sought by school officials cooperatively and peacefully before a search is conducted. This guide recommends a search strategy that begins with a request for cooperative surrender of the item and escalates to more intrusive methods only as necessary. Students should be given as much opportunity as practical to cooperate with officials and thereby limit intrusions on their privacy.

The elements of this search strategy are summarized here. More specific details are given in the section immediately following. Student searches should conform with the following sequence as much as possible:

(1)   First, the school officials should name the item sought, indicate its suspected location, and ask the student to relinquish possession cooperatively. Recall that if the item or its location cannot be specified with a reasonable degree of certainty, it may be questionable whether the officials have sufficient particularity for a valid search (see Section 3:4).

If the student refuses to cooperate or produces something that is not the item sought, school officials may escalate to the next level of intrusiveness.

(2)   If the suspected location of an object is the student's person, the school officials should conduct a visual inspection (without touching the student) to locate suspicious bulges and to isolate

specific areas where an intrusion or physical contact may eventually take place. They should point to the area and ask the student to produce whatever is causing the suspicious bulge. *See* Section 4:3 for further discussion.

When the suspected location is a small confined place or thing (such as a container), the officials should point out the location and ask the student to empty its contents for visual inspection. For example, the student might be asked to empty pockets or a purse or a small opaque container (so long as the officials reasonably suspect that the item may be located in those places). If the sought-after item is among the contents, school officials should ask that it be handed to them.

If the suspected location is a locker, assigned area, vehicle, or similar place, the officials should ask the student to provide access by, for instance, unlocking a locker or vehicle door, to permit a visual inspection. If the sought-after item is discovered during that visual examination, the officials should ask the student to hand it over.

If the student refuses to cooperate at any point or the item sought is not found, school officials may escalate to the next and highest level of intrusiveness.

(3) At this point, they may physically search for the item as carefully, thoroughly, and intensely as is reasonably consistent with the initial justification for the search. They may also take forcible action to compel the search if necessary. A more detailed discussion of applicable scope, intensity, duration, and force limits is presented immediately below.

§ 4:3 Procedures for a reasonable search: Scope and intensity limits

The Supreme Court required in New Jersey v. T.L.O., 469 U.S. 325, 342 (1985), that a search as actually conducted must be consistent with its original justification and cannot be excessively intrusive in relation to the nature of suspected infractions or the student's age and sex. Otherwise the search will be considered unreasonable and unlawful.

These requirements impose practical limits on the scope, intensity, and methods of the search. A reasonable justification to search does not confer unrestricted authority to use every means at the officials' disposal to look wherever and as closely as they please. The limits of a reasonable and lawful search are determined by the nature of the initial reasonable suspicions (i.e., what the officials suspect concerning the nexus between infraction, item, and place (*see* Section 3:3)).

(1) *Scope limits (where officials can search).* The scope of a search is determined by the description of the suspected location of sought-after items. In general, officials may search the entire area so described, extending to any inner place or receptacle that might conceivably contain the item. Once officials have valid access to search an area, additional acts of entry or opening are permitted to complete a search of that place. United States v. Ross, 456 U.S. 798, 820–21 (1982).

School officials must be careful with any property that obviously belongs to someone else. Officials cannot automatically search such property just because it happens to be discovered among the personal effects of or in a place controlled by the suspected student. If the school official has no way of knowing the property belongs to someone else, however, the search will not be held invalid. State v. Nabarro, 55 Haw. 583, 525 P.2d 575, 576–77 (1974) (if police are not aware of the ownership of an item, the court will not expect them to avoid a search; in this case, however, the owner of a purse police searched had made it clear that the purse belonged to her and that she was a visitor and not a resident of the premises being searched).

To illustrate, suppose officials reasonably suspect that illicit substances are to be found in a particular student's locker. This suspicion would permit them to search and open any box, container, tin, book, bag, or other receptacle found there that might hold the contraband. State v. Davenport, 55 Haw. 90, 516 P.2d 65, 72

(1973). It would not be reasonable to search through personal papers, small diaries, or calendars and the like if these could not plausibly contain the quantity of illicit substance sought. State v. Shinault, 120 Ariz. 213, 584 P.2d 1204, 1206 (1978).

Similarly, if officials reasonably suspect that a gun has been hidden somewhere in a particular student's car, all areas of the car and its contents can be searched. They could open the glove compartment and trunk, look under and behind seats, carpets, and the dashboard, into hidden crevices and recesses; they could open any container that could hold the gun and search any other likely place. United States v. Kralik, 611 F.2d 343, 345 (10th Cir. 1979). A monogrammed jacket obviously belonging to another student should not, however, be searched unless there are clear indications that the weapon may be concealed there. (Recall that student automobiles are treated as protected places in the school setting.)

In another case, assume the officials were searching for a baseball bat used to commit an assault. The trunk and other large hidden areas of a car could be searched but not the glove compartment, personal papers, or small flight bag found on the back seat (because these areas could not possibly contain the bat).

Finally, suppose officials have narrowly described the place to be searched as a gray metal toolbox contained in a particular student's locker. The locker can be entered only for purposes of gaining access to the toolbox. They can then search the toolbox but not the locker.

School officials cannot normally extend a search into any other protected area that was not reasonably suspected at the inception of the search. For example, having initially suspected that evidence was to be found in a student's purse, a school official could not proceed to search the student's car or locker after finding nothing in the purse. See Jenkins v. Talladega City Bd. of

Educ., 95 F.3d 1036 (11th Cir. 1996), aff'd en banc, 115 F.3d 821 (11th Cir. 1997), cert. denied, 118 S. Ct. 412 (1997) (holding that an accusation that two eight-year-old female students had stolen $7 and put it in a backpack did not justify a strip search of the girls, but also holding by an 8-3 vote that because the law regarding strip searches of eight-year-olds was not sufficiently clearly established the teacher and counselor who engaged in this activity had qualified immunity from a damage suit). *But see* In re P.E.A., 754 P.2d 382 (Colo. 1988) (based on a report from a student informer, two students suspected of selling marijuana were subjected to a pat-down search, their lockers were searched, and when no evidence was found, questioned as to their method of transportation to school; upon learning the two students arrived with P.E.A. in his car, school officials conducted a pat-down search of P.E.A., searched his locker, and then searched his car, finding drug paraphernalia in the console and marijuana in a closed duffel bag in the trunk; the court held these subsequent searches to be reasonable).

It should also be obvious that the special regime established by the T.L.O. case allowing more flexible warrantless searches in schools does not allow school officials and school personnel to escort the students to their homes and search the homes without a warrant. Ianson v. Zion-Benton Township High School, 2001 WL 185021 at *4 (N.D.Ill. 2001) ("In light of the fact that the opinion in T.L.O. turned on the need for 'maintaining security and order in the schools,' this court declines defendant's invitation to extend the protection of T.L.O. out from the schoolyard and into the home.").

(2) *Intensity limits (how closely officials can search).* The determination that a search as actually conducted is reasonable in terms of its intensity and methods will depend on the description of the sought-after items. As a general rule, officials may search as carefully and meticulously as is

consistent with the nature of the objects they are seeking to find. In most cases, the limits will be governed by the physical properties of the item— particularly its size. Thus, the level of fine scrutiny permitted in searching for a threatening extortionary note will not be considered reasonable for a stolen basketball. *See, e.g.,* T.J. v. State, 538 So. 2d 1320 (Fla. App. 1989) (a search for a knife did not justify searching a small zippered side pocket inside a purse); Blair v. Commonwealth, 225 Va. 483, 303 S.E.2d 881, 886 (1983) (a search for stolen coins allows officials to look in very small boxes); United States v. Chadwell, 427 F. Supp. 692, 696 (D. Del. 1977) (a search for stolen mag wheels does not allow police to search the top shelf of a closet, since the wheels could not fit into such a small space).

To illustrate, if a student's locker were being searched for an extortionary note, officials could open and examine journals, files, books, boxes, calendars, folders, or virtually any other similar item that might hold the note (they probably could not, however, open a tiny pill box or other such small item). Conversely, journals, files, books, calendars, folders, and such could not be searched if they were looking for a handgun. A possible exception might be if the student was suspected of selling arms and the officials were seeking receipts or a client list related to that crime. But even then it would not be proper to read through all of the correspondence, notes, and miscellaneous papers found in a student's appointment book.

If school officials are searching for several items, any container found in the prescribed area may be opened and examined so long as it could possibly contain any one of the items. For example, virtually any container or area in a student's car could be examined if they were searching for *both* illegal pills and a stolen classroom television monitor. This broad scope would not exist if they were only searching for the television monitor. In that case, it would not be reasonable to look into the glove compartment, or under the seat, or to inspect papers and files found in a box on the floor. *See, e.g.,* State v. Tinkham, 719 A.2d 580, 583 (N.H. 1998) (permitting a search for a plastic bag containing marijuana to include the student's pockets, socks, and shoes "given that these are obvious places where one might hide contraband").

(3) *Methods.* The law does not require that specific detailed procedures be followed to conduct a reasonable search. General guidelines do exist, however, to guide school officials:

- Begin the search in areas or containers that are most likely to contain the object sought. State v. Mollberg, 310 Minn. 376, 246 N.W.2d 463, 468 (1976) (when searching for a fresh deerskin, there is no reason to begin in a clothes closet). For example, it would be more reasonable to search for a knife by opening small containers found in a student's locker before examining a personal calendar that may have a hidden compartment concealing the weapon.

- Exhaust all prior possibilities before damaging any property in the search. It would not be reasonable to begin disassembling the dashboard of a student's car before searching the glove compartment for a gun. State v. Sierra, 338 So. 2d 609, 616 (La. 1976).

- Avoid unnecessary property damage. State v. Sierra, 338 So. 2d 609, 616 (La. 1976).

- An unproductive search cannot be prolonged indefinitely. The search can continue only for a period that is consistent with its original objectives. Longer periods may be consistent with a search for small contraband items or documents (especially if intermingled with other documents); only short searches are allowed for large objects in confined spaces.

- Delays in commencing a search cannot be excused if caused by any lapse of the school officials, such as not having necessary witnesses or experts available at the time the search is conducted.

- Do not attempt to isolate suspected documents, journals, ledger entries, or diaries intermingled with other documents or papers by reading through the material. This activity may be viewed an invalid ransack search because the officials indiscriminately exposed all of the student's papers to scrutiny.

This limitation creates a serious problem when specific papers are sought. One possible approach is to impound and seal all papers and documents among which the suspected item may be mingled. Before searching any of these impounded materials, the school principal should then convene a hearing where persons having proper standing in relation to the papers may petition for their return or specify conditions for a search that will protect their privacy.

- If the student being searched attempts to minimize any intrusion by revealing the location of items sought, officials should begin by looking in those places. This requirement is especially important if the place identified would be a plausible repository for the item. *But see* United States v. Chadwell, 427 F. Supp. 692, 696 (D. Del. 1977) (the court held that the police had no obligation to believe occupant when he told them the objects of their search, mag wheels, were in his garage, and the police searched the house first).

Note that this guideline does not involve consent (with its attendant restrictions, Section 2:14). As long as the student indicates a location within the prescribed area of the search or a public place, school officials have lawful access without any need for consent.

Consent is involved, however, when the indicated location is a protected place that was not originally suspected and described for search. For example, suppose the officials suspected that evidence was to be found in a student's purse but she indicates that the item is actually hidden in her locker. Any intrusion into the locker must comply fully with all requirements for a consent search (Section 2:14). The only way to avoid this is by re-examining the information available and establishing proper grounds for an independent search of the locker.

- During a search, school officials may be accompanied by persons who can assist in locating or identifying the sought-after item. Such persons might include victims, witnesses, or experts qualified to identify illicit substances. Commonwealth v. Farrar, 271 Pa. Super. 434, 413 A.2d 1094, 1100 (1979) (the sister of a victim of theft was able to identify the stolen property); People v. Poole, 48 Cal. App. 3d 881, 122 Cal. Rptr. 87, 89 (1975) (experts).

The actions of any person who accompanies or assists in a search are governed by the same standards that regulate the school officials' conduct. Thus, anyone who accompanies the officials cannot violate a student's privacy by opening containers or searching places that are off limits to the officials. The entire search can be invalidated if this happens. State v. Klostermann, 317 N.W.2d 796, 803 (N.D. 1982).

(4) *The use of force.* Students do not have a right to resist or prevent lawful searches. If resistance is encountered, school officials may use a reasonable degree of force against property or in some restricted instances against persons to compel the search.

Any application of force must be regarded as a very serious matter, but some use of reasonable force is permitted to support the authority of the school officials. It would be demoralizing and confusing if officials had no means whatsoever of enforcing or compelling searches that they are authorized to conduct. United States v. Harrison, 432 F.2d 1328, 1330 (D.C. Cir. 1970) (reasonable force can be used to prevent the destruction of evidence); State v. Lewis, 115 Ariz. 530, 566 P.2d 678, 681 (1977) (the use of force must be reasonable).

Several general principles are relevant to the application of force:

- School officials may never use deadly force or force that is designed to cause or create any substantial risk of death, serious bodily injury, disfigurement, extreme pain, or other such physical harm. *But see* Tennessee v. Garner, 471 U.S. 1, 11 (1985), for a discussion on when deadly force can be used by police.

- School officials may never use any force designed to cause extreme mental distress or which subjects any student to gross degradation.

- The decision to use force as well as how much force to exercise should be evaluated against the severity of any threat presented by the suspected infraction. Rochin v. California, 342 U.S. 165, 172 (1952) (the use of medical procedures to induce vomiting in order to recover possible evidence is an unreasonable use of force).

  There can be little justification for applying force when the suspected infraction being investigated presents only a marginal threat.

  If there is a significant threat, however, it may be incumbent on the school officials to use some measure of reasonable force to alleviate the threat. This matter is discussed further below.

- If there are indications that the student might violently resist a search, school officials should not escalate this precarious situation by attempting to overpower the student. There are several important points here.

  If the suspected infraction presents only a minimal threat to health or safety, it is unlikely that the application of any force would be justified.

  A threat that is already significant can be exacerbated by an unrestrained exercise of force. Any irrational application of excessive force can place the student, innocent bystanders, and school officials in jeopardy of physical harm. In situations of this sort, it is much better to notify the police.

- Although broad generalizations are impossible, perhaps the most extreme level of force one should ever normally use against a student would be physical restraint. This action could involve physically holding or restraining a student who attempts to block access to a place or possession.

  Beyond this, any attempt to push, shove, punch, trip, apply choke holds, threaten belligerently, challenge, or engage in other similar conduct would not be a reasonable application of force. Conduct of this kind can easily escalate the situation to a point where there is an even greater threat to health or safety than that presented by the infraction being investigated, a situation that would clearly be unacceptable and unwarranted. State v. Williams, 16 Wash. App. 568, 560 P.2d 1160, 1162 (1977); People v. Trevino, 72 Cal. App. 3d 686, 691, 140 Cal. Rptr. 243, 246 (1977).

- When directing force against a student's possessions, avoid as much property damage as possible. For example, try to obtain keys or combinations before cutting off the lock securing a locker. Be especially careful of a student's vehicle. Try to obtain keys or use a lock "jimmy" or secure the services of a locksmith to avoid breaking window glass or pulling a door lock. If property damage appears necessary and reasonable in relation to the severity of a threat to health or safety, inform the student of the intended action. This approach may elicit cooperation.

  Again, school officials must carefully evaluate the extent to which there is a threat to health or safety before engaging in conduct that may result in some form of property damage. Breaking into a student's car to find a can of spray paint (a potential fire hazard under some conditions) used to vandalize school property may not be considered reasonable.

- Naturally, school officials can defend against any attack by a student to the fullest extent necessary.

(5) *Search of the student's person.* The search of a student's person includes any exploration into his or her clothing. Proceed very cautiously when conducting any search of the student's person because this conduct is regarded as highly intrusive by nature. Doe v. Renfrow, 475 F. Supp. 1012, 1024–25 (N.D. Ind. 1979), aff'd in part, remanded in part, 631 F.2d 91 (7th Cir. 1980), cert. denied, 451 U.S. 1022 (1981).

There is no doubt that students have reasonable expectations of privacy for their own bodies. Consequently, any intrusion on those expectations is likely to offend the sense of decency and reasonableness which forms the basis for Fourth Amendment protective principles (*see* Section 1:5). Flores v. Meese, 681 F. Supp. 665, 667 (C.D. Cal. 1988); Daniel S. v. Bd. of Educ. of York Community High School, 152 F.Supp.2d 949 (N.D.Ill.2001) (holding that conduct by a gym teacher requiring two male 17-year-old student to stand naked in front of their male classmates for 16 minutes (in a school where "the custom of the boys . . . was to shower with their swim suits on") presented a claim for damages as an unreasonable seizure under the Fourth Amendment); Thomas v. Roberts, 261 F.3d 1160 (11th Cir. 2001), remanded, 536 U.S. 953 (2002), on remand, 323 F.3d 950 (11th Cir. 2003) (holding that strip searches of fifth graders, without individualized suspicion, in search of a missing $26 constituted an unreasonable search under the Fourth Amendment, but ruling nonetheless that the school officials had qualified immunity from suit because their action was not in violation of constitutional standards that were clearly defined at the time of the incident).

The special character of searches directed at a student's person is recognized in Hawaii's implementing regulations, which explicitly prohibit any exploratory conduct that exposes the genitals or the female breasts (Subsection 8-19-17(a) of Hawaii Department of Education Regulations, Chapter 19, Subchapter 4) and any search involving body contact with a person of the opposite sex except in a case presenting an imminent threat to health or safety.

If the fruits, instruments, contraband, or other evidence of a suspected infraction are reasonably suspected of being on a student's person, school officials should proceed with a strategy of escalating intrusiveness, as described in Section 4:2. Specifically:

(a) The officials who conduct the search of a student's person must be of the same sex as that student. M. Gardner, "Student Privacy in the Wake of T.L.O.," 22 Ga. L. Rev. 897, 923 (1988). This requirement would be relieved only when there is an imminent threat to health or safety, such as when the student is reasonably suspected of being presently armed and dangerous.

(b) The officials should name the sought-after item, indicate its suspected location, and ask the student to relinquish it cooperatively. If the student refuses to cooperate or produces something other than the item sought, the officials may escalate to the next level of intrusiveness.

(c) The officials should conduct a visual inspection (without touching the student) to isolate suspicious areas or likely locations of the item where an intrusion or contact may eventually take place. These sites would include inner and outer pockets, large folds of material, cuffs, and any unusual or suspicious bulges.

The officials should point to these areas and ask the student to empty out all contents for inspection. Wilcher v. State, 876 S.W.2d 466 (Tex. App. 1994) (reasonable search where school officials discovered contraband after asking student to turn pants pockets inside out). The officials may then search the contents and open any closed opaque containers that could conceal the sought-after item.

Under very unusual circumstances, school officials may request that the student open his or her mouth for a visual inspection only. *Officials may not probe or explore the student's mouth in any way whatsoever. They are also prohibited from asking the student to expose any other body cavity for their inspection (including ears and nostrils).* If the suspected item is discovered in the student's mouth, the officials should ask that it be removed and surrendered. *They should never attempt to reach in or otherwise remove something from a student's mouth*—such conduct is not only excessively intrusive but dangerous as well.

If the student refuses to cooperate or the sought-after item is not found, the officials may escalate to the next and highest level of intrusiveness.

(d)   Before actually making any physical contact, the officials should evaluate carefully the nature of the infraction and properties of the item sought. This review will determine whether a highly intrusive search of the student's person would still be reasonable. New Jersey v. T.L.O., 469 U.S. at 342 ("a search will be permissible in its scope when the measures adopted are reasonably related to the objectives of the search and not excessively intrusive in light of the age and sex of the student and the nature of the infraction").

Nature of the infraction. In considering the nature of a suspected infraction, school officials should look at (i) how serious it is and (ii) the extent to which health or safety is threatened. Giles v. Ackerman, 746 F.2d 614, 617 (9th Cir. 1984), cert. denied, 471 U.S. 1053 (1985) (arrestees charged with minor offenses can only be strip searched if police hold a reasonable suspicion that they are carrying weapons or contraband). Relatively minor infractions that only marginally threaten health or safety may not justify subjecting suspected students to the physical search of their person.

Nature of the item. School officials should assess carefully the properties of the item sought, especially its size, weight, density, and other pertinent physical characteristics. Officials are permitted to search the student's person only for things that could reasonably be hidden there (i.e., comparatively small objects). Although a search of the student's person for drugs might be permissible, for example, a search for stolen shop equipment like an electric drill would be unlawful in most cases.

An assessment of physical properties will also serve two other purposes. First, if the student has cooperated with requests to produce items so far, it is quite likely that only very small or thin items could still remain undiscovered. If the item sought is not very small or thin, therefore, it may not in fact be hidden on the student's person.

If there is still a reasonable possibility that something small and thin may be found, its physical properties will help to isolate and limit the search accordingly. For example, suppose an official reasonably suspected that a stolen wallet was hidden on the student's person. In that case, it might not be reasonable to reach into the back pockets of a student's jeans when a visual inspection would be just as effective.

The search. Officials should use the two-stage pat down and search procedure described in Section 5:10.

They should begin by patting down the outer surface of a student's garments. The scope and intensity of the pat-down should be consistent with the seriousness of a suspected infraction and the nature of the item sought. An intense exploration of every possible area of the body would not be consistent with minor infractions or a search for relatively large items. By this time, it should be possible to focus and confine any pat-down to clearly suspicious areas where the item might be concealed. A pat-down of genital areas or female breasts is *extremely intrusive* and should almost always be avoided.

The primary purpose of a pat-down is to obtain tactile information that would justify further searching beneath the surface of outer garments. School officials may intrude below the surface of outer garments to retrieve any object revealed by a pat down whose size, shape, and density are consistent with those of the item sought. They may also retrieve, open, and examine any container that might plausibly contain the item. Cason v. Cook, 810 F.2d 188, 193 (8th Cir. 1987) (a pat-down search for stolen currency was not excessively intrusive when a stolen coin purse was already found in the student's purse); Wynn v. Board of Educ., 508 So. 2d 1170, 1172 (Ala. 1987) (a search of a student's shoes and socks for stolen currency was not excessively intrusive even though the search was carried out in front of the whole class).

There is no requirement to re-evaluate the sensory data continuously while retrieving objects. Thus, officials can proceed to remove an object for examination even if it becomes immediately apparent upon directly feeling something that it is not the item sought.

See Section 5:10 for additional discussion.

(6) *Strip and body cavity searches.* In the usual case, school officials are prohibited from conducting any strip or body cavity search for fruits, instruments, contraband, or other evidence related to a suspected infraction.

School officials can, however, render emergency assistance in accordance with the provisions of Section 2:9. They can also conduct strip or body cavity searches in exceptional situations involving threats to health or safety. Searches should not be "excessively intrusive in light of the age and sex of the student and the nature of the infraction." New Jersey v. T.L.O., 469 U.S. at 342. "In fact, strip searches are probably only permissible in the school setting, if permissible at all, where there is a threat of imminent serious harm." Jenkins v. Talladega City Bd. of Educ., 95 F.3d 1036, 1047 n.20 (11th Cir. 1996), aff'd en banc, 115 F.3d 821 (11th Cir. 1997), cert. denied, 118 S. Ct. 412 (1997). First, they must have a reasonable suspicion that the student possesses weapons or contraband. Flores v. Meese, 681 F. Supp. at 668. Second, the reasonable suspicion standard should be strictly applied. *Id.* at 669. Examples of strip searches conducted in the school setting where the courts found no reasonable suspicion include requiring 14- and 15-year-old students to strip to their underwear during a search for a diamond ring (Kennedy v. Dexter Consolidated Schools, 10 P.3d 115 (N.M. 2000), requiring two eight-year-old girls to strip twice because of allegations they stole $7 from another student (Jenkins v. Talladega City Bd. of Educ., 95 F.3d 1036 (11th Cir. 1996) aff'd en banc, 115 F.3d 821 (11th Cir. 1997), cert. denied, 118 S. Ct. 412 (1997)), asking a student to pull open his underwear both in front and back to discover a missing $100 (State ex. rel. Galford v. Mark Anthony B., 443 S.E.2d 41 (W. Va. 1993)), requiring a student to pull down his pants when he was being investigated for skipping school (Coronado v. Texas, 835 S.W.2d 636 (Tex. Crim. App. 1992)), a strip search for drugs when a search of pockets produced no contraband (State v. Sweeney, 782 P.2d 562 (Wash. App. 1989)), requiring a 15-year-old girl who was hiding in a parking lot during school to remove her jeans (Cales v. Howell Pub. Sch., 635 F. Supp. 454 (E.D. Mich. 1985)), a strip search of an entire fifth grade class for $3.00 (Bellnier v. Lund, 438 F. Supp. 47, 54 (N.D.N.Y. 1977)), a strip search of a male student to find a stolen $100 (State ex rel. Galford v. Mark Anthony B., 433 S.E.2d 41 (W. Va. 1993)), and a search of a student who had been under observation for suspected drug-dealing, had entered the rest room twice in one hour, and had lunch with another student suspected of drug-dealing. People v. Scott D., 34 N.Y.2d 483, 315 N.E.2d 466, 470–71 (1974). And *see* New Jersey v. T.L.O., 469 U.S. at 382 n.25 (Stevens, J., dissenting and concurring) ("strip searches have no place in the school house").

A strip search was found reasonable in Singleton v. Board of Educ. USD 500, 894 F. Supp. 386, 390–91 (D. Kan. 1995). A school official searched a student for $150 the student allegedly had stolen. The search involved the school official patting the student's crotch, unbuttoning and lowering the student's cut-offs and searching the inside band of his boxers, and removing the student's shirt. Because the search was conducted in private and the student was never required to remove his underwear, the district court found the search to be reasonable. *Id.* at 391.

Another example where a student was required to remove his clothes is the case of Cornfield v. Consolidated High Sch. Dist. 230, 991 F.2d 1316 (7th Cir. 1993), where the student was believed to be concealing drugs in the crotch of his sweat pants. The court felt that requiring the student to remove his clothes was the least intrusive means, and that "[u]nder the circumstances, a pat-down would have been very invasive." *Id.* at *9. Other decisions permitting an intrusive strip search are Williams v. Ellington, 936 F.2d 881 (6th Cir. 1991), where the court permitted a search of a high school student's undergarments by a school official looking for a vial of cocaine based on an allegation by a fellow student; Widener v. Frye, 809 F. Supp. 35 (S.D. Ohio 1992), where school officials were allowed to remove the jeans (but not the undergarments) of a 15-year-old male thought to be in possession of marijuana; Rinker v. Sipler, 264 F. Supp. 2d 181, 178 Ed. Law Rep. 730 (M.D. Pa. 2003) (ruling that a search requiring a male student to lower his pants to his knees, followed by a school security officer running his hands around the interior of the student's boxer shorts to determine if anything was hidden inside, was justified to find out if the student possessed drugs); Rudolph ex rel. Williams v. Lowndes County Bd. of Educ., 242 F. Supp. 2d 1107 (M.D. Ala. 2003) (ruling that requiring a student to remove his underwear down to his knees did not constitute a constitutional violation in the context of a search for drugs); Phaneuf v. Cipriano, 330 F. Supp. 2d 74 (D. Conn. 2004) (concluding that a strip search of Phaneuf for marijuana was reasonable based on a tip from a credible student that Phaneuf was storing marijuana in her underpants, and because the school officials summoned Phaneuf's mother to conduct the search).

An example of an unreasonable strip search is found in Oliver v. McClung, 919 F. Supp. 1206 (D. Ind. 1995), where the court ruled that a strip search of seventh-grade girls conducted in an effort to find $4.50 that had been stolen was unreasonable. This opinion discusses and distinguishes Cornfield, Williams, and Widener and emphasizes that a strip search for illegal drugs can be defended much more easily than a strip search for a modest sum of money.

Reaching the same conclusion was Konop v. Northwestern School District, 26 F. Supp.2d 1189 (D.S.D. 1998), which denied a motion to dismiss claims brought by two eighth-grade female students against the school district, the principal, and a female music teacher who took them into the bathroom and searched their bodies in an effort to find $200 thought to have been stolen. The music teacher pulled the girls' underwear away from their bodies and touched one in the process. One girl "was menstruating at the time and the students were embarrassed and humiliated but did not think they had the right to say 'no.' Both students were crying during the search . . . " *Id.* at 1203. The court felt this highly intrusive search was unjustified, given that "[t]here was no imminent serious harm of any kind," *id.*, and that the school officials "did not have any reasonable cause to believe the plaintiffs stole the missing $200" or even "whether, in fact, $200 was missing." *Id.* at 1206.

Similar facts produced a similar result in Kennedy v. Dexter Consolidated Schools, 10 P.3d 115 (N.M. 2000), where students were individually taken to the restroom, told to strip to their underwear, and examined (with their underwear pulled away from their bodies to facilitate inspection) in an attempt to find a missing diamond ring. The court ruled that such a search was unconstitutional, particularly in light of the absence of any grave or imminent danger to health or safety, and the absence of any individualized reasonable suspicion. *See also* Bell v. Marseilles Elementary School, 160 F. Supp. 2d 883, 888–90, 156 Ed. Law Rep. 1066 (N.D. Ill. 2001) (holding that requiring 30 students in a gym class to remove their shirts and/or lower their pants to mid-thigh for a visual inspection or waist band check of their underwear to search for a "relatively small amount of money" was "undoubtedly intrusive" and unreasonable, and that the officer did not have qualified immunity because "there is no question that plaintiffs' Fourth Amendment rights were clearly established in the factual context of student searches by school agents"); Holmes v. Montgomery, 2003 WL 1786518 (Ky. Ct. App. 2003) (characterizing a search requiring female high school students to raise their shirts above their bras and lower their pants below their knees as a "strip search" - "exposing partially clad midriffs, thighs, and undergarments for visual inspection in the backdrop of an accusatory ambiance" - and ruling that the search was unjustified in the context of an effort to find a missing pair of shorts); Watkins v. Millennium School, 290 F. Supp. 2d 890, 183 Ed. Law Rep. 454 (S.D. Ohio 2003) (ruling that the taking of a second or third grade student into a supply closet and requiring her to pull out her waistband so that the teacher could look underneath her pants, in a search for a missing $10, constituted a significant intrusion that could not be justified, in the absence of individualized suspicion and any emergency situation).

(7) *Frisk for weapons.* If officials reasonably suspect that the student whose possessions are being searched may be armed, the student can be frisked for weapons. The initial frisk must be limited to an outer garment pat-down, and any further search or seizure must be confined to hard objects that could reasonably be weapons. *See* Section 5:7 for specific procedural details. Giles v. Ackerman, 746 F.2d at 617–18.

§ 4:4 Plain view

School officials may seize any incriminating item inadvertently discovered during the course of a lawful search even if the item was not particularly described as a basis for the search. To make a lawful seizure of this kind, all requirements for a valid plain view seizure must be satisfied (Section 6:5).

§ 4:5 Duration limits

Once the purpose of a search has been achieved, any authority to search immediately ends. Typical examples are:

(1) A student promptly surrenders the sought-after item upon the notice and announcement of an intention to search. The officials cannot then continue with the intended search.

(2) The sought-after item is discovered during the search. Once the item is found officials must discontinue searching regardless of any prior discovery of other unexpected objects related to the suspected infraction. Simply finding additional related items does not broaden the authority to extend a search for more evidence.

If an unspecified quantity of the item is sought, however, such as an unknown quantity of an illicit substance, officials may search the prescribed area exhaustively regardless of how much has already been found.

A related point is that the justification to conduct a search is valid for only *one* search episode. Officials cannot use a given statement of facts to justify conducting repeated harassing searches of a student on several different occasions. In order to search a student again lawfully, they must clearly articulate additional facts that would support a more precise reasonable suspicion. (See Section 3:1.)

Chapter 5

Investigative Stops

Research References

West's Key Number Digest

Arrest ⌐63.5; Constitutional Law ⌐254.2; Criminal Law ⌐394, 394.4; Searches and Seizures ⌐36, 37

KeyCite®: Cases and other legal materials listed in KeyCite Scope can be researched through West's KeyCite service on Westlaw®. Use KeyCite to check citations for form, parallel references, prior and later history, and comprehensive citator information, including citations to other decisions and secondary materials.

---

§ 5:1   Elements of an investigative stop

Overview

Many conceivable situations can raise a reasonable suspicion that something illicit is afoot. Not all of these sets of facts will, however, provide sufficient justification to conduct a student search. Suppose, for instance, school officials observe a furtive gesture or see a student at a location where the student should not normally be. Although the official may logically have reason to connect the student with some specific infraction, other necessary facts of sufficient quantity and certainty may not be immediately evident to justify a search (*see* Sections 3:2–3:4). For example, the officials might not be able to particularize the suspected item or specify the place to be searched.

Even if school officials cannot lawfully conduct a search under these circumstances, they can detain the suspected student briefly and conduct a limited investigation. This action is called an investigative stop. Such a stop allows officials to maintain the status quo temporarily by freezing suspicious situations for purposes of gathering more information. They can obtain the student's identity and an explanation of the student's conduct or reasons for being in the area.

If the student offers a plausible explanation dispelling the officials' suspicions, the investigative stop must come to an end and the student allowed to proceed. If their suspicions are not satisfied, the officials must then carefully examine whether they have proper grounds for a valid student search. They may not have such grounds if no other articulable facts emerged from the investigation (even if the officials remain suspicious).

A student may be frisked for weapons incident to a valid and lawful investigative stop if school officials come to reasonably suspect that the student may be presently armed and dangerous. Frisks for weapons may be conducted for this protective purpose only.

Even if an official has no suspicion whatsoever, reasonable or not, the official can always request information from any student and seek the student's consent to a search. Florida v. Bostick, 501 U.S. 429, 111 S. Ct. 2382 (1991). As explained in Section 2:14, searches conducted pursuant to "consent" are valid only if the consent is truly voluntary.

§ 5:2   Elements of an investigative stop— Reasonable suspicion requirement

No search is permitted if school officials lack the factual details to establish all the necessary incriminating relationships for a student search as explained in Section 3:1. The officials can, however, investigate situations when they believe that illegal activity is occurring. If they have facts of sufficient quantity and certainty to reasonably suspect that a particular student has recently committed, is committing, or is about to commit an infraction, an investigative stop is permitted to detain briefly and question that student. United States v. Hensley, 469 U.S. 221, 227 (1985). To undertake such a stop, school officials must demonstrate a sufficient probability of specific illicit conduct by the particular suspected student based on articulable facts in combination with rational inferences from those facts (Terry v. Ohio, 392 U.S. 1, 21 (1967)) and any special training or expertise the officials possess (United States v. Oates, 560 F.2d 45, 59–60 (2d Cir. 1977)). *See* Sections 3:2 and 3:3. In other words, the officials must show how and why a particular student is reasonably suspected of being involved with an infraction.

Investigative stops are not permitted on the basis of mere hunches. Students may be detained and questioned to investigate suspicious situations only if the officials have (at least) a reasonable suspicion connecting a particular student with a specific infraction. *See* Alabama v. White, 496 U.S. 325 (1990). But a tip from an anonymous informer is usually sufficient to justify an investigative stop "because teachers must immediately address rumors concerning the possession of weapons on school premises to ensure the safety of the students for whom they are responsible." In re D.E.M. v. Commonwealth, 727 A.2d 570, 575 (Pa. Super. 1999); *see also* In the Matter of C.S., 1998 Tex. App. LEXIS 7436 at *6–7 (Tex. App. 1998).

Keep in mind that a student search is not immediately permitted for situations discussed here because all the necessary objective and factual preconditions for a search are not yet available. The results of an investigative stop may eventually provide that basis. The degree of suspicion necessary to justify an investigative stop is less than that necessary to conduct a search.

§ 5:3 Elements of an investigative stop—Purpose and function of investigative stops

Investigative stops may be used only for specific purposes under prescribed conditions. These are discussed in turn below.

(1) *Prevention and apprehension.* The purpose of an

investigative stop is to *prevent* illicit conduct from occurring and to apprehend persons who are in the process of violating the law. Terry v. Ohio, 392 U.S. at 22. School officials can therefore investigate infractions that may then be occurring or are about to occur based on less evidence than required for a student search. Investigative stops aimed at infractions suspected of having been committed in the *immediate* past are also consistent with this line of reasoning.

The question whether investigative stops are permitted in connection with infractions that have occurred some time in the past cannot be answered precisely. But in United States v. Hensley, 469 U.S. 221 (1985), the Supreme Court unanimously permitted an investigative stop of a person identified in a "wanted flyer" as a suspect in an armed robbery that occurred two weeks previously. The court used a balancing test. It ruled that the "wanted flyer" was credible and established the requisite "reasonable suspicion." It then concluded that "the strong government interest in solving crimes and bringing offenders to justice" justified the brief stop. *Id.* at 229. Once Hensley was stopped, the police found guns in his possession, thus establishing "probable cause" for his arrest. The Court does not say whether he could have been detained if the guns had not been found, nor does the opinion address whether such a stop would be permitted if a longer period had passed since the crime was committed. *See* In the Matter of C.S. v. State of Indiana, 735 N.E.2d 273 (2000) (permitting a school police officer to conduct a "pat down search for officer safety" of a student that had previously been adjudicated a delinquent child and was on probation attending summer school).

(2) *Nature of the suspected infraction.* School officials should avoid investigative stops related to very minor infractions, because the detention and questioning of persons during a public encounter is regarded as quite intrusive. United States v. Oates, 560 F.2d at 59. Courts have scrutinized

specific investigative stops carefully because they entail significant possibilities for abuse.

As noted above, it is the value of an investigative stop as a tool to prevent and solve crimes that balances or offsets its intrusiveness. The less serious the crime, the more difficult it is to justify the stop, because intrusions of this sort can easily assume the character of roving exploratory harassment.

(3) *Who may be stopped.* Two separate issues can be identified here: (a) whether investigative stops are permitted only if based on a reasonable suspicion that excludes all but a single student; and (b) whether witnesses or other persons not suspected of any infraction may be detained and questioned.

- Any student reasonably suspected of an infraction can be stopped and questioned even if the facts that underlie the stop do not absolutely exclude all other students. Officials can thus stop and question several students when it is uncertain which one is actually guilty, if for instance they have a suspect's description that is sufficiently detailed to permit selective nonarbitrary stops. Another example of a situation lacking an exclusive suspicion but permitting a stop would be when several students have been observed near a recent crime scene.

  Note that this provision cannot be interpreted to allow a roving dragnet interrogation. Although some indeterminacy affecting only a few students may be tolerated, the detention and questioning of many students would not be justified.

- Current case law does not indicate definitively whether officials can detain witnesses for questioning during public encounters. *See, e.g.,* United States v. Ward, 488 F.2d 162, 163 (9th Cir. 1973) (police stopped defendant to question him regarding fugitives in surrounding area and then arrested him for showing false identification; court found that detaining defendant for questioning was not a violation of

Fourth Amendment); Baxter v. State, 274 Ark. 539, 626 S.W.2d 935, 936–37 (1982) (police stopped defendant to ask whether he had seen anyone in a park following a jewelry store robbery and arrested two people lying down in the back seat of defendant's car; court found no violation of the Fourth Amendment); United States v. Dunbar, 470 F. Supp. 704, 708 (D. Conn. 1979) (police cannot stop a driver to assist him and then arrest him for a bomb found in the car in plain view). In what they described as "a close case," "based on the totality of the circumstances," the Ninth Circuit permitted the Anchorage Police Department to conduct an investigative stop and search of a suspicious high school student slowly circling the school ground in a car, based on a report from a reliable school official that the student had a weapon, even though the official had not seen any weapon. United States v. Donnelly, 2001 WL 247591 (9th Cir. 2001) (unpublished).

§ 5:4   Elements of an investigative stop—Factors that can lead school officials to reasonably suspect a particular student of specific illicit conduct: The student-infraction nexus

These factors are the same ones discussed extensively for student searches (Section 3:5). Basically, they relate to the student's conduct, appearance, or location. It is worth repeating that all of the relevant surrounding circumstances must be examined to establish a reasonable suspicion. In most cases, officials will need a cluster of complementary factors.

A list of relevant factors is provided below; refer to Section 3:5 for details. Valid informational sources are also indicated; *see* Section 3:7 for further discussion.

Factors Indicating Illicit Conduct

(1)   Suspicious conduct and furtive gestures;
(2)   Demeanor;
(3)   Unusual physical state;
(4)   Resemblance to a suspect's description;

(5)   Attempts to flee from school officials;

(6)   Nature of the area: "Suspect" locations;

(7)   Proximity to the scene of an infraction; and

(8)   A student's prior history.

Valid Sources of Information

(1)   The official's personal observations and knowledge;

(2)   Reliable reports of other school officials;

(3)   Reports of eyewitnesses and victims; and

(4)   Informant tips.

§ 5:5   Elements of an investigative stop— Conducting the investigative stop

Investigative stops, like student searches, must be conducted within prescribed limits according to consistent procedural guidelines. The scope, intensity, and duration limits of a lawful stop as well as proper methods and other related concerns are discussed below.

(1)   *Detaining suspected students for questioning.* An investigative stop does not occur whenever a school official addresses some questions to a student. An investigative stop occurs when a student is briefly and temporarily *detained* for questioning. This key factor is met when, after all the surrounding circumstances are considered, a rational student would believe that he or she was not free to ignore the official's questions and leave. Florida v. Royer, 460 U.S. 491, 501–02 (1983); California v. Hodari D., 499 U.S. 621, 643 (1991).

In the school setting it is very likely that a student would feel detained when: (a) there is a show of authority (in this case simply through a school official's position); (b) several officials are present and surround the student; (c) the official's language or tone of voice indicates that compliance would be compelled (United States v. Berryman, 717 F.2d 651, 655 (1st Cir. 1983)); (d) the officials pursue a student who attempts to terminate the encounter by leaving (State v. Saia, 302

So. 2d 869, 870 (La. 1974); *but see* California v. Hodari D., 499 U.S. 621 (1991) (when a police officer is chasing a person, a seizure does not occur until the person is actually apprehended)); (e) they demand or order the student to do something (Johnson v. United States, 468 A.2d 1325, 1327 (D.C. App. 1983)); (f) they block the student's path (United States v. Berryman, 717 F.2d at 655); (g) they summon or remove the student to another place (e.g., their office) for questioning (Florida v. Royer, 460 U.S. at 502); or (h) they use some type of physical restraint (Johnson v. United States, 468 A.2d at 1327).

The foregoing list is illustrative and not exhaustive. The key is that some official conduct or other circumstantial cues must convey to the student that he or she is not free to leave.

(2) *Scope and intensity limits.* During an investigative stop, officials are permitted to obtain the student's identity and ask for an explanation of the student's activities. Florida v. Royer, 460 U.S. at 502. Officials cannot intensely question the student in a general exploratory manner or inquire about other unrelated matters. J.R.H. v. State, 428 So. 2d 786, 787 (Fla. App. 1983).

If the student provides satisfactory and plausible answers to these questions, the student must be allowed to leave. Florida v. Royer, 460 U.S. at 502. Officials cannot expand the scope or intensity of their inquiry and continue to question the student.

A stop may be prolonged and its scope expanded if the student is evasive or provides improbable or obviously false answers. Thus, officials may explore and follow significant new facts and suspicions that may emerge during the brief questioning. Even if the original suspicions of wrongdoing are not completely dispelled, however, the investigative stop cannot be turned into a general interrogation.

(3) *Duration limits.* Investigative stops based on a reasonable suspicion of wrongdoing *must be brief.* In general, they should be no longer than reason-

ably necessary to obtain the student's identity and an explanation of the student's activities. United States v. Place, 462 U.S. 696, 709–10 (1983).

No definitive rules have been established to determine what is a reasonably brief or unduly long investigative stop. Nevertheless, it is clear that if the student furnishes plausible and satisfactory answers, the stop must end. State v. Watson, 165 Conn. 577, 345 A.2d 532, 537 (1973).

The question of duration is most relevant when a student responds in a way that does not dispel suspicions. Although it is permissible to prolong the stop in this case, officials cannot continue indefinitely until their suspicions are completely and totally resolved. State v. Watson, 165 Conn. 577, 345 A.2d 532, 537, 539 (1973).

What constitutes a reasonable extension will depend on specific circumstances. Investigative stops are reasonably prolonged when: (a) a diligent effort is being made to resolve the matter (e.g., officials pursue a directly related line of questioning or summon a nearby witness) (United States v. Sharp, 470 U.S. 675, 687–88 (1985)); or (b) the student's continued presence is necessitated by the nature or seriousness of a suspected infraction (e.g., because there is good reason to believe that evidence for which officials cannot yet validly search may be destroyed or dissipated) (State v. McFarland, 4 Ohio App. 3d 158, 446 N.E.2d 1168, 1172 (1982)).

(4) *Investigative method limits.* During a stop, various techniques may be used to investigate suspicions. Officials should keep in mind that the scope, intensity, and duration limits set forth above will govern the application of any technique. For example, although none of the following are inherently improper, any one could invalidate a stop if its use (or manner of use) caused the period of detention to be unreasonably long:

● *Brief interrogation.* Officials may ask the suspected student for identification and an explanation of the student's conduct or reason for being in the area. Their questions must remain focused on the initially suspected infraction and cannot extend to other matters.

During the interrogation, officials may request that the student *voluntarily* consent to a search (*see* Section 2:14 for requirements). But they should be aware of the risks presented by consent searches in the school setting (Section 2:21).

- *Open public view examination of the student.* During a stop, officials may view and use other senses to observe the student. They may request that the student display his or her hands, shoes, or other nonintimate areas generally exposed to public view. They may even ask to view the exterior (but not examine or search the interior) of possessions carried by the student. State v. Dirk, 364 N.W.2d 117, 122 (S.D. 1985) (hands); Green v. State, 461 N.E.2d 108, 112 (Ind. 1984) (shoes).

  This technique can provide information about any injuries the student may have suffered, and even about the student's immediate prior location or activity.

- *Verification.* Officials can verify the student's identification or explanation, especially if they are highly improbable or known to be false. It is also possible to determine quickly whether an infraction actually has occurred by inspecting the immediate area or checking with other officials. State v. Fauria, 393 So. 2d 688, 690 (La. 1981).

- *Viewing by witnesses or victims.* If witnesses or victims are readily available they may be summoned for purposes of viewing the suspected student. This practice can be used for a recently committed infraction. Davis v. United States, 498 A.2d 242, 245 (D.C. App. 1985).

- *Removing the suspected student to another location.* Under unusual circumstances, a student may be removed to another more private or secure location for questioning (e.g., an office). Considerations of safety, security, or a desire to spare the student undue embarrassment might motivate such a move. Florida v. Royer, 460 U.S. at 504–5. It is also sound practice to use this technique anytime the stop occurs in an isolated or remote area. Normally, however, officials should avoid moving the student to another area because it can unduly prolong the stop.

It is worth repeating that the foregoing is not a routine list of techniques officials can successively implement to conduct an exhaustive and comprehensive investigation. Investigative stops must be brief and focused on the initial suspicions. Once the student has satisfactorily explained the suspicious conduct, the stop must end. Officials cannot prolong the stop by going from one investigative technique to another in hopes that something incriminating will eventually turn up.

(5) *Plain view.* Officials may seize any incriminating items discovered inadvertently during the course of a valid and lawful investigative stop, provided that all necessary requirements for a plain view seizure are satisfied first (*see* Section 6:5).

(6) *Relation to student searches.* It should be clear that during an investigative stop officials cannot engage in any conduct amounting to a search (Section 2:1). There would be no reason to use this more restricted method of investigation if they already had proper grounds for a valid student search.

The results of an investigative stop may of course provide additional facts which can then serve as the basis for a lawful student search. School officials must determine carefully whether all requirements for a valid search are satisfied before proceeding (Section 3:1).

§ 5:6 Elements of an investigative stop—Detention to investigate alleged child abuse

School officials are frequently required by statute to

detect and report child abuse cases involving students under their care. In light of the seriousness and gravity of child abuse, courts may grant school officials greater leeway in investigating these cases.

It is not a per se violation of the Fourth Amendment for a school official to question a student about potential child abuse, especially where a statute requires such an investigation. Picarella v. Terrizzi, 893 F. Supp. 1292 (M.D. Pa. 1995). The questioning must still, however, be reasonable under the Fourth Amendment. Reasonableness in the school context may be measured under the standard set forth recently in Vernonia Sch. Dist. v. Acton, 515 U.S. 646 (1995), discussed in Chapter 12, where the United States Supreme Court reviewed state action under the Fourth Amendment by comparing (1) a student's legitimate expectation of privacy, (2) the character of the intrusion, and (3) the nature and concern of the government concern at issue, and the efficacy of this means for meeting it. Picarella, 893 F. Supp. at 1301.

In Picarella, school officials took a student from her classes and brought her to a private office where they questioned the student in a "suggestive manner" about possible physical abuse at home. The student cried, asked that the questioning stop, and requested to see her brother or parents. Even after running from the office to the ladies room to regain her composure and escape the questioning, she was escorted back to the office and interrogated again. Several students and others witnessed the events that took place outside the office. Picarella v. Terrizzi, 893 F. Supp. 1292, 1296 (M.D. Pa. 1995). After weighing the state's interest and the manner of the questioning against the student's privacy interest, the district court found no Fourth Amendment violation.

Following Vernonia School District, the district court determined that a public school student has a reduced expectation of privacy because of the responsibility of the school as custodian and educator. Picarella v. Terrizzi, 893 F. Supp. 1292, 1301 (M.D. Pa. 1995). Because the questioning of the student was conducted in private and because the events witnessed by other students occurred when the student left the private room and were not due to any conduct on the part of the school officials, the detention and questioning was legitimate. The court stated that there was "no question" of the state's interest in preventing and punishing child abuse, an interest that outweighed the interests of the student. Picarella v. Terrizzi, 893 F. Supp. 1292 (M.D. Pa. 1995). In sum, under Vernonia School District and Picarella, where a student's expectations of privacy are diminished and where the prevention and punishment of child abuse are extremely important state interests, school officials may have considerable freedom to investigate allegations of child abuse as long as their manner of questioning is not overly intrusive. At the very least, school officials must conduct the questioning discreetly and in private away from other students and any other uninvolved parties. For a discussion of what constitutes a "seizure" of a student, *see* Section 6:14.

§ 5:7 Frisk of the student's person for weapons— Purpose and general requirements

School officials may frisk a student for weapons during the course of a valid and lawful stop if they believe that their safety or that of others may be endangered because the student is presently armed and dangerous. Terry v. Ohio, 392 U.S. at 24; In the Interest of Angelia D.B., 564 N.W.2d 682 (Wis. 1997). Specific requirements related to the purpose and basis of a weapons frisk are discussed here; methodological considerations are treated separately below.

(1) *The frisk must be coincident with a valid and lawful stop.* The right to frisk for weapons exists only if the school officials have proper constitutional grounds for detaining and questioning the student pursuant to an investigative stop. Adams v. Williams, 407 U.S. 143, 146 (1972). In the usual case, however, if school officials have reason to believe a student is armed, they would have proper grounds for an investigative stop.

(2) *Protective purpose.* The usual purpose justifying a frisk is to neutralize weapons in order to protect school officials and others from grave physical injury or death. Adams v. Williams, 407 U.S. 143, 146 (1972).

Frisks connected with valid investigative stops cannot be used more generally for the prevention and detection of other infractions. It is also improper to conduct a frisk for purposes of preserving evidence that might be destroyed or to search for anything but weapons.

(3) *The student must be reasonably suspected of being both armed and dangerous.* In the school setting, any student suspected of being armed may be viewed as presumptively dangerous and capable of using the weapon against others. This assumption is proper because there is virtually no innocent or lawful reason for students to possess a weapon while in school.

§ 5:8   Frisk of the student's person for weapons— Reasonable suspicion requirement

School officials cannot routinely frisk students for weapons as part of every investigative stop. In order to conduct a lawful frisk for weapons, officials must at least reasonably suspect that the student is armed and dangerous or "whether a reasonably prudent [officer] in the circumstances would be warranted in the belief that [her] safety or that of others was in danger." In the Matter of the Welfare of P.J.K., a Child, 1998 Minn. App. LEXIS 1142 at *6 (Minn. App. 1998) (quoting from State v. Gilchrist, 299 N.W.2d 913, 916 (Minn. 1980), and Terry v. Ohio, 392 U.S. 1, 27 (1968)). This standard requires school officials to have specific articulable facts and rational inferences which in combination with their special training and expertise demonstrates a substantial possibility that the student is armed and dangerous (*see* Section 3:2).

It should be mentioned that although a frisk for weapons obviously cannot be arbitrary or based on mere hunches, the reasonable suspicion requirement is not as strictly interpreted in a frisk situation as it is for initiating a stop.

(1) *The right to frisk is immediate and automatic if a student is suspected of a violent infraction.* School officials can *immediately* frisk a student reasonably suspected of a violent infraction based on that suspicion alone. Under this circumstance, no other indication that the student may be armed and dangerous is required. In the school setting violent infractions may include:

- Assault;
- Burglary;
- Possession or use of weapons or dangerous items;
- Extortion;
- Possession of firearms;
- Murder;
- Robbery;
- Sexual offenses;
- Terroristic threatening; and
- Fighting or other threatening behavior.

(2) *Other factors sufficient to give a reasonable suspicion that the student is armed.* When a student is stopped for questioning on a suspicion of being involved with a nonviolent infraction, some indication that the student may be armed and dangerous is needed before officials can conduct a lawful frisk. The U.S. Supreme Court said in Florida v. J.L., 528 U.S. 1134 (2000), that an anonymous tip that a person is carrying a gun is not, without more, sufficient to justify a police officer's stop and frisk of that individual. An illustrative list of factors that have been found to provide the additional suspicion that would justify a frisk includes:

- Information from a teacher that the suspected student possessed a weapon (Minner v. State, 1994 WL 605761 (Tex. App. 1994)).
- Suspicious or characteristic bulges in the student's clothing suggesting the possibility of a concealed weapon (State v. Allen, 93 Wash. 2d 170, 606 P.2d 1235, 1236 (1980)).
- Directly observing all or part of an object that could be a weapon (Commonwealth v. Wascom, 236 Pa. Super. 157, 344 A.2d 630, 632 (1975)).
- Sudden inexplicable moves toward a pocket or other place that might conceal a weapon (United States ex rel. Griffin v. Vincent, 359 F. Supp. 1072, 1076 (S.D.N.Y. 1973)).
- Knowledge that the suspected student has previously been involved in serious or violent

infractions (People v. Allen, 50 Cal. App. 3d 896, 901, 123 Cal. Rptr. 80, 82 (1975)).

- Knowledge that the suspected student has previously been found to be armed (State v. Hobart, 94 Wash. 2d 437, 617 P.2d 429, 433 (1980)).

- The discovery of any weapon on the student's person (Commonwealth v. Wascom, 344 A.2d at 632 (after finding a knife openly exposed to public view in the student's pocket, officials can conduct a frisk on the assumption that there may be other weapons)).

As noted earlier, the reasonable suspicion requirement for a frisk is not interpreted strictly, but officials should not assume incorrectly that no standards at all apply. Because the intent of this provision is to protect officials during investigative encounters, they may frisk if the surrounding circumstances indicate that their safety or that of others may be endangered.

§ 5:9   Frisk of the student's person for weapons—Scope and intensity limits

The lawful scope of a weapons frisk is very narrowly defined.

(1) *Strictly limited to a search for weapons.* The only justification for a weapons frisk is personal protection. Consequently, there are two restrictions on the scope and intensity of a frisk.

- The frisk must be restricted to finding weapons or implements that could be grasped easily by the student to assault an official during a brief face-to-face investigative encounter. Examples include guns, large knives, clubs, and other similar implements. Terry v. Ohio, 392 U.S. at 29.

  In most cases the scope and intensity of a lawful frisk cannot encompass very small or cleverly concealed implements that the student could not reach without considerable difficulty and delay. The premise is that officials can easily summon help or neutralize the student if the student attempted to remove a razor blade cleverly hidden in a pocket.

Similarly, officials should avoid "fanciful speculation" about what might be a potential weapon. The term "weapon" as used here refers to guns, large knives, clubs, and the like, but not a cigarette lighter that could be used as a torch, or a plastic water pistol that may be filled with acid. There would be virtually no limit on the scope and intensity of a frisk if such speculation were permitted. People v. Collins, 1 Cal. 3d 658, 663, 83 Cal. Rptr. 179, 183, 463 P.2d 403, 407 (1970).

- Officials may not frisk the student for anything but weapons. A weapons frisk cannot be used as an opportunity to search for contraband, to preserve evidence, or for any other evidentiary purpose. Such items may be lawfully seized, however, if they are inadvertently discovered during the course of a lawful frisk (see the Plain View discussion in Sections 6:5 and 6:9). State v. Hobart, 94 Wash. 2d 437, 617 P.2d at 433–34.

(2) *Search of possessions.* School officials may search any closely held possession of the suspected student if they reasonably suspect that the item may conceal a weapon. Examples include bags, purses, knapsacks, and packages that can be readily opened (but not those sealed with tape or string), and any other closed opaque containers. United States v. McClinnhan, 660 F.2d 500, 504 (D.C. Cir. 1981). The only restriction is that the possessions searched must be plausible repositories for weapons. Thus, officials could not normally search small envelopes, diaries, calendars, and similar items for weapons.

A search of immediately held property is allowed as part of a weapons frisk, because simply removing possessions that might conceal a weapon from the student's immediate control will not dissipate the threat to safety. If the frisk of the student's person were fruitless, those possessions would have to be returned. The student could then use any weapon concealed in the returned items against the official. United States

v. McClinnhan, 660 F.2d 500, 504 (D.C. Cir. 1981).

(3) *Frisk of companions.* Occasionally, circumstances may justify frisking the companions of a student who is suspected of being armed. This action can sometimes be justified even if the school officials would not otherwise have had any grounds to stop and question the companions. Again, the purpose is self-protection. The following circumstances illustrate when a frisk of companions might be justified:

- When the student is suspected of a very serious or violent infraction (United States v. Vigo, 487 F.2d 295, 298 (2d Cir. 1973) (narcotics dealer found with a gun on his person justifies search of his companion's purse for additional weapons)).

- When the official is in an isolated or remote location (United States v. Tharpe, 536 F.2d at 1100).

- When there are several companions whose numerical advantage might be multiplied if they are armed (United States v. Tharpe, 536 F.2d at 1100).

- When the companions make any defiant, menacing, or otherwise threatening gesture (United States v. Gonzalez, 319 F. Supp. 563, 564–65 (D. Conn. 1970)).

- When the companions attempt to intrude or otherwise interfere with the stop and frisk (People v. Roach, 15 Cal. App. 3d 628, 632, 93 Cal. Rptr. 354, 356 (1971)).

School officials must proceed carefully in these situations. Merely being in the vicinity of a suspected student does not necessarily imply illegal conduct.

§ 5:10   Frisk of the student's person for weapons— Method: Frisk of the student's person for weapons

It is worth emphasizing again that any frisk of the student's person will be highly intrusive and must not be undertaken routinely or without strong justification.

Normally, the frisk process will involve two steps. First, an external pat-down of the student's outer garments for indications that a weapon may be present. If and only upon having such indication, officials may then intrude beneath the surface of the student's clothing to search for and remove any weapon.

(1) *Patting-down students of the opposite sex.* Ideally, school officials should refrain from patting-down students of the opposite sex.

This restraint is not strictly obligatory, however, because weapons frisks invariably occur in settings where the school officials have reason to believe that they are in immediate or imminent danger. Consequently, there will seldom be any opportunity to secure assistance from another official of appropriate sex to conduct the frisk. *See, e.g.,* In the Interest of Angelia D.B., 564 N.W.2d 682, 692 (Wis. 1997), where the court ruled that it was reasonable and only "a relatively minor intrusion" for a male police liaison to pat down a 15-year-old female student, and then lift her shirt to observe her waistline, when she was suspected of possessing a knife in school.

(2) *The pat-down.* Patting-down the surface of a student's outer garments can take many different forms and vary in scope and intensity. The important point is that it must be consistent with finding weapons that a student could readily grasp to assault an official during a face-to-face interrogation. The pat-down may, therefore, be as thorough as necessary to detect guns, large knives, clubs, and other similar implements but not so meticulous as to discover hidden razors, needles, or other items that have only a remote possibility of being used as weapons. State v. Woodford, 26 Ohio Misc. 51, 269 N.E.2d 143, 148 (1971).

In most cases, it is not deemed necessary or appropriate to touch and scrutinize every possible area of the student's body. Normally, officials would be justified in using their hands and fingers to pat-down and feel around the *armpits, pockets,* and *waist band area* of a student's body.

School officials will have virtually no occasion to conduct a full-scale pat-down. In the exceptional case when such a highly intrusive procedure can be justified, they can use their hands and fingers to explore and feel the surface of every part of the student's body, including the arms, armpits, waist and back, groin area, legs, and feet. *This is not a normal procedure; it can only be used in exceptional circumstances.*

The primary purpose of conducting a pat-down is to prevent further unnecessary intrusions on the student's person. Conversely, a pat-down can furnish the necessary justification for searching below the surface of a student's clothing.

Under certain limited circumstances, officials may dispense with the pat-down and immediately conduct a search for weapons. This procedure might be justified if they believe that the student may already be going for the weapon (e.g., the student makes a sudden move toward a pocket which might conceal a weapon) or they see part of the weapon protruding from some area.

Tactile sensations that justify a search for weapons. School officials may proceed to search beneath the surface of a student's outer garments upon feeling a hard object whose size and density is such that it might be a weapon, such as a metallic item shaped like a gun or knife.

Officials need not be certain that such items are in fact weapons; a reasonable possibility is sufficient.

Officials are allowed greater leeway in deciding whether something might be a weapon when the student is wearing heavy or bulky clothing, because the nature of such clothing can hamper that determination.

A search is not normally permitted if officials feel something soft (even if they cannot determine what it might be). This is consistent with the earlier proscription against "fanciful speculation" about what might potentially be a weapon. Guns, knives, or clubs are not soft and if concealed in heavy padding would be very difficult to reach and use in face-to-face encounters. People v. Collins, 1 Cal. 3d at 662, 83 Cal. Rptr. at 182, 463 P.2d at 406.

(3) *Search of the student's person after pat-down.* Upon feeling a hard object whose size and density suggests a weapon, school officials may intrude below the surface of clothing to remove the item for examination. If the object turns out to be a weapon, they may seize it. Commonwealth v. Hawkes, 362 Mass. 786, 291 N.E.2d 411, 413 (1973). Officials must return to the student any item that is not a weapon or that could not plausibly be used as a weapon.

Note that the right to search for a weapon does not give officials the authority to conduct a full search of the student's person. They may only reach below the surface of clothing to remove suspicious hard objects detected by a frisk.

In most cases, officials will not know exactly what the suspected object is before removing it for examination. Sometimes, as the suspected object is being removed, they may immediately determine that it is not a weapon by direct feel, if, for example, they reach into a pocket for the hard rectangular object thought to be a knife and find that it is a comb. In such cases officials can proceed to remove the object and look at it. There is no expectation that they must finely divide the stages of the search to accommodate this sort of re-evaluation.

If the suspected object is found to be a closed opaque container, officials may open and examine it so long as a weapon might reasonably be concealed within. The size, weight, and feel of such containers is relevant to that determination. People v. Ortiz, 67 Haw. 181, 683 P.2d 822, 826–27 (1984).

As mentioned above, officials may also search for other closely held possessions that might conceal a weapon.

(4) *Plain view.* Although it is not legitimate to search for anything but weapons in this situation, officials may seize any incriminating item inadvert-

ently discovered as a result of a weapons frisk provided that all necessary requirements for a plain view seizure are satisfied (Section 6:5).

Chapter 6

Seizure

Research References

West's Key Number Digest
Schools ⊕139.5; Searches and Seizures ⊕13, 30

KeyCite®: Cases and other legal materials listed in KeyCite Scope can
be researched through West's KeyCite service on Westlaw®. Use
KeyCite to check citations for form, parallel references, prior and
later history, and comprehensive citator information, including citations to other decisions and secondary materials.

Three types of seizure occur in the school setting: (1)
seizures incident to lawful student searches; (2) plain view
seizures; and (3) open public view seizures. Although each
type of seizure has distinct antecedent requirements, they
all require lawful access to the item before it can be seized.
In most cases, lawful access will originate with a valid
student search. Sometimes lawful access is given by virtue
of the surrounding circumstances.

§ 6:1   Seizures incident to lawful student searches

This section details what actions are permitted upon discovering any sought-after items during a student search. Much of the material is also applicable to plain view and open public view seizures.

§ 6:2   Seizures incident to lawful student searches—What is a seizure?

Seizures present considerably fewer problems of interpretation and implementation than searches. This difference exists because a search will generally precede any seizure and thus offers significantly greater opportunities to intrude unjustifiably upon individual privacy expectations.

Under the Fourth Amendment, a seizure is any government action that materially interferes with a student's possessory interests in tangible property. United States v. Jacobsen, 466 U.S. 109, 113 (1984). In the school setting, something is "seized" when school officials confiscate or take it away from a student. A seizure can occur even if the student hands the item to the official if the transfer cannot be reasonably characterized as being voluntary.

§ 6:3   Seizures incident to lawful student searches—What may be seized?

School officials may seize any item discovered during a valid and lawful student search that has been:

(1)   Properly connected beforehand with a specific infraction (Section 3:3);

(2)   Properly connected beforehand with the place to be searched (Section 3:3); and

(3)   Described with sufficient particularity to assure a reasonable certainty of proper identification (Section 3:4).

Any fruits, instruments, contraband, or other evidence related to the suspected infraction and meeting these three criteria may be seized.

Plain view exception. Under some conditions, it is also possible to seize incriminating items that were not initially particularized as objects of the search. This action is permitted if the items are discovered in "plain view" (*see*

Section 6:5). Thus, if school officials inadvertently see something incriminating during a lawful search that was not initially expected, it can be seized if all requirements for a plain view seizure are satisfied. Coolidge v. New Hampshire, 403 U.S. 443, 465 (1971).

Private papers: Special considerations. The seizure of private papers such as books, journals, records, or diaries poses special problems because no matter how precisely such items are described, their seizure may nonetheless be seen to be the equivalent of a "ransack search." For example, the only way to isolate sought-after documents that are intermingled with other personal papers and records may be to read and expose all of the student's papers indiscriminately. Such conduct could easily raise objections that the officials engaged in a general roving exploratory search (i.e., an unlawful search).

No completely satisfactory solution has been found for this problem. One possibility is to have the student pick out and hand to the officials specifically described documents that may be intermingled with other papers. If the student refuses to cooperate, the officials might impound and seal all of the papers that may contain the sought-after documents. A hearing could then be held so that persons with proper standing can petition for the return of certain papers or specify conditions and limitations that would protect their privacy interests during any subsequent search.

§ 6:4   Seizures incident to lawful student searches—Inventory, receipt, custodial, and reporting requirements

Once school officials have seized something pursuant to a lawful student search, good management practice requires them to: (1) prepare an accurate list describing the items; (2) provide the student with a receipt documenting the seizure; (3) implement appropriate custodial procedures to preserve the evidentiary value of any seized items that may be used in disciplinary proceedings; (4) transfer any requested evidence to the police; and (5) arrange for the final disposition or return of seized items. In addition, special procedures are necessary for seizures related to very serious crimes or which involve extremely hazardous or deadly items.

(1) *Inventory of items seized.* All items should be listed and described in terms of their quantity, condition, and any distinguishing characteristics such as color, size, and serial numbers. This good management practice will facilitate any subsequent disciplinary proceeding. It also serves to protect school officials against any false claim for damage or loss.

(2) *Receipt.* An item identification tag should be made for each seized item and a *receipt* given to the student. This practice documents and formalizes the seizure and provides a mechanism by which evidentiary items can eventually be reclaimed.

(3) *Custodial requirements to protect evidence.* Once something is seized, school officials must take precautions to preserve its evidentiary value. Otherwise the evidence may be of no use in subsequent disciplinary proceedings. In order for evidence to be admissible during a disciplinary proceeding, it must be authenticated or identified through testimony showing: (a) that the item introduced as evidence is the same item that was lawfully seized; (b) that the item is in substantially the same condition as when it was originally seized and has not been altered; and (c) that any tangible change in the item has a valid and plausible explanation (e.g., that some laboratory testing altered the item's shape).

Generally, an unbroken "chain of custody" must be established to support these facts. The evidence must be in continuous possession of known officials who can testify to that custody. This requirement assures the identity and integrity of evidence by precluding any opportunity for unknown or unauthorized persons to have access to it (no matter how briefly). An unbroken chain of custody can be established by:

- Individually tagging each item seized with an item identification tag.
- Maintaining constant physical possession of the item so that it is never left unattended even for a brief moment.

- Depositing the item in a secure and locked storage area where access is controlled by and restricted to known officials. This area must be locked at all times, its keys or combinations must be secured, and some sort of sign-in/sign-out procedure must be in force.
- Assuring that any official who must withdraw evidence for a valid purpose such as laboratory testing does so by first signing the item out.
- Assuring that the chain of custody remains unbroken during any period when the evidence is withdrawn from storage. For example, laboratory technicians conducting a test of an item should be reminded that they must never leave it unattended.

(4) *Transfer of requested evidence to police.* Police may request the transfer of certain evidence related to offenses for further investigation. Any such transfer should be handled by the school principal who will arrange for proper receipts of transfer and subsequent school access during disciplinary proceedings.

(5) *Final disposition or return of seized items.* Weapons, illegal substances, and similar items should not be returned to students.

Evidence may be retained until its evidentiary value has been exhausted completely. If evidence used in one disciplinary proceeding may be useful in some other proceeding or context, it can be retained.

- *Fruits.* Fruits of an infraction such as stolen property may be returned to their rightful owners at the conclusion of the disciplinary proceeding. School officials should send a written notice to the owner indicating that the property can be reclaimed after providing proper identification and showing some acceptable claim of ownership. This notice should include a date after which any unclaimed property will be discarded or destroyed. The person claiming the item should sign a receipt acknowledging the return, and school officials should retain and file all signed receipts.

● *Instruments, contraband, and other evidence.*
School officials will generally transfer criminally unlawful items such as firearms and
large quantities of drugs to the police. In that
case, students or their parents must attempt
to reclaim the items under police rules.

School officials should send a written notice
to the student's parents indicating that they
may reclaim the property after identifying
themselves and showing some acceptable claim
of ownership. This notice should include a date
after which any unclaimed property will be
discarded or destroyed. Parents claiming the
property should sign a receipt which should be
retained by the school.

(6) *Special procedures for very serious crimes and
extremely hazardous or deadly items.* Additional
precautions are needed when officials seize evidence of very serious crimes or if the item is
extremely hazardous or deadly. Steps should be
taken to preserve the evidentiary value of such
items for criminal court proceedings.

The Supreme Court has not yet considered
whether evidence seized by school officials pursuant to or in violation of a T.L.O.-type search is
admissible in criminal court proceedings (*see*
Chapter 7). New Jersey v. T.L.O., 469 U.S. at
333, n.3 (declining to determine whether evidence should be excluded from a criminal
proceeding). This question is complicated because
juvenile proceedings are not usually considered
criminal in nature, although some courts are
reevaluating this issue. School officials will inevitably come into contact with evidence that may
be relevant to criminal proceedings. Because it is
not always possible to avoid such contact or to
alert police beforehand, some attempt must be
made to preserve the admissibility of this
evidence.

When school officials seize weapons, drugs, or
evidence of a serious crime such as murder, and
these items will be transferred to police for even-
tual criminal prosecution, they should:

- avoid handling the items in a manner that could destroy fingerprints, residues, or other potentially useful indicia of the crime;
- seal the items individually in *clear* plastic bags; and
- label the bags as follows:

ATTENTION: Do Not Examine Until Warrant Requirements Satisfied.

This action will help to prevent police from inadvertently tainting the evidence.

If school officials have lawfully opened any closed opaque container during a valid student search, they should *leave the container open* before sealing it in a clear plastic bag. In some cases the police cannot lawfully open such containers without a warrant or they will taint the evidence. If they are unable to view the contents of such containers, they may not be able to arrest a student immediately. If the incriminating containers are left open, the police can make an immediate determination about whether proper grounds exist for an arrest.

§ 6:5 Plain view seizures

Incriminating evidence discovered unexpectedly during a search or other justified intrusion may be seized even if this evidence was not originally particularized as the proper object of a search (Sections 3:3 and 3:4), provided:

(1) The underlying search or intrusion is valid and lawful;

(2) The evidence is discovered inadvertently; and

(3) The incriminating character of the evidence is immediately apparent (Coolidge v. New Hampshire, 403 U.S. at 466).

These plain view rules apply regardless of whether the unexpected evidence may relate to some other unrelated infraction. The purpose of these rules is to allow for the seizure of an incriminating item under prescribed conditions even when the item was not originally anticipated or specified.

The only exceptions are that school officials may not undertake a plain view seizure of any material protected by the First Amendment (Roaden v. Kentucky, 413 U.S. 496, 502 (1972)) (Section 3:4) and they may not seize any item located on the student's person unless proper grounds exist for searching the student's person (Section 3:1).

§ 6:6 Plain view seizures—Prior valid intrusion

An essential precondition for plain view seizure is that the access to the object and the view must be fundamentally lawful. This requirement means that the school officials must come upon unexpected incriminating evidence while engaged in a valid and lawful search or other justified intrusion. Texas v. Brown, 460 U.S. 730, 738 n.4 (1983). This condition is satisfied in the school setting when:

    (1) *There is a prior valid intrusion.* School officials must have established the proper grounds for and be in the midst of a lawful:

      — student search (Section 3:1);

      — emergency intrusion (Section 2:9);

      — consent search (Section 2:14);

      — automobile search (Section 3:12); or

      — investigative stop/frisk for weapons (Chapter 5).

Nothing may be seized if the search or intrusion is unlawful or invalid.

    (2) *The item is actually in plain view.* The unexpected incriminating evidence must be uncovered during a search or justified intrusion whose scope, intensity, and duration are properly limited as actually conducted. The plain view provision thus permits school officials to seize incriminating evidence that is exposed to detection when they are looking in a manner authorized by law. *See, e.g.,* Bundick v. Bay City Ind. School Dist., 140 F.Supp.2d 735, 738 (S.D.Tex. 2001) (upholding a seizure of a machete from a toolbox in a student's truck after the toolbox had been opened following an "alert" on the truck by a dog trained to detect narcotics, gunpowder, alcohol and medications).

School officials cannot seize any such evidence if it is discovered only by exceeding the reasonable and lawful scope, intensity, and duration limits prescribed for a search or justified intrusion. People v. Hill, 12 Cal. 3d 731, 117 Cal. Rptr. 393, 528 P.2d 1, 13 (1974). For example, suppose school officials have valid grounds to search a student's locker for stolen shop equipment such as pliers or wrenches. In this situation, the plain view provision cannot be used to seize a small packet of drugs discovered while looking through an appointment calendar found in the locker. In this example, the reasonable scope and intensity limits of a search for stolen shop equipment would have been exceeded. Pliers and wrenches cannot possibly be hidden in an appointment calendar and the school officials should not have been looking there without any other justification. The drugs would not therefore actually have been in plain view if the scope and intensity of the search had been lawfully confined.

Similarly, incriminating evidence uncovered after the primary objective of the search or justified intrusion has been achieved cannot be seized under the plain view provisions. If school officials unlawfully continue to search after finding the item originally justifying a search or after an emergency is dissipated, the plain view doctrine could not be validly used to seize any incriminating evidence subsequently discovered. Again, if they had properly concluded the search or intrusion as required, the incriminating evidence would not actually have been in plain view.

It is important to understand that not only must the view of unexpected incriminating evidence be lawful, but the school officials must have had lawful access as well. Illinois v. Andreas, 463 U.S. 765, 771 (1983). Having a lawful view does not immediately imply lawful access. Certain open public view observations (Section 2:4) provide the clearest illustration of this fact. Suppose school officials unexpectedly observe some obviously incriminating item such as a gun through the wire mesh door of a student's locker. Their view of the gun is unquestionably lawful, but because the locker is a protected place, they do not have immediate lawful access. In this case the officials must carefully determine whether their view of the gun provides the proper justification for a search (in this instance, it probably does).

§ 6:7 Plain view seizures—Inadvertent discovery

A second requirement for plain view seizures is that the incriminating evidence must be uncovered inadvertently. The school officials must not have anticipated discovering the evidence or known of its location in advance. This limitation is designed to protect students from unjustified searches that circumvent Fourth Amendment standards. If the location of incriminating evidence (not originally particularized as a basis for the search or intrusion) was known beforehand and if the school officials had an intention to seize it, they cannot justify a seizure under the plain view doctrine. Coolidge v. New Hampshire, 403 U.S. at 470–71. Dangerous contraband, stolen property, or lethal items are generally considered to be exceptions to the inadvertent discovery rule. *Id.* at 471–72. Such items may be validly seized in plain view even with prior knowledge. *See* United States v. Vargas, 621 F.2d 54, 56 (2d Cir. 1980) (contraband can be seized without reference to inadvertence); United States v. Cutts, 535 F.2d 1083, 1084 (8th Cir. 1976) (weapons or contraband seizure does not require inadvertence).

The inadvertent discovery requirement remains controversial, because the Supreme Court has never clearly specified what degree of expectation officials are permitted to have and still claim an inadvertent discovery. Moreover, the purpose of this requirement seems less clear in the school setting where search warrants are not required. Consequently, the inadvertent discovery requirement is probably not as critical to plain view seizures in schools as the requirements of a prior valid intrusion and an immediately apparent incriminating character.

To the extent that some specification is possible, it is safe to say that complete ignorance of the evidence is not demanded as a condition for inadvertent discovery. Texas v. Brown, 460 U.S. 730, 743–44 (1983) (officials can hold a generalized suspicion or an expectation that evidence will be found). A valid claim can generally be made if the school officials do not have sufficient information beforehand to know reliably that unspecified evidence is in the particular place that will be lawfully searched or intruded into. For example, they may have a general idea that drug paraphernalia will usually be found in the presence of drugs. But if they do not have sufficient information to particularize such items as part of the basis for their search, any subsequent discovery (during a lawful search for drugs) would be considered inadvertent.

Avoid pretext searches. Sometimes school officials may know the location of important evidence and wish to make a seizure, but lack the proper grounds for a search. In that case, they cannot search for some inconsequential item in hopes of being "lawfully" positioned to seize the otherwise inaccessible evidence in plain view. It does not matter that the search for the inconsequential item may be technically correct under Fourth Amendment standards. The key question is whether that search would normally have been conducted even if there was no desire to seize the inaccessible evidence. If such a search would not have taken place, it will be viewed as an invalid pretext for the real objective (i.e., the seizure of otherwise inaccessible evidence). Any evidence seized in connection with a pretext search must be excluded. Amador-Gonzalez v. United States, 391 F.2d 308, 313–14 (5th Cir. 1968) (an arrest cannot be used as a pretext for an unlawful search); State v. Blair, 691 S.W.2d 259, 262 (Mo. 1985) (an arrest for a parking violation cannot be used as a pretext to search).

To illustrate, a search for a cigarette lighter might be considered a pretext if school officials would not normally bother with such trivial searches and the real objective appears to be to seize otherwise inaccessible evidence of major vandalism. In this case, a convincing argument can be made that the search for the lighter only serves as a means of circumventing Fourth Amendment protection to gain access to the inaccessible vandalism evidence.

The pretext objection does not apply to any search that would normally have been conducted, regardless of the underlying motivation. In the example above, no pretext is likely to be found if school officials seized the otherwise inaccessible vandalism evidence while searching for evidence of assault (a very serious offense which must be investigated). The assault presents a valid and lawful purpose, and the search would have been conducted regardless of whether officials knew of the vandalism evidence.

§ 6:8   Plain view seizures—Incriminating character of the evidence is immediately apparent

As a general rule, the Fourth Amendment does not permit a search for unspecified items. The purpose of this restriction is to protect against roving exploratory searches. The incriminating character of inadvertently discovered evidence seized in plain view must therefore be immediately apparent without any need for detailed inspection or scrutiny. There are two aspects of this rule:

(1)   *The nexus between item and infraction.* School officials cannot seize something under the plain view doctrine simply because it seems suspicious or might prove useful later. They must have sufficient facts to reasonably suspect (Section 3:2) that the inadvertently discovered item is a fruit, instrument, contraband, or other evidence of some specific infraction (Section 3:3). United States v. Hillyard, 677 F.2d 1336, 1341–42 (9th Cir. 1982). Recall that the infraction may either be the one originally justifying the search or intrusion or it may be an unrelated infraction. Chambers v. State, 508 S.W.2d 348, 352 (Tex. Crim. App. 1974).

When something is discovered *inadvertently,* its incriminating character can be established by, among other things:

- Any special knowledge or expertise the school officials possess. Officials can, for example, make a valid plain view seizure of "drug paraphernalia," including such innocent items as plastic bags or scales, if they have had special drug enforcement training or experience. But even with such expertise, they could not seize a closed plastic vial of generic looking pills because they would have no basis to decide whether the pills might actually be legal (assuming they had no other evidence). Eisenman v. Superior Court, 21 Cal. App. 3d 342, 350, 98 Cal. Rptr. 342, 347 (1972).

- Indications that an item might be the fruit of a

crime. For example, officials might reasonably suspect that an item inadvertently discovered is stolen property because its serial number has been obliterated, or because they know a similar item was recently stolen in the area, or because they find unusually large quantities of the item.

- A clear determination that the item is contraband which students are prohibited from possessing.
- The collective determination of other officials who may be present or corroboration by an expert, witness, or victim.

(2) *The "immediately apparent" requirement.* The main question here is how closely school officials may look to determine whether inadvertently discovered items might be incriminating evidence. To be consistent with the purpose of protecting against illegal exploratory searches, the Supreme Court allows no more than a "mere inspection" under very limited conditions.

The main concern here is to protect from inspection items that fall outside the reasonable scope of the search or intrusion. Any item within the proper limits of a search or intrusion can be scrutinized as closely as is reasonable and necessary to find the object originally justifying the search or intrusion. If any conspicuously incriminating evidence is inadvertently discovered during such an acute examination, its seizure will not be invalidated by the intensity of the inspection.

Occasionally, the incriminating character of an item may be self-evident, requiring not even a casual inspection. A gun discovered during a search, for example, is obviously seizable as contraband. *See, e.g.,* Bundick v. Bay City Ind. School Dist., 140 F.Supp.2d 735, 738 (S.D.Tex. 2001) (upholding a seizure of a machete from a toolbox in a student's truck after a dog trained to detect narcotics, gunpowder, alcohol and medications had "alerted" on the truck, because "it was 'immediately apparent' that the machete was an illegal knife under the school district rules; therefore, taking possession of the machete constituted a valid 'plain view seizure'").

Sometimes the incriminating character of an item may be established by mere inspection, or a cursory examination which amounts to nothing more than picking something up and noting physical properties such as a brand name or serial number. United States v. Marbury, 732 F.2d 390, 399 (5th Cir. 1984); Basham v. Commonwealth, 675 S.W.2d 376, 383–84 (Ky. 1984). This inspection is permitted only when the item gives some indication of being a fruit, instrument, contraband, or other evidence of an infraction. School officials cannot validly inspect, no matter how superficially, everything that comes into view during a lawful search or justified intrusion. In order to inspect an item that falls outside the reasonable scope of a search or justified intrusion, some fact or circumstance must indicate that it might be incriminating evidence.

Indications of this sort are generally more apparent and persuasive when unexpected evidence appears related to the infraction originally justifying the search or intrusion. Chambers v. State, 508 S.W.2d at 352–53. Incriminating clues are easier to justify in that case because the school officials should be more familiar with the surrounding circumstances. For example, there might be reason to believe that something unexpectedly found near other evidence of the infraction being investigated could be an instrument or other evidence customarily connected with such infractions. Suppose while searching for a stolen radio, school officials find not only the particular radio but also observe several other radios nearby. Under this circumstance, it is reasonable to suspect that the other radios might also be stolen, and school officials could superficially inspect them for confirmation (e.g., to see if their serial numbers are obliterated) and possible plain view seizure.

School officials must keep in mind, however,

that the plain view doctrine is not intended as a general grant of authority to examine everything in sight. This provision is meant only to accommodate the inadvertent discovery of conspicuously incriminating evidence. That is, it offers a chance to avoid passing up something that is clearly incriminating but was not particularized as an object of the search.

One final point of clarification is required. The casual inspection allowed under this rule does not permit any disassembly, close detailed reading, minute scrutiny, or other forms of intense examination. Commonwealth v. Bowers, 217 Pa. Super. 317, 274 A.2d 546, 548 (1970) (police called television repairer to dismantle a television in an attempt to locate the serial number). Casual inspections can, however, involve the use of other senses such as smell or hearing. See Section 2:5. For example, if school officials have special training in drug detection (Section 3:7) and detect the distinctive odor of marijuana plainly emanating from a closed opaque plastic bag, they could validly examine and seize it under the plain view doctrine.

§ 6:9 Open public view seizures

This form of seizure originates with open public view observations (Section 2:4). If school officials lawfully observe some conspicuously incriminating evidence that is openly exposed to public view and scrutiny, they may seize it provided the evidence is not located in a protected place (Section 2:3).

Open public view observations are not considered to be searches under the Fourth Amendment. Consequently, officials may seize even nonthreatening contraband items that are openly exposed and not located in protected places—subject to the restrictions specified in Section 6:11. In other words, even if officials cannot lawfully search for certain nonthreatening contraband (assuming no misuse or connection with a threatening infraction), these items may be seized under proper conditions.

§ 6:10   Open public view seizures—Requirements for an open public view seizure

Open public view seizures are most closely related to plain view seizures. The two are distinguishable in that lawful and proper open public view seizures do not involve any prior intrusion under the Fourth Amendment. School officials simply come upon and observe a situation without any preceding suspicions or intention to search or seize. That observation may or may not subsequently justify the seizure of something as incriminating evidence.

Despite this difference, the requirements for lawful open public view seizures parallel those for lawful plain view seizures in several important respects. First, the "view" of the item must be lawful according to standards for an open public view (Section 2:7). In the absence of a lawful view, any resulting seizure would be invalid. Illinois v. Andreas, 463 U.S. at 771.

A second parallel requirement is that only items reasonably suspected (Section 3:2) of being the fruit, instrument, contraband, or other evidence of some specific infraction (Section 3:3) may be seized under provisions for open public view seizures. The item-infraction nexus is a necessary precondition for open public view seizures. Officials cannot seize something simply because it seems suspicious or may prove useful later. Illinois v. Andreas, 463 U.S. 765, 771 (1983).

The circumstances for establishing a reasonable nexus between item and infraction under open public view conditions are like those for a plain view seizure (Section 6:8). Because the encounter is brief, school officials will initially have only very limited data. Accordingly, the incriminating character of an item will usually come from:

(1) An official's special knowledge and expertise;

(2) Indications that something may be the fruit of a crime because the officials observe unusual quantities or have some other knowledge;

(3) A clear indication that something is contraband which students are prohibited from possessing, such as a gun or radio, but not some white powdery substance that might be talc; or

(4) The collective determination of other officials present or corroboration by an expert, witness, or victim.

See Section 6:8 and, more generally, Sections 3:6 and 3:7.

§ 6:11   Open public view seizures—Restrictions and limitations

A number of notable exceptions and limitations follow from the fact that open public view seizures are not based on any valid prior search or intrusion:

(1)   School officials cannot physically inspect suspicious items, even in a cursory manner, to establish their incriminating character. That determination must be made only on the basis of sense data allowed under provisions for a lawful open public view (Section 2:6).

(2)   School officials cannot seize and search or examine any item or closed opaque container simply because it is in open view and not located in a protected area. United States v. Chadwick, 433 U.S. 1, 6 (1977). The only exceptions are for emergencies (Section 2:9), consent (Section 2:14), or abandonment (Section 2:23).

Officials may seize closed opaque containers only if articulable facts lead them to reasonably suspect that they may contain fruits, instruments, contraband, or other evidence. Esco v. State, 668 S.W.2d 358, 361–62 (Tex. Crim. App. 1982). Any subsequent opening and examination of the container's contents would amount to a search. Consequently, officials must carefully determine whether they have proper grounds for a lawful search (Section 3:1).

School officials may seize and search items and containers when their contents are plainly visible (e.g., a clear plastic bag) and they have a reasonable suspicion that some of the contents are incriminating evidence. Arkansas v. Sanders, 442 U.S. 753, 764 (1979) (officials can also seize the contents of a container when the contents can be inferred from the container (e.g., a gun case)); Holland v. State, 1997 WL 7025 (Tex. App. 1997) (holding that a small piece of tin foil that fell out of a wallet and later was acknowledged to contain LSD could be viewed as a plain view situation, when evidence from a previously reliable informant also provided reasonable suspicion that the student possessed LSD).

The rule allowing open public view seizures must not be misused to furnish a means of circumventing the Fourth Amendment protection against unreasonable government searches.

(3) In the absence of an emergency (Section 2:9) or consent (Section 2:14), school officials cannot automatically seize an item exposed to open public view if it is located on the student's person. It does not matter that the item may be conspicuously incriminating or that it can be seized without interfering with the student.

To seize an item from a student's person, school officials must carefully determine whether they have proper grounds for a lawful search (Section 3:1), and they must pay particular attention to the special requirements for searching the student's person (Section 4:3). It is doubtful, for instance, that a contraband radio observed sticking out of a student's shirt pocket could be seized lawfully, although it might be seizable if observed in an open knapsack. On the other hand, school officials could lawfully seize a gun seen sticking from a student's waist band under the emergency search provisions (Section 2:14). In a decision indicating greater deference to law enforcement officials, the South Carolina Court of Appeals allowed police on school grounds to seize a cigarette pack that could be seen in a 16-year-old student's pocket, and then to seize a marijuana roach that could be seen inside the clear cellophane wrapper of the cigarette pack. In re Thomas B.D., 486 S.E.2d 498 (S.C. App. 1997). Similarly, a Florida court ruled that a school official could require a student who had recently been in an altercation with another student to empty his pocket after noticing a "bulge in his right pocket" of a "hard surfaced" object, although acknowledging that "the circumstances here are, at best, marginal." R.C. v. State, 852 So. 2d 311 (Fla. Dist. Ct. App. 4th Dist. 2003).

(4)   School officials may possibly seize allegedly obscene material openly exposed to public view, but because serious First Amendment considerations are involved in this kind of seizure, it should be based on the judgment of several school officials (*see* Section 3:4).

(5)   It is worth emphasizing that absent an emergency (Section 2:9) or consent (Section 2:14), school officials may only seize incriminating evidence observed in open public view if it is not located in a protected area. If the evidence happens to be publicly exposed but located in a protected place, the school officials must comply with all requirements for a lawful student search (Section 3:1) before a valid seizure is possible. For example, even if some obviously incriminating evidence is seen through the wire mesh door of a student's locker, officials cannot immediately seize it. The proper grounds for a student search must first be established to give lawful access, and then a seizure would be valid. Illinois v. Andreas, 463 U.S. at 771.

School officials can seize the item without prior grounds for a search if it is something imminently dangerous like a bomb or weapon. In that case an emergency intrusion would be justified (Section 2:9).

§ 6:12   Open public view seizures—Relation to student searches

School officials cannot seize or search something simply because it is exposed to public view and scrutiny. Even if their view may be lawful, the act of seizing or searching through something can violate justified privacy expectations. In order to intrude lawfully on those expectations, officials must obtain valid access by establishing proper grounds for a student search. Sometimes these grounds may be obtained by an open public view observation. For example, if officials witnessed an assault, they would have valid grounds to search the suspected student who might try to hide a weapon on his or her person upon seeing an official approach.

It is therefore advisable to determine carefully whether

any public view observations might satisfy requirements for a lawful student search, even when they would not support an immediate seizure.

§ 6:13 "Plain feel" seizures

In 1993, the Supreme Court ruled that if a police officer feels a weapon underneath clothing during a pat-down search conducted according to Terry v. Ohio, 392 U.S. 1 (1968), the officer can seize the weapon without a warrant if the contour or mass of the weapon makes its incriminating character immediately apparent and the Terry frisk is otherwise conducted properly. Minnesota v. Dickerson, 508 U.S. 366 (1993). Other types of contraband can also be seized under this rule if the pat-down clearly reveals their existence.

In the Dickerson case itself, however, the Court ruled that the seizure was unconstitutional, because the officer could not immediately determine that the lump he felt was crack cocaine and came to that realization only after squeezing and manipulating the contents of Dickerson's jacket pocket. A similar situation occurred in In re S.D., 633 A.2d 172 (Pa. Super. 1993), where the Superior Court of Pennsylvania held that an officer's retrieval of fifty plastic vials of crack cocaine from a juvenile after feeling a "large hard object" in the minor's pocket during a pat-down search was unconstitutional in the absence of any evidence that the officer believed that what he felt was weapons or contraband. This new "plain feel" rule thus applies only when the item's identity is immediately apparent. Further intrusive feeling is not permitted absent a warrant for a police officer or a "reasonable suspicion" for a school official. It is unclear at this point what exactly will be required to meet the "reasonable suspicion" standard in the school context. *See* Patman v. State, 537 S.E.2d 118 (Ga.App. 2000) (ruling that the conclusion of a police officer, after a pat-down search of a student, that it "felt as though" the student had marijuana in his pocket was not sufficient to meet the "immediately identifiable" standard required by the plain-feel doctrine).

Moreover, S.D. raises yet another issue with respect to the applicability of the Dickerson "plain feel" doctrine pursuant to state constitutions. In S.D., the court stated its lack of enthusiasm to use the "plain feel" rationale to justify a search of an individual where probable cause cannot exist. In re S.D., 633 A.2d 172, 176 (Pa. Super. 1993) (quoting Commonwealth v. Marconi, 597 A.2d 616 (Pa. Super. 1991), alloc. denied, 611 A.2d 711 (1992)). Underlying the court's concern was the doctrine's reliance on the sense of touch, which is "not so definitive as the recognition of certain sounds, smells, or tastes." Under the "plain feel" doctrine, the police could assume that any small object felt in a pocket could be drugs. Under the facts of the case, the court did not have the opportunity to test the validity of Dickerson as applied to the Pennsylvania state constitution; it did state, however, that it would do so when the proper facts were presented.

In 2000, the U.S. Supreme Court rejected the idea of a blanket "plain feel" rule, when it ruled that a federal immigration official's squeezing of a bag in the overhead bin of a bus violated the passenger's Fourth Amendment rights. Bond v. United States, 120 S. Ct. 1462 (2000).

§ 6:14   Seizure of a student

What actions constitute a "seizure," or "custodial confinement" or "detention" or "arrest" of a student? This question can be difficult because students are in a constant state of confinement, at least to some extent, when they are at a public school. A school official or safety officer, for instance, always has the right to "approach someone who look[s] like a student [on school grounds] and ask him for his identification card," and then to require the individual to go a dean's office for further questioning if the person cannot provide adequate identification. People v. Butler, 725 N.Y.S.2d 534, 539–40 (N.Y.Sup. 2001); see also In re Joseph F., 102 Cal.Rptr.2d 641 (Cal.App. 2000) (same result). More significantly, the California Supreme Court has ruled that no seizure at all occurs when school officials detain students as part of an investigation: "we conclude . . . that the broad authority of school administrators over student behavior, school safety, and the learning environment requires that school officials have the power to stop a minor student in order to ask questions or conduct an investigation even in the absence of reasonable suspicion, so long as such authority is not exercised in an arbitrary, capricious, or harassing manner." In re Randy

G., 28 P.3d 239 (Cal. 2001). The Massachusetts Supreme Judicial Court has ruled similarly that interrogation of 13–14 year old students in the assistant principal's office for 15–20 minutes was not "custodial interrogation." Com. v. Ira I., 439 Mass. 805, 791 N.E.2d 894, 178 Ed. Law Rep. 491 (2003). The court explained that: "It is unrealistic to expect school officials who are responsible for addressing student behavioral issues to refrain from investigating allegations of students' harming each other, and the mere fact that such officials are in positions of authority over students does not transform every interview of a student into a custodial interrogation." Com. v. Ira I., 439 Mass. 805, 791 N.E.2d 894, 178 Ed. Law Rep. 491 (2003). *See also* Milligan v. City of Slidell, 226 F.3d 652, 655 (5th Cir. 2000) ("it is not at all clear that [students] have some privacy right not to be summoned to and detained in a school official's office for questioning on matters of school discipline"); Ianson v. Zion-Benton Township High School, 2001 WL 185021 (N.D.Ill. 2001) ("In light of the special relationship between teachers and students, the diminished protection of the Fourth Amendment for public schoolchildren and need to maintain discipline and order in the schools, the individuals' actions in detaining and interrogating plaintiffs was reasonable."); Shuman ex rel. Shertzer v. Penn Manor School Dist., 2004 WL 1109506 (E.D. Pa. 2004) (ruling that holding a student in the principal's office for 3.5 hours while an incident was investigated did not violate his Fourth Amendment rights: "It is difficult to imagine the state of American high schools if a call to the principal's office or a detention in which a student is permitted to complete school assignments and eat lunch in the school cafeteria constitutes a deprivation of that student's Fourth Amendment rights").

Some other courts that have examined this question, however, have applied the same standards that determine when an adult has been arrested or confined in other contexts. In ruling that an emotionally disabled ninth grader had been seized when he was put into a small "time out room," even though he walked into the room on his own, the court said that "[a]n encounter becomes a seizure when its circumstances 'become so intimidating as to demonstrate that a reasonable person would have believed he was not free to leave if he does not respond . . . '" Rasmus

v. State, 939 F. Supp. 709, 713 (D. Ariz. 1996). Because
the ninth grader had seen others physically thrown into
the room when they refused to enter on their own, he felt
he had no choice be to proceed into it. Similarly, a New
York court upheld a $75,000 jury verdict against a school
district that had forcibly confined a second grader with a
learning disability in a small padded "time-out room" on
75 separate occasions, some times for periods in excess of
one hour. Peters v. Rome City School Dist., 298 A.D.2d
864, 747 N.Y.S.2d 867, 170 Ed. Law Rep. 351 (4th Dep't
2002).

A federal court in Kansas ruled that a Fourth Amendment seizure occurred, if the evidence were construed most
favorably to the plaintiff, in an incident involving a
struggle between a ninth grade student and a school security officer because the student "was not free to leave the
school building during the physical struggle" and the security officer's "use of force may not have been reasonable
under the circumstances." Nicol v. Auburn-Washburn USD
437, 231 F. Supp. 2d 1107, 1117 (D. Kan. 2002).

In People v. Parker, 672 N.E.2d 813 (Ill. App. 1996), a
16-year-old saw that a metal detector had been set up at
the entrance to his high school. When he turned to walk
away, he was told by a police officer that he was obliged to
walk through the detector. The court ruled that this action constituted an "illegal seizure," saying that "[a] person
is seized within the meaning of the fourth amendment
when, by a show of authority or use of physical force, his
freedom of movement is restrained." Id. at 815 (citing
United States v. Mendenhall, 446 U.S. 544, 553 (1980)).

A student in the high school marching band alleged that
she was seized in violation of her Fourth Amendment
rights when she was forced to participate in a week-long
retreat which included being locked into the auditorium
during a "mandatory pizza party," being locked in her
room, and being forced to participate in a knighting
ceremony during which she was "forced to kneel." The
federal district court ruled that these allegations were sufficient to allege a seizure under the Fourth Amendment,
but that once the factual evidence was developed it may
appear that the actions of the school officials were reasonable under the circumstances. Hilton v. Lincoln-Way High
School, 1998 WL 26174 (N.D. Ill. 1998).

What about pulling a student out of class to question them about an infraction or criminal matter being investigated? Does that constitute a "seizure"? The opinion in Bills v. Homer Consolidated Sch. Dist. No. 33-C, 967 F. Supp. 1063 (N.D. Ill. 1997), suggests that it might, but that school officials would have qualified immunity to protect their conduct unless the student could show "a clearly established constitutional right" to be free from such seizures.

Similarly, the U.S. Court of Appeals for the Second Circuit held that removing a five-year-old student from school to have her inspected for evidence of sexual abuse in a nearby hospital constitutes a "seizure" that triggers Fourth Amendment requirements. Tenenbaum v. Williams, 193 F.3d 581 (2d Cir. 1999). The court ruled that the welfare workers who ordered the removal had qualified immunity from suit, because the constitutional principles were unclear at the time the incident occurred, but upheld a $15,000 verdict against the City of New York, because the removal without judicial approval was City policy. *See also* Daniel S. v. Bd. of Educ. of York Community High School, 152 F.Supp.2d 949 (N.D.Ill.2001) (holding that conduct by a gym teacher requiring two male 17-year-old student to stand naked in front of their male classmates for 16 minutes — in a school where "the custom of the boys . . . was to shower with their swim suits on" — presented a claim for damages as an unreasonable seizure under the Fourth Amendment); Doe ex rel. Doe v. State of Hawaii Dept. of Educ., 334 F.3d 906, 178 Ed. Law Rep. 677 (9th Cir. 2003) (ruling that a vice-principal's taping the head of an eight-year-old to a tree for five minutes constituted a seizure for Fourth Amendment purposes); Samuels ex rel. R.J. v. Independent School Dist. 279, 2003 WL 23109698 (D. Minn. 2003) (ruling that even though the "relaxed Fourth Amendment standards" applicable to school searches under *T.L.O.* also apply to school seizures, the handcuffing of a ninth-grader involved in a scuffle was not justified). *But see* Doe v. S. & S. Consolidated I.S.D., 149 F.Supp.2d 274, 287 (E.D.Texas 2001) (ruling that the Fourth Amendment is not implicated by "school officials restraining a 'raging' child or placing her in a timeout room"); In the Matter of V.P., 55 S.W.3d 25 (Tex.App. 2001) (ruling that the continued questioning of a 14-year-old student by an assistant principal after the student had requested to see his attorney was not a "custodial interrogation" requiring that questioning stop when an attorney is requested); In re Harold S., 731 A.2d 265 (R.I. 1999) (ruling that when a school principal questions a student about his or her possible involvement in alleged misconduct on school property that may amount to a violation of a criminal statute, Miranda warnings need not be given to the student); State v. J.T.D., 851 So. 2d 793 (Fla. Dist. Ct. App. 2d Dist. 2003) (ruling that the questioning of a middle-school student about lewd molestation of another student by an assistant principal in the presence of a police officer - serving as the school's resource officer - was not a custodial interrogation requiring *Miranda* warnings); J.D. v. Com., 42 Va. App. 329, 591 S.E.2d 721, 184 Ed. Law Rep. 1049 (2004) (acknowledging that *Miranda* warnings might be necessary when a questioning of a student is conducted by a police or security officer, but ruling that such warnings are not required when the questioning is conducted by a principal or other school official).

Chapter 7

Exclusion of Illegally Obtained Evidence

Research References

West's Key Number Digest
Criminal Law ⚷394, 394.4

> **KeyCite®:** Cases and other legal materials listed in KeyCite Scope can be researched through West's KeyCite service on Westlaw®. Use KeyCite to check citations for form, parallel references, prior and later history, and comprehensive citator information, including citations to other decisions and secondary materials.

This chapter outlines briefly some general principles of the exclusionary rule. Although school officials are not expected to conduct a judicial analysis of evidence, a good faith effort to protect privacy expectations is required.

§ 7:1   Exclusionary rule

According to Supreme Court holdings, evidence that a person can show was obtained by means of an illegal search or seizure must be suppressed and cannot be considered or used against the individual in a criminal proceeding or in a noncriminal proceeding where penalties of some kind are sought to be imposed. This exclusionary rule applies not only to primary evidence gained directly from illegal searches or seizures, but also to any derivative evidence obtained as a result of knowledge or information discovered through an illegal search or seizure. Derivative evidence that must be suppressed because of its illegal origins is often referred to as the "fruits of the poisonous tree."

The Court has stressed that its primary objective in prohibiting the use of illegally obtained evidence is to remove incentives for the government to engage in any future conduct that may be either technically or intentionally unconstitutional. United States v. Calandra, 414 U.S. 338, 347 (1974). This approach assumes that governmental officials will refrain from conduct they know will inevitably lead to the suppression of evidence.

Clarifying remarks by the Court also make it clear that the exclusionary rule is not a constitutional right. United States v. Calandra, 414 U.S. 338, 348 (1974). Nor does the Court regard the rule as a form of redress for any injuries to the privacy expectations of a person. The Court's position is that once such expectations are violated they cannot be effectively restored. United States v. Calandra, 414 U.S. 338, 347 (1974).

Because the exclusionary rule is viewed as a judicial deterrent rather than a form of redress it has not been interpreted as proscribing the use of illegally seized evidence in all proceedings or against all persons. United States v. Calandra, 414 U.S. 338, 348 (1974). Its application has been restricted to those areas where deterrent effects are most pronounced. The rule is thus applied in noncriminal proceedings when: (a) the agency that commits the illegal search or seizure is the same one seeking to use the tainted evidence; and (b) the tainted evidence is used to impose a penalty that is not merely ministerial or procedural in character. Thus, it is proper to apply the exclusionary rule in any school disciplinary proceeding where some type of penalty may be imposed on a student, and some states have adopted the exclusionary rule in school settings. See State v. M.A.L., 765 P.2d 787, 790 (Okla. Crim. App. 1988); In re Pima County Juvenile Action, 733 P.2d 316, 318 (Ariz. App. 1987); In re Dumas, 515 A.2d 984, 988 (Pa. Super. 1986); People v. Pruitt, 662 N.E.2d 540 (Ill. App. 1996), appeal denied, 667 N.E.2d 1061 (Ill. 1996); State ex rel Juvenile Dep't v. Finch, 925 P.2d 913 (Or. App. 1996).

In 1996, however, the U.S. Court of Appeals for the Eighth Circuit reached the opposite conclusion and concluded that the exclusionary rule should not apply to a school disciplinary proceeding. Thompson v. Carthage Sch. Dist., 87 F.3d 979 (8th Cir. 1996). School officials had found crack cocaine in a pocket of a ninth grader's jacket and expelled him based on that finding. The court of appeals agreed that imposing the exclusionary rule would deter school officials from violating the constitutional rights of their students. But the court then argued that because school officials "are not law enforcement officers," and "do not have an adversarial relationship with students," and because "children's legitimate expectations of privacy are somewhat limited at school," "there is little need for the exclusionary rule's likely deterrent effect," and that "[i]n any event, any deterrence benefit would not begin to outweigh the high societal costs of imposing the rule." *Id.* at 981–82. (This conclusion is "dicta" rather than a "holding" in a formal sense, because the court of appeals held later in the same opinion that the Fourth Amendment rights of the student had not been violated— and hence the applicability of the exclusionary rule was irrelevant—but the court's views on the inapplicability of the exclusionary rule were nonetheless strongly and clearly stated.).

Another important decision rejecting the application of the exclusionary rule in a school disciplinary setting is In the Matter of Juan C. v. Cortines, 679 N.E.2d 1061 (N.Y. 1997). A school security aide searched a student because he suspected the presence of a gun in the student's jacket based on the way the jacket was being pulled down. When the student was prosecuted for criminal possession of a weapon, the Family Court ruled that the gun had been illegally seized because "the outline of the gun was not visible [in the jacket], the slight bulge was not in any particular shape or form and was not remotely suspicious." 647 N.Y.S.2d 491, 492 (Sup. Ct. App. Div. 1996). Because the school security aide did not have a reasonable suspicion to search the student, the gun could not be used as evidence under the exclusionary rule in the criminal court, and the four-member panel of the Appellate Division of the Supreme Court ruled unanimously that it also could not be used in the school disciplinary proceeding because the exclusionary rule applied there. The court of appeals unanimously reversed, however, ruling that the collateral estoppel rule should "not be rigidly or mechanically applied," 679 N.E.2d at 1065, and that the school officials should be able to make their own determination about whether the search was reasonable, whether evidence is credible, and whether it should be considered in determining whether to suspend a student. The court of appeals acknowledged that its decision created "a seeming paradox" whereby school authorities were allowed to use evidence deemed to have been seized illegally even though they were required by "their constitutional and pedagogical obligations" to respect "the rights of the many thousands of law-abiding students yearning to learn about school subjects and life in society," and that its decision should not be interpreted as investing "the Chancellor and school officials or employees and their actions with immunity from appropriate scrutiny of the Judicial Branch when circumstances not now before us may warrant." *Id.* at 1070.

Other courts that have ruled that the exclusionary rule does not apply in school disciplinary proceedings include D.R.C. v. State, 646 P.2d 252, 258 n.10 (Alaska App. 1982), and James v. Unified Sch. Dist. No. 512, 899 F. Supp. 530, 533–34 (D. Kan. 1995). The Supreme Court did not resolve this issue in New Jersey v. T.L.O., 469 U.S. at 333 n.3.

§ 7:2 Application of the exclusionary rule

School officials who conduct hearings where evidence from a student search or seizure is introduced must be prepared to consider objections to that evidence and to exclude any evidence shown to be obtained illegally. Although a full-scale judicial hearing on the issue is not expected, the decision to admit or exclude evidence must be made in good faith. If the issue is significant, it may be litigated and the question of admissibility ultimately settled in court. A bad faith determination by school officials can have unknown adverse consequences.

The following material is not intended as a complete procedural guide. For specific requirements concerning the use and admissibility of evidence, reference should be made to the regulations developed for the particular proceeding involved. Only a brief sketch of factors relevant to Fourth Amendment validity is presented here.

§ 7:3 Application of the exclusionary rule—The student's burden of proof in seeking to suppress evidence

The student who wishes to exclude evidence obtained from a search or seizure has a lower burden of proof compared to that of the school. This reduced burden exists because student searches and seizures occur without the benefit of any prior magistrate review or search warrant. Consequently, the student must simply show a causal link between an illegal search or seizure and the evidence in question. To demonstrate this link, the student must:

(1) *Establish proper standing as an "aggrieved person."* The student must show a justified expectation of privacy in the place or thing searched or seized (Sections 1:3 and 2:3) (Rawlings v. Kentucky, 448 U.S. 98, 104–5 (1980)); and

(2) *Establish that the evidence was obtained by an illegal search or seizure.* For primary evidence, the student must show that standards applicable to the particular type of search or seizure in question were not satisfied fully. For example, a student might demonstrate coercion in a consent search, show how the valid scope of a search was exceeded, point to the absence of a necessary nexus link, or prove any number of other defects detailed in earlier sections of this guide. United States v. Parker, 722 F.2d 179, 182–83 (5th Cir. 1983).

To exclude secondary or derivative evidence, the student must show that the evidence is tainted because it was obtained by exploiting a primary illegality, that is, by demonstrating that derivative evidence was obtained mainly because of information or facts that came to light only as a result of an illegal search or seizure (the "fruit of the poisonous tree"). Wong Sun v. United States, 371 U.S. 471, 487–88 (1963).

§ 7:4 Application of the exclusionary rule—The school officials' burden of proof in refuting a claim of illegality

School officials bear the ultimate burden of proof whenever evidence is alleged to have been obtained by an illegal search or seizure. If they wish to use evidence that has been challenged, they must show by a preponderance of relevant facts that charges of illegal conduct are unfounded. For primary evidence, they must show that the search was conducted lawfully; for derivative evidence, they must show that they did not exploit a primary illegality.

If the search was conducted illegally, any primary evidence seized during the illegal search or seizure must be *automatically excluded* and not considered in any proceeding against the student.

Derivative evidence allegedly obtained by exploiting a primary illegality is said to be tainted and therefore excludable. That determination is not final, however, as is the case for primary evidence. Derivative evidence must be subjected to an "attenuation analysis" before deciding whether it must be excluded. Derivative evidence can be purged of the taint from an illegal search or seizure if it was obtained by means sufficiently distinct from the primary illegality. School officials can show this attenuation by several methods:

(1) *Establishing an independent source.* The causal link between a primary illegality and derivative evidence can be severed by establishing an independent source. An independent source is said to exist whenever the discovery of derivative evidence is based on information or facts that do not originate with an illegal search or seizure. United States v. Crews, 445 U.S. 463, 472–73 (1980). For example, suppose the school officials had proper grounds to search a student's locker but they illegally detained the student for questioning prior to initiating the search. Any evidence seized in connection with the legal search of the locker is not tainted by the illegal investigative stop, because the search has a basis that is independent of any information obtained during the illegal stop.

It is not yet certain whether the basis for discovering derivative evidence must be entirely independent from any primary illegality to purge a taint effectively. At this time, the safest interpretation seems to be that if information and facts from an illegal search or seizure merely corroborates or reinforces other sufficient information and facts already known, there is no taint. Wong Sun v. United States, 371 U.S. 471 (1963).

A somewhat different application of this provision holds when the derivative evidence is the identity of a live witness. The Supreme Court is much less inclined to exclude witness testimony regardless of prior illegalities. This different rule applies because the decision of a live witness to testify can occur voluntarily and independently of any illegal search or seizure that reveals the witness' identity or extent of knowledge. United States v. Ceccolini, 435 U.S. 268, 276–77 (1978).

(2)   *Showing an attenuated connection.* In many cases it may not be possible to sever the causal link between a primary illegality and derivative evidence. School officials can then attempt to show that intervening factors have attenuated the connection so much that any taint has been dissipated. Support for this conclusion occurs when the causal link between an illegality and derivative evidence can only be made by sophisticated and obscure reasoning.

The determination that a primary taint has been dissipated by an attenuated connection must consider all relevant circumstances. Brown v. Illinois, 422 U.S. 590, 603–4 (1975). Deterrence objectives of the exclusionary rule are also very cogent and germane here. The critical question is whether a causal link is so attenuated that excluding the evidence would have no meaningful deterrent effect. If there is no deterrent lesson for the government to learn, there is no reason to exclude the evidence. Among the factors to be considered are:

- *Temporal proximity.* Whether substantial passage of time has passed between a primary illegality and the discovery of derivative evidence. As the temporal connection between illegal conduct and derivative evidence becomes more remote, fewer reasons justify the exclusion of the evidence, because any possible deterrent effect will have diminished with time.

The passage of time is less important for physical evidence than for witness testimony. This difference exists because a witness has more opportunity to exercise free will in deciding to testify if some time passes between the illegal discovery of the witness's identity and the giving of testimony.

- *Intervening circumstances.* If a critical event occurred between school officials' illegal conduct and the discovery of derivative evidence, then there may be no deterrent value in excluding the tainted evidence. The argument is that the evidence was discovered based on this intervening event and not because of the illegal conduct. Obviously, the event must be quite substantial or it will not interrupt the causal chain.

  One example might be when a student pulls out a gun and threatens a school official after being illegally detained on a weak hunch that the student might be armed. In this case, the taint of the illegal investigative stop is purged by the student's act of displaying a weapon.

- *Nature of the illegality.* The deterrent effect of excluding tainted evidence is arguably diminished when the illegality is of a technical or inadvertent nature or was committed in good faith (i.e., in the belief that the search was legal). These circumstances might contribute to an argument against applying the exclusionary rule. United States v. Leon, 468 U.S. 897, 919–21 (1984); Massachusetts v. Sheppard, 468 U.S. 981, 987–88 (1984).

  The converse is also true. When officials flagrantly and deliberately commit an illegality to obtain evidence, the deterrent effect of excluding evidence is clear, direct, and particularly appropriate. Thus, if the illegality appears intentional, it is not likely to be excused.

(3) *Claiming inevitable discovery.* This defense is not yet sanctioned by the Supreme Court, although

it is generally recognized in lower courts. *But see* Nix v. Williams, 467 U.S. 431, 444 (1984) (deterrence has little value when the evidence in question would have been inevitably discovered by other police action; here, a volunteer search for a missing body would have resulted in discovery of the body, and police interrogation of the suspect as to the body's whereabouts, although illegal, should not result in exclusion of the evidence since discovery was inevitable). The argument is that certain illegalities connected with a search or seizure are irrelevant because the allegedly tainted evidence would inevitably have been discovered by other lawful conduct that is normal and routine. In other words, it does not matter that an illegality may have advanced the discovery of evidence if it would almost certainly have been found by legal means anyway.

Unlike the two preceding arguments, a claim of inevitable discovery relies on supposition and speculation rather than factual argument. Nardone v. United States, 308 U.S. 338, 341 (1939) (recognizing the need for sophisticated argument to prove inevitable discovery); United States v. Romero, 692 F.2d 699, 704 (10th Cir. 1982) (acknowledging the dangers of a judge's speculation that discovery would be inevitable).

An example will serve to illustrate several important points connected with making this claim. Suppose school officials have sufficient information to reasonably suspect that evidence is located somewhere in a student's car and they also have proper grounds for a search. Prior to the search, they illegally detain the student for questioning and learn that the evidence is hidden in a sealed box under the front seat. A claim of inevitable discovery might be made if it is a normal routine practice to look under car seats in search of such evidence and officials can convincingly explain why the box would have been examined.

The main point in this example is that the evidence would have been discovered by normal routine lawful conduct during a search of the car, even absent the illegal stop. Thus, it is necessary to inquire about the normal search and seizure practice of school officials and the nature of the investigation (serious or perfunctory).

Caution: This argument cannot be used to rehabilitate a fundamentally illegal search or seizure (i.e., a search or seizure that was unjustified at its inception). A claim of inevitable discovery is relevant only to the refutation of an intervening illegality.

It is worth repeating that the attenuation analysis discussed here applies only to derivative evidence. Primary evidence obtained directly as a result of illegal searches or seizures must be excluded automatically.

Chapter 8

Special Procedures for Very Serious Infractions

§ 8:1   In general

Research References

West's Key Number Digest

Schools ⚬169.5

> **KeyCite®:** Cases and other legal materials listed in KeyCite Scope can be researched through West's KeyCite service on Westlaw®. Use KeyCite to check citations for form, parallel references, prior and later history, and comprehensive citator information, including citations to other decisions and secondary materials.

§ 8:1   In general

The Supreme Court has not yet specifically decided whether evidence seized by school officials in a T.L.O.-type search is admissible in criminal court proceedings. Consequently, it may be wise to report all serious crimes to the principal who will then refer the matter directly to the police for investigation. This approach gives the police an opportunity to seize any evidence under a warrant issued by a magistrate using the probable cause standard, and thereby preserve admissibility for criminal prosecution.

Whenever possible, school officials should avoid conducting a search or seizure to investigate a very serious crime, because if the search or seizure is unlawful, the evidence may be tainted and criminal prosecution obstructed. If a search or seizure cannot be avoided or was conducted inadvertently, school officials should attempt to preserve the evidentiary value of any seized items by observing the special procedures outlined in Section 6:4.

School officials may of course cooperate with police. The Supreme Court has not yet ruled, however, on the question of whether the standard of reasonable suspicion would apply in such joint action or whether the higher standard of probable cause would be more appropriate. New Jersey v. T.L.O., 469 U.S. at 341 n.7. State decisions vary on this issue. *See, e.g.,* State v. D.T.W., 425 So. 2d 1383, 1385 n.2 (Fla. App. 1983) (reasonable suspicion standard does not apply to joint action); Cason v. Cook, 810 F.2d 188, 191 (8th Cir. 1987) (reasonable suspicion is the proper standard); Shade v. City of Farmington, Minnesota, 309 F.3d 1054, 170 Ed. Law Rep. 529 (8th Cir. 2002) (same). *See also* Section 10:4. School officials should have proper authority to consent before assisting with opening school property assigned for a student's exclusive use (*see* Section 2:16). For example, they should normally avoid opening a student's locker for the police. It is better that the suspected student be served with a warrant or that the police break into the locker under their own authority instead.

Chapter 9

Civil Liability for Illegal Searches or Seizures

Research References

West's Key Number Digest

Civil Rights ⚷192, 198(1); Constitutional Law ⚷319, 319.5; Federal Courts ⚷511; Schools ⚷89; Searches and Seizures ⚷55

> **KeyCite®:** Cases and other legal materials listed in KeyCite Scope can be researched through West's KeyCite service on Westlaw®. Use KeyCite to check citations for form, parallel references, prior and later history, and comprehensive citator information, including citations to other decisions and secondary materials.

---

§ 9:1   Liability generally

All school officials who conduct student searches or

seizures must be aware that they may face civil suits if they violate the Fourth Amendment rights of students. Students can file actions in state or federal court under 42 U.S.C.A. Section 1983 if they are deprived of any right, privilege, or immunity guaranteed by the U.S. Constitution. Students can also file state law tort actions against officials in state court, and they can combine state tort claims with Section 1983 claims in both state and federal court. Suits can be brought for declaratory or injunctive relief and for recovery of compensatory and punitive damages. In some cases, students can even recover attorney fees.

§ 9:2 Liability under 42 U.S.C.A. Section 1983

Section 1983 of title 42 of the U.S. Code states:

Every person who, under color of any statute, ordinance, regulation, custom, or usage, of any State or Territory . . . subjects, or causes to be subjected, any citizen of the United States or other person within the jurisdiction thereof to the deprivation of any rights, privileges, or immunities secured by the Constitution and laws, shall be liable to the party injured in an action at law, suit in equity, or other proper proceeding for redress.

§ 9:3 Liability under 42 U.S.C.A. Section 1983— Elements of 42 U.S.C.A. Section 1983

The first element of Section 1983 of title 42 of the U.S. Code is the deprivation of rights, privileges, or immunities secured by the Constitution and laws. Specific intent to deprive a person of constitutionally protected rights is not required to hold a wrongdoer civilly liable. The official need only have caused the deprivation. Monroe v. Pape, 365 U.S. 167, 187 (1961). A gym teacher's conduct requiring two male 17-year-old student to stand naked in front of their male classmates for 16 minutes (in a school where "the custom of the boys . . . was to shower with their swim suits on") was, for instance, found to present a claim for damages as an unreasonable seizure under the Fourth Amendment. Daniel S. v. Bd. of Educ. of York Community High School, 152 F.Supp.2d 949 (N.D.Ill.2001).

The second element is that the action must have been performed under color of law. Officials act under color of state law when they act with the appearance of authority and use their state power to deprive a protected right. Under this reading of Section 1983, even if state officials act outside the scope of their authority or in violation of state law, they could be held liable if they carried out their conduct under the cloak of state authority. Monroe v. Pape, 365 U.S. 167, 184 (1961).

"Under color of law" has also been interpreted as state involvement through laws, policies, or regulations. For example, in Bellnier v. Lund, 483 F. Supp. 47, 51 (N.D.N.Y. 1977), the court held that "New York State is inextricably entwined in its various municipal school systems" because of compulsory education embodied in state law, state regulation of teachers, and a state law provision that "requires that a board of education indemnify a teacher for all costs and attorneys' fees resulting from an action, civil or criminal, growing out of an attempt to discipline a student." Thus school officials may act under color of law when carrying out a student search pursuant to a government policy. Even parents of students can act under color of law under this definition. "It is enough that [a private person] is a willful participant in joint action with the State or its agents." Kuehn v. Renton Sch. Dist. No. 403, 694 P.2d 1078, 1082 (Wash. 1985) (quoting Dennis v. Sparks, 449 U.S. 24, 27–28 (1980)).

The third element is that the officials must meet the definition of "person." Individuals meet this definition, and they may be sued in their individual or official capacities. In suits in an individual capacity, plaintiffs sue to "impose personal liability upon a government official for actions he takes under color of state law." Kentucky v. Graham, 473 U.S. 159, 165 (1985). The plaintiff has to show that the official, acting under color of state law, caused a violation of constitutional rights. If the officials are sued in their official capacities, the offices they hold are, in essence, being sued. The plaintiff must show that the "entity itself is a 'moving force' behind the deprivation." Id. at 166. A policy or custom must be implicated. If an official retires or resigns while the suit is in progress, it will continue against the new office holder. Owen v. City of Independence, 445 U.S. 622 (1980).

States and some state agencies are not considered to be "persons" under Section 1983 and are thus protected from suit in both federal and state court. These entities are protected from suit in federal court by the Eleventh Amendment, which prohibits suits against states in federal courts unless the state consents or Congress abrogates the protection.

This immunity does not, however, include local government bodies, including municipalities and school boards, which have been held to meet the definition of "person" under Section 1983. *See* Monell v. Department of Social Servs., 436 U.S. 658 (1978). School boards "can be sued directly under § 1983 . . . where . . . the action that is alleged to be unconstitutional implements or executes a policy statement, ordinance, regulation, or decision officially adopted and promulgated by that body's officers." *Id.* at 690. In other words, the policy itself must be unconstitutional, and the policymakers may be liable for acts that it "officially sanctioned or ordered." Pembauer v. Cincinnati, 475 U.S. 469, 480 (1986). Students can also sue school boards when an act by a teacher, principal, or other school employee in accordance with a "custom or usage" violates a constitutional right. Monell, 436 U.S. at 691.

In Landstrom v. Illinois, 699 F. Supp. 1270 (N.D. Ill. 1988), a school principal conducted an illegal search of a student in a child abuse investigation. The court held that the board was not liable because the principal had acted in contravention of the school district's policy. If, in following the policy, he had violated the student's constitutional rights, the district would have been liable. *See also* Riddick v. School Bd. of Portsmouth, Va., 230 F.3d 1353 (4th Cir. 2000) (ruling that the school board was not liable for the track coach's secret videotaping of his female team-members in various states of undress even though he had been reprimanded for different improper conduct several years earlier, because the school board cannot be held liable for the earlier decision of the superintendent not to fire the coach).

Similarly, in Moore v. Florence Sch. Dist. No. 1, 444 S.E.2d 498 (S.C. 1994), a school principal searched a student's automobile for drugs. The student sued the school district under Section 1983, claiming that the search was unreasonable and therefore violated his constitutional rights. The court held that even if the search was unreasonable, the school district would not be liable under Section 1983 because an unreasonable search could not (by definition) be conducted pursuant to official school district policy, which allows only reasonable searches to be conducted.

In Muhammed v. Chicago Bd. of Educ., 1995 WL 89013 (N.D. Ill. 1995), the court dismissed a Section 1983 action against the Board of Education in a case involving a charge that a security guard twice used unreasonable force in removing a member of the local school council from a classroom. Because two incidents do not "constitute a pattern of violations sufficient to put the school on notice of potential harm to students," the evidence did not show "an official policy or custom," which is needed for an action against a municipal agency. The action was also dismissed against the security guard in his official capacity, but it could continue against him in his individual capacity. *See also* Oliver v. McClung, 919 F. Supp. 1206 (D. Ind. 1995) (three searches do not establish a "pattern" sufficient to impose liability on the school board).

The New Mexico Court of Appeals, in Kennedy v. Dexter Consolidated Schools, 955 P.2d 693, 702–03 (N.M. App. 1998) revised on other grounds, 10 P.3d 115 (N.M. 2000), explained that school boards can be held liable for unconstitutional searches only if based on policy or custom, but ruled that because the school board had not changed its policies after a strip search had occurred in 1989, it impliedly endorsed the practice and thus could be held liable for a 1992 strip search. Similarly, a federal judge in Illinois ruled that the conduct of a week-long retreat for high school band members including ritual hazing that had taken place for more than 30 years was sufficient to show a pattern or series of incidents sufficient to implicate a municipal defendant. Hilton v. Lincoln-Way High School, 1998 WL 26174 (N.D. Ill. 1998).

Supervisors or principals may be sued if they have authorized or approved an unconstitutional search. Cales v. Howell Pub. Sch., 635 F. Supp. 454, 456 (E.D. Mich. 1985), *quoting* Ghandi v. Police Dep't, 747 F.2d 338, 351 (6th Cir. 1984). "Supervisory indifference or tacit authorization of subordinates' misconduct, if demonstrably a causative factor in a constitutional injury, is actionable under 42 U.S.C.A. Section 1983." Burnham v. West, 681 F. Supp. 1160, 1162 (E.D. Va. 1987). The plaintiff must also show that the supervisor failed to "take reasonable remedial steps to prevent the injury." *Id.* at 1162, *quoting* Orpiano v. Johnson, 632 F.2d 1096, 1101 (4th Cir. 1980). The court in Burnham ruled that the principal's supervisor was not liable because she promptly investigated the searches in question, inquired into the principal's policies concerning searches, discussed the searches with legal counsel, and recommended to the principal that he narrow the scope of future searches by more extensive presearch investigations. *Id.* at 1163. A "failure to train" claim can be brought where the failure "amounts to deliberate indifference" the student's rights and "actually caused" a violation of these rights. Evans ex rel. Evans v. William Penn School Dist., 2002 WL 1001068 (E.D. Pa. 2002).

A federal court in Kansas ruled that a Section 1983 claim could be brought against a school district and school officials for an allegation that a school security officer had used force against a ninth grade student in a manner that constituted punishment for inappropriate behavior and that may have reached "the 'shock the conscience' standard necessary to take her claim to trial." Nicol v. Auburn-Washburn USD 437, 231 F. Supp. 2d 1107, 1115–16 (D. Kan. 2002). Quoting from Harris v. Robinson, 273 F.3d 927, 930, 159 Ed. Law Rep. 533 (10th Cir. 2001), the court said that a claim must allege that force had been used that was "so severe, . . . so disproportionate to the need presented, and was so inspired by malice or sadism rather than merely careless or unwise excess of zeal that it amounted to a brutal and inhumane abuse of official power literally shocking to the conscience." In the Nicol case, the plaintiff alleged that the security guard had pushed her into a file cabinet, shoved her through a door, put her into a headlock, dragged her across the hallway, and pinned her against the wall, and then when she had grabbed a water fountain, the fountain came off the wall when the security guard pulled her away from it. 231 F.Supp.2d at 1116. *See also* Bisignano v. Harrison Central Sch. Dist., 113 F.Supp.2d 591 (S.D.N.Y. 2000) (refusing to dismiss a claim brought for violation of constitutional rights under Section 1983 by a 13-year-old who was pushed into a dark closet for 30 seconds by her gym teacher during a dispute over a $20 bill); Ianson v. Zion-Benton Township High School, 2001 WL 185021 (N.D.Ill. 2001) (ruling that a school security guard who escorted students to their homes and then seized their home computers, without a warrant, was not entitled to qualified immunity from their lawsuit alleging violation of their Fourth Amendment rights).

§ 9:4 Liability under 42 U.S.C.A. Section 1983— Immunity from suit

As explained above, school districts and officials do not have absolute immunity from suits brought under 42 U.S.C.A. Section 1983. *See, e.g.,* Howlett v. Rose, 496 U.S. 356 (1990). This potential liability underscores the critical importance of strict compliance with procedures discussed in this guide.

School officials may, however, under some circumstances, have qualified immunity when they are sued in their individual capacities. "[G]overnment officials performing discretionary functions . . . generally are shielded from liability for civil damages insofar as their conduct does not violate clearly established statutory or constitutional rights of which a reasonable person would have known." Harlow v. Fitzgerald, 457 U.S. 800, 818 (1982).

Officials who conduct searches will be immune if their actions were reasonable in light of clearly established law in place at the time of the search. Williams v. Ellington, 936 F.2d 881, 885 (6th Cir. 1991); M.W. ex rel. T.W. v. Madison County Bd. of Educ., 262 F. Supp. 2d 737, 177 Ed. Law Rep. 1095 (E.D. Ky. 2003). If their action was reasonable, they may escape liability even if the court finds that they violated a student's constitutional rights. In Saucier v. Katz, 121 S.Ct. 2151 (2001), the Supreme Court clarified the responsibilities of courts in adjudicating these claims, explaining that the key question is whether it should be clear to an official that the conduct was unlawful in the situation at hand. If the law was not clear enough to put the official on notice that the conduct was clearly unlawful, then the court should grant summary judgment based on qualified immunity, and the official should not face the burdens of litigation. In the Eleventh Circuit, qualified-immunity protection for school officials is high because a principle is "clearly established" only if it has developed "in such a concrete and factually defined context to make it obvious to all reasonable government actors . . . that 'what he is doing' violates federal law." Thomas v. Roberts, 261 F.3d 1160 (11th Cir. 2001), aff'd on remand, 323 F.3d 950 (11th Cir. 2003); Lassiter v. Alabama A&M University, 28 F.3d 1146, 1149 (11th Cir. 1994). Furthermore, "[l]aw can be clearly established in this circuit only by decisions of the U.S. Supreme Court, this court, or the highest court of the state from which the case arose." Thomas, supra. Officials may be granted qualified immunity if they reasonably believed that the search met the reasonable suspicion standard, even if that belief was mistaken. *See,* for example, Cornfield v. Consolidated High Sch. Dist. 230, 991 F.2d 1316, 1324 (7th Cir. 1993), where individuals conducting a search were held to have qualified immunity because their search was "reasonable under the circumstances." The court held that school officials would be protected by the doctrine of qualified immunity for their discretionary acts unless "their conduct violates clearly established statutory or constitutional rights of which a reasonable person would have known." *Id.* at 1323–24 (*quoting* Doe v. Bobbitt, 881 F.2d 510, 511 (7th Cir. 1989), and *citing* Harlow v. Fitzgerald, 457 U.S. 800, 818 (1982)). The court reached a similar result in James v. Unified Sch. Dist. No. 512, 959 F. Supp. 1407 (D. Kan. 1997), dismissing a claim brought under Section 1983 by a male high school student whose car was searched by a police officer after he had received an anonymous phone call that a gun was in the car. The court ruled that the student had the burden of establishing that this conduct violated a clearly established law, but had failed to produce any authoritative appellate decision with analogous facts. *See also* DesRoches v. Caprio, 974 F. Supp. 542, 552 (E.D. Va. 1997), rev'd on other grounds, 156 F.3d 571 (4th Cir. 1998), where the court held that the school principal had qualified immunity and was not obliged to pay damages, even though a blanket search of student backpacks for stolen sneakers was deemed to be a violation of the students' Fourth Amendment rights, because the law was not "so clear that a school official would have known he was violating clearly established law": "Surely a school principal cannot be charged with full and comprehensive knowledge of subtle aspects of constitutional law." The Maryland Court of Appeals ruled that under the rules promulgated by the Maryland State Board of Education, lockers are not the personal property of the student, but rather are school property, and can be searched at will, without any probable cause or reasonable suspicion whatsoever. In re Patrick Y., 746 A.2d 405 (Md. 2000). *See generally* Chapter 13.

On the other hand, officials are not immune under Section 1983 if they "knew or reasonably should have known" their official actions would violate students' constitutional rights, or if they acted "with the malicious intention to cause a deprivation of constitutional rights or other injury to the student." Bellnier v. Lund, 438 F. Supp. at 54. In Bilbrey v. Brown, 738 F.2d 1462 (9th Cir. 1984), school officials who conducted a strip search of fifth graders to look for lost money were *not* immune from suit because they should have known about students' Fourth Amendment rights, which had been clearly established through school regulations and case law. The court noted that the more intrusive the search, the harder it is to prove a good faith belief. Superintendents of schools will be given immunity if they are not directly involved in the search. Bellnier, 438 F. Supp. at 55. In a similar fact situation involving two strip searches of two eight-year-old girls accused of stealing $7, the U.S. Court of Appeals for the Eleventh Circuit ruled by an 8-3 vote that the teacher and counselor had qualified immunity from suit because the law regarding such highly intrusive searches was not clearly established at the time of their action. Jenkins v. Talladega City Bd. of Education, 115 F.3d 821 (11th Cir. 1997), cert. denied, 118 S. Ct. 412 (1997). But two 1998 decisions rejected claims of qualified immunity and allowed civil actions for damages to go forward against school officials in intrusive searches requiring students to strip and pull out their underwear for inspection. Konop v. Northwestern School District, 26 F. Supp. 2d 1189 (D.S.D. 1998), and Kennedy v. Dexter Consolidated Schools, 10 P.3d 115 (N.M. 2000), discussed in Section 4:3. The Konop decision concluded that the school officials had not acted in an "objectively reasonable" fashion, and that their conduct "may have been extreme or outrageous." 26 F. Supp.2d at 1207. "It does not require a constitutional scholar to conclude that a nude search of a thirteen-year-old child is an invasion of constitutional rights of some magnitude." *Id.* at 1206 (quoting from Doe v. Renfrow,

631 F.2d 91, 92 (7th Cir. 1980)). The New Mexico Supreme Court has also ruled, based on common sense as well as related caselaw, that "the unlawfulness of conducting a strip-to-undergarments search without individualized suspicion was clearly established in 1992." Kennedy v. Dexter Consolidated Schools, 10 P.3d 115, 121 (N.M. 2000). *See also* Bell v. Marseilles Elementary School, 160 F. Supp. 2d 883, 890, 156 Ed. Law Rep. 1066 (N.D. Ill. 2001) (ruling that a school officer did not have qualified immunity to conduct a partial strip search of 30 students in a gym class, because "there is no question that plaintiffs' Fourth Amendment rights were clearly established in the factual context of student searches by school agents"); Fewless ex rel. Fewless v. Board of Educ. of Wayland Union Schools, 208 F. Supp. 2d 806, 819–20, 167 Ed. Law Rep. 153 (W.D. Mich. 2002) (ruling that school officials did not have qualified immunity to conduct a strip search of a special education 14-year old who had been accused by other students of having marijuana in his "butt crack," because the officials did not have enough evidence to form reasonable suspicion, the search was conducted in an unnecessarily intrusive fashion, and was at the same time pointless, because it was not designed to discover "marijuana placed deeply between the buttocks"); Doe ex rel. Doe v. State of Hawaii Dept. of Educ., 334 F.3d 906, 178 Ed. Law Rep. 677 (9th Cir. 2003) (denying immunity to a vice principal who taped an eight-year-old head's to a tree for five minutes, and explaining that the right of a student to be free of excessive physical punishment or restraint was clearly established as early as 1990).

In Hope v. Pelzer, 122 S.Ct. 2508, 153 L.Ed.2d 666 (U.S. 2002), involving a prison inmate tied to a hitching post for seven hours in the sun, the Supreme Court reaffirmed that officials can be on notice that their conduct violates established law even in novel factual situations. Based on that decision, the Court remanded back to the Eleventh Circuit for reconsideration the case of Thomas v. Roberts, 122 S.Ct. 2653, 153 L.Ed.2d 829, 166 Ed.Law.Rep.415 (U.S. 2002), where the Eleventh Circuit had previously ruled that an assistant principal in Georgia had qualified immunity from a suit brought by fifth graders who had been strip-searched without individualized suspicion in her effort to solve the apparent theft of $26, because the illegality of such action had not been "clearly established" in the Eleventh Circuit as of the time of the action: "Although a reasonable school official might have paused before strip searching a class of fifth graders, the best she could have discovered from a reading of the available caselaw was that a court may later determine that the searches were unreasonable." Thomas v. Roberts, 261 F.3d 1160 (11th Cir. 2001). On remand, the Eleventh Circuit ruled "that Hope does not dictate a change in the outcome of this case," but substituted a new discussion of the qualified immunity issue. Thomas ex rel. Thomas v. Roberts, 323 F.3d 950, 952, 174 Ed. Law Rep. 874 (11th Cir. 2003). In this new discussion, the court reiterated that constitutional principles can become "clearly established" in the Eleventh Circuit only as a result of decisions of the U.S. Supreme Court, the Eleventh Circuit itself, or of the relevant state supreme court. Thomas ex rel. Thomas v. Roberts, 323 F.3d 950 at 955, 174 Ed. Law Rep. 874 (11th Cir. 2003). Because no case from any of these courts had ruled that strip searches are always unconstitutional as of 1996, when the incident occurred, and because the search did "not rise to a level so egregious as to alert the officials that such conduct is unconstitutional even without caselaw," the school officials who conducted the search had qualified immunity from suit. Thomas ex rel. Thomas v. Roberts, 323 F.3d 950 at 956, 174 Ed. Law Rep. 874 (11th Cir. 2003); Watkins v. Millennium School, 290 F. Supp. 2d 890, 183 Ed. Law Rep. 454 (S.D. Ohio 2003) (ruling that a genuine issue had been raised whether a teacher had qualified immunity, after the teacher required a young student to pull back her waistband in a supply closet in a search for a missing $10, because the search violated the procedures established at the school); Doyle v. Rondout Valley Cent. School Dist., 3 A.D.3d 669, 770 N.Y.S.2d 480 (App. Div. 3d Dep't 2004) (granting qualified immunity to a member of the state police who turned over two students to a school principal and remained present while the principal instructed each student "to drop his pants and turn around in a 360" in his underwear" pursuant to a search for marijuana, because of "the somewhat ambiguous state of the law regarding mixed police/school searches" and the possibility that a reasonable police officer could have concluded that "probable cause was unnecessary if the search was conducted by school officials, albeit in his presence"). (For additional cases addressing the constitutionality of strip searches, see Section 4:3.)

The Third Circuit ruled that a high school swim coach who forced a student swimmer to take a pregnancy test in violation of her rights of personal privacy and freedom from illegal searches did not have qualified immunity from her lawsuit under 42 U.S.C.A. section 1983 because her rights were clearly established and the coach's action was objectively unreasonable. Relying on Anderson v. Creighton, 483 U.S. 635 (1987), the Third Circuit concluded that the specific conduct at issue need not have been previously found to be unlawful if it is beyond the boundaries of reasonableness. Gruenke v. Seip, 225 F.3d 290 (3rd Cir. 2000).

Municipalities and school boards do not have qualified immunity based on the good faith of their officers. Owen v. City of Independence, 445 U.S. 622 (1980). The threat of suit encourages policy makers to promulgate constitutional policies and procedures, serves as deterrent to unconstitutional acts, and deters abuses of power. Additionally, if governmental entities were immune from suit, plaintiffs would have no remedies, given the qualified immunity of officials.

School officials can also be found liable if they fail to train their subordinates regarding the proper way to conduct searches of students. Kennedy v. Dexter Consolidated Schools, 10 P.3d 115, 122 (N.M. 2000).

§ 9:5 Liability under 42 U.S.C.A. Section 1983— Defenses

As the section above explains, reasonableness is a defense to a 42 U.S.C.A. Section 1983 action, and most civil liability cases brought under this section have been unsuccessful because courts take a generous view of the type of information needed to justify the "reasonable suspicion" standard required for a search. In a 42 U.S.C.A. Section 1983 action, defendant school officials have the burden of showing that they had a reasonable suspicion that the search was necessary to maintain discipline and a safe educational environment. The grounds for the search and the search itself must both be reasonable, and the courts assess reasonableness on a case-by-case basis.

In Martinez v. School Dist. No. 60, 852 P.2d 1275 (Colo. App. 1992), the behavior and appearance of a student led a school monitor to believe that the student was under the influence of alcohol. Subsequently, the monitor required two other students who had been with the first student previously at a party to blow in the monitor's face so he could smell their breath. The school officials argued that this activity was not a "search," but the court said that even if it was a search it was justified because the monitor had a reasonable suspicion that the other students had also consumed alcohol. The court thus dismissed the students' Section 1983 claim.

Similarly, when two students implicated the defendant in a bomb threat that had been made to the school by telephone, the seizure and interrogation of the plaintiff by the school principal was held to be justified at its inception. Because of the serious nature of the suspected offense, the scope of the interrogation was held to be reasonable, and the plaintiff's Section 1983 claim failed. Edwards v. Rees, 883 F.2d 882 (10th Cir. 1989).

Another case involved a sixteen-year-old high school student who was subjected to a search of his person because he was suspected of concealing drugs in the crotch of his sweatpants. He was obliged to remove his clothes in the locker room so that his naked body could be visually inspected. The court found the search to be based on reasonable suspicion because it was motivated by a series of tips associating the student with drug use, and accompanied by an apparent admission made by the student, an unusual bulge in his crotch area, and furtive behavior. The dismissal of the student's Section 1983 action was affirmed on appeal because the search was reasonable in scope and the school officials were found to have qualified immunity because their actions were not shown to be outside a "'clearly established' constitutional norm." Cornfield v. Consolidated High Sch. Dist. 230, 991 F.2d 1316, 1324 (7th Cir. 1993).

Other cases where Section 1983 actions have failed are Webb v. McCullough, 828 F.2d 1151 (6th Cir. 1987), where the court ruled that a warrantless search of a high school band member in her hotel room during a school trip to Hawaii was justified under the in loco parentis doctrine; Jennings v. Joshua Indep. Sch. Dist., 877 F.2d 313 (5th

Cir. 1989), where the court ruled that conducting an automobile search in a school parking lot pursuant to a search warrant did not violate any constitutional guarantees; Williams v. Ellington, 936 F.2d 881 (6th Cir. 1991), where the court ruled that a warrantless intrusive strip search was justified based on relatively unparticularized allegations against the plaintiff. The Williams decision is questionable, particularly in light of the intrusiveness of the search (her undergarments were examined in an attempt to find a vial of cocaine).

§ 9:6 Liability under 42 U.S.C.A. Section 1983— Remedies

When student plaintiffs are successful, courts may award declaratory relief, issue an injunction, or award monetary damages.

Declaratory relief is a statement by the court that clarifies the rights and liabilities of the parties and "afford[s] relief from the uncertainty, insecurity, and controversy giving rise to the proceeding." Bilbrey v. Brown, 738 F.2d 1462, 1470 (9th Cir. 1984). In Section 1983 cases, declaratory judgments are used to warn and educate school officials and to define and establish Fourth Amendment rights and responsibilities. *Id.* at 1471.

An injunction is designed to force the defendant to stop the illegal activity. If a search policy is found to be unconstitutional, for example, a court might issue an injunction to compel the school district to promulgate a new one.

Monetary damages are the usual remedy for constitutional violations, and can include compensatory and punitive damages. Compensatory damages provide payment to the plaintiff for the actual injury resulting from the deprivation of constitutional rights. These damages can include out-of-pocket losses and losses from injury to reputation, humiliation, mental anguish, and emotional distress. Memphis Community Sch. Dist. v. Stachura, 477 U.S. 299, 307 (1986). *See also* Carey v. Piphus, 435 U.S. 247, 264 (1978) (damages for mental and emotional distress are compensable as long as there is proof that such injuries occurred). Courts generally do not award damages absent actual injury because it is so difficult to put monetary value on constitutional rights. Memphis Community Sch.

Dist., 477 U.S. at 310. If a plaintiff wins damages against officials in their individual capacities, the officials must pay the award from their personal assets unless the employer has agreed to indemnify them. If the suit is against individuals for actions taken in their official capacities, the governmental entity pays the award. Kentucky v. Graham, 473 U.S. 159, 166 (1985).

When a court finds a constitutional violation but no actual injury, it usually awards nominal damages because "the law recognizes the importance to organized society that those rights be scrupulously observed." Carey v. Piphus, 435 U.S. at 266.

Punitive damages are intended to punish defendants when their "conduct is shown to be motivated by evil motive or intent or when it involves reckless or callous indifference to the federally protected rights of others." Smith v. Wade, 461 U.S. 30 (1983). Punitive damages are designed both to punish and to deter, and courts can assess punitives against officials sued in their individual capacities when the conduct is outrageous. School boards and other government entities are immune from punitive damages under Section 1983. Newport v. Fact Concerts, 453 U.S. 247 (1981).

The New Mexico Supreme Court upheld jury-determined punitive damage awards of $50,000 against a school principal in favor of two students forced to strip to their underwear in a search for a diamond ring without any individualized suspicion, and also upheld awards of $25,000 each against other school officials. The court approved the trial court's jury instruction, which told the jury it could award punitive damages for "willful, wanton, or reckless" conduct. The award was warranted because one school official had "administered a particularly humiliating search to Crystal, requiring not only that she strip nude, but that she urinate while Ms. Rodrigues observed her," and hence that she had "acted intentionally with 'utter indifference' toward the rights of the students." Kennedy v. Dexter Consolidated Schools, 10 P.3d 115, 125–26 (N.M. 2000).

§ 9:7 Liability under 42 U.S.C.A. Section 1983—Attorney Fees

Under 42 U.S.C.A. Section 1988, the court has the

discretion to award attorney fees to the prevailing party in Section 1983 actions. Section 1988 says in part: "In any action or proceeding to enforce . . . section . . . 1983 . . . of this title . . . , the court, in its discretion, may allow the prevailing party, other than the United States, a reasonable attorney's fee as part of the costs."

Courts award prevailing plaintiffs attorney fees "to ensure effective access to the judicial process." Hensley v. Eckerhart, 461 U.S. 424, 429 (1983). To prevail, a plaintiff must "succeed on any significant issue in litigation which achieves some of the benefit the parties sought in bringing suit." *Id.* at 433. Plaintiffs may also prevail if there is a settlement in their favor or if the defendant takes action that moots the case. Smith v. Thomas, 725 F.2d 354, 356 (5th Cir. 1984). Reasonable attorney fees are calculated by multiplying the number of hours spent on the successful claim times a reasonable hourly rate. Hensley, 461 U.S. at 440. The court in Burnham v. West, 1988 U.S. Dist. LEXIS 17997 (E.D. Va. Apr. 4, 1988), entered a declaratory judgment in favor of the plaintiffs and ordered the defendants to pay $36,865.22 in attorney fees.

Defendants successfully sued in their individual capacities must pay attorney fee awards from their personal assets; only in official-capacity actions are government entities liable to prevailing plaintiffs for attorney fees. Kentucky v. Graham, 473 U.S. at 172. If the defendants are immune from liability, courts will not award the plaintiffs attorney fees even if a constitutional violation is found. *Id.* at 165.

Courts rarely award attorney fees to prevailing defendants because it would discourage plaintiffs from bringing suit and undermine enforcement of 42 U.S.C.A. Section 1983. Hughes v. Rowe, 449 U.S. 5, 14–15 (1980). In cases brought under Title VII of the 1964 Civil Rights Act, defendants "may recover attorney's fees . . . only if the District Court finds 'that the plaintiff's action was frivolous, unreasonable, or without foundation, even though not brought in subjective bad faith.'" *Id.* at 14, *quoting* Christianburg Garment Co. v. EEOC, 434 U.S. 412, 421 (1978). The court cannot force the plaintiff to pay the defendant's attorney fees just because the plaintiff lost the case. *Id.*

§ 9:8 Tort liability generally

In addition to pursuing the federal remedy provided in 42 U.S.C.A. Section 1983, students may pursue tort claims under state law when they are deprived of any right, privilege, or immunity guaranteed by the U.S. Constitution. Students may sue for compensatory and punitive damages, but they are unlikely to recover attorney fees for state law claims. Students usually file state law claims in state court, but they may file state tort claims in federal court under the doctrine of pendent jurisdiction at the same time they file their Section 1983 case.

§ 9:9 Causes of action

The claims or causes of action available to students after they are subjected to an illegal search or seizure include actions for infliction of emotional distress, false imprisonment, and battery.

§ 9:10 Causes of action—Infliction of emotional distress

Students may sue school officials for intentional or negligent infliction of emotional distress. To sustain a claim of intentional infliction of emotional distress, the students must prove that the officials intended to cause them severe emotional distress. To prove negligent infliction of emotional distress, the students must show that the officials' conduct falls below the standard established by law for the protection of others against unreasonable risk of harm, or that the actions fell below the standard of care a reasonable school official would have taken in carrying out a search. In other words, the plaintiffs must show that the officials' actions caused an unreasonable risk of harm.

In both negligent and intentional infliction situations, the officials' conduct must be outrageous or "beyond all possible bounds of decency," and it must cause emotional injury to the student. Landstrom v. Barrington Sch. Dist., 699 F. Supp. 1270, 1281 (N.D. Ill. 1988). Interrogation would never rise to the level of outrageous conduct, for example, but a nude search would. The emotional distress must be severe. "[H]orror, grief, shame, humiliation,

221

worry, etc. . . . are not actionable . . . . [I]t must be so severe that no reasonable man could be expected to endure
it." *Id. See also* Konop v. Northwestern School District, 26
F. Supp. 1189, 1207 (D.S.D. 1998) (allowing a claim based
on an intrusive semi-nude search to go forward because
"there is sufficient evidence that defendants' conduct may
have been extreme or outrageous" and "there is a genuine
issue of material fact whether plaintiffs suffered an
extreme disabling emotional response to defendants'
conduct"). In some jurisdictions, the plaintiff must show
that the intentional infliction of emotional distress caused
physical injury; in others, severe mental distress alone is
sufficient to create liability.

A Kansas federal court ruled that allegations of physical
force by a security officer against a ninth grade student
met the requirement of involving "extreme and outrageous
conduct" that produced "extreme and severe" emotional
distress. Nicol v. Auburn-Washburn USD 437, 231 F.
Supp. 2d 1107, 1118–19 (D. Kan. 2002). To meet this standard, the emotional distress must be so severe that "no
reasonable person should be expected to endure it," and
the conduct must "beyond the bounds of decency and ut-
terly intolerable in a civilized society." Nicol v. Auburn-
Washburn USD 437, 231 F. Supp. 2d 1107 at 1118 (D.
Kan. 2002) (*citing* Roberts v. Saylor, 230 Kan. 289, 637
P.2d 1175 (1981). The level of distress is determined, in
part, by "whether a plaintiff needed mental counseling."
Roberts v. Saylor, 230 Kan. 289, 637 P.2d 1175 (1981).

§ 9:11   Causes of action—False imprisonment

Students may sue officials for false imprisonment when
the officials use their authority to restrain the students'
freedom of movement without reasonable suspicion of a
violation of the law or school rules. The officials need not
necessarily restrain the students physically; words, body
language, or threats of physical force can be sufficient. Of
course, the students must be aware that they have been
restrained for a suit to succeed. *Id.* at 47–51. The court in
In re Robert B., 218 Cal. Rptr. 337, 340 (Cal. App. 1985),
held that a security guard had acted reasonably in detaining a student after the guard saw him exchanging money
with another student in a group of students known to use
marijuana. *See also* Hassan v. Lubbock Ind. Sch. Dist., 55

F.3d 1075 (5th Cir.), cert. denied, 516 U.S. 995 (1995), Wojcik v. Town of N. Smithfield, 76 F.3d 1 (1st Cir. 1996), Oliver v. McClung, 919 F. Supp. 1206 (D. Ind. 1995), and Harris v. County of Forsyth, 921 F. Supp. 325 (M.D.N.C. 1996), all rejecting deprivation of liberty and related false imprisonment claims in situations where students were detained for limited periods. *See generally* Chapter 5 ("Investigative Stops").

§ 9:12   Causes of action—Battery

If officials touch a student without consent in the course of a search, the student may sue them for battery if the search is not based on a reasonable suspicion, even if no overt injury occurred. All that is necessary is harmful or offensive contact with the student's body or clothing and an intent to touch. In Jarrett v. Butts, 379 S.E.2d 583 (Ga. App. 1989), a teacher intentionally touched a student while taking her picture. The court noted that "any unlawful [and unconsented to] touching is a physical injury to the person and is actionable. . . . Thus even the minimal touching in this case can support a cause of action for assault and battery." *Id.* at 585–86. *See also* Oliver v. McClung, 919 F. Supp. 1206 (D. Ind. 1995) (allowing a battery claim to proceed to trial in a case where three seventh-grade girls were touched by female employees during a strip search); Dubbs v. Head Start, Inc., 336 F.3d 1194, 179 Ed. Law Rep. 92 (10th Cir. 2003) (ruling that nonconsensual medical examinations constitute a "technical battery"). In contrast, Wallace v. Batavia Sch. Dist., 68 F.3d 1010 (7th Cir. 1995), ruled that a disruptive student forcibly escorted out of a classroom could not maintain a civil rights action, even if the teacher's action were viewed as corporal punishment. In Konop v. Northwestern School District, 26 F. Supp.2d 1189, 1206–07 (D.S.D. 1998), the court allowed a female eighth-grader's claim for battery to go to trial based on a touching by a teacher while the teacher was pulling the waist band of the student's panties away from the student's body.

§ 9:13   Causes of action—Duty to protect students from assault

In addition to these common-law causes of action, it also

needs to be mentioned that many states now emphasize the duty imposed on school officials to provide safe schools and a drug-free environment, and that school officials may be liable if they fail to meet this responsibility. *See, e.g.,* T.J. v. State, 538 So. 2d 1320, 1321 (Fla. App. 1989) ("In this state, school boards have potential civil liability if school officials fail to take reasonable steps to protect students from assaults by other students."); In re Frederick B., 237 Cal. Rptr. 338, 342 (Cal. App. 1987) ("Failure to ensure student safety can result in civil liability for educational authorities."). *See also* Horton, 690 F.2d at 481.

§ 9:14 Immunity

States and state agencies have traditionally been immune from tort suits in state courts, but states have waived this immunity in many situations. State agencies and officials usually retain their immunity for their policy or "discretionary" decisions which require them to exercise their sound judgment, but not for their "ministerial" actions, when they are carrying out established policy. Municipal corporations and school boards also traditionally had absolute immunity, but again many states have modified this immunity. Some states have enacted statutes making municipalities qualifiedly immune. *See, e.g.,* Pritchard v. Arvon, 413 S.E.2d 100 (W. Va. 1991). Municipalities and school boards are also qualifiedly immune for their discretionary decisions. *See also* Section 9:4.

School officials are qualifiedly immune when they carry out discretionary actions within their scope of authority and in good faith. To show bad faith, the official must exhibit "malicious or intentionally unlawful behavior." Willoughby v. Lehrbass, 388 N.W.2d 688, 701 (Mich. App. 1986). Willoughby held that a principal was immune from liability for false imprisonment because his acts were discretionary: "the real decision . . . was how to discipline." *Id.* at 701. Searches and seizures generally require an exercise of judgment and are thus "discretionary," but the carrying out of the search—the "ministerial" aspect—may not qualify for immunity if conducted improperly. *See, e.g.,* Oliver v. McClung, 919 F. Supp. 1206 (D. Ind. 1995), where the court denied qualified immunity to three school employees who engaged in an unreasonable strip search, looking for $4.50 that had been stolen. In Holmes v. Montgomery, 2003 WL 1786518 (Ky. Ct. App. 2003), the court explained that state officials would be immune under Kentucky law if they were "performing an activity commonly held to be within the traditional role or scope of government *and* [were] called upon to exercise discretion rather than merely . . . performing ministerial tasks." *Id.* at *7 (emphasis in original; *citing* Yanero v. Davis, 65 S.W.3d 510, 161 Ed. Law Rep. 1058 (Ky. 2001)). Applying this test to a search requiring high school females to reveal their undergarments, the court denied immunity because the Board of Education "had in place a written policy categorically prohibiting strip searches of students." *Id.*

§ 9:15 Liability

Officials may be liable for a tort if their acts are operational and require no independent judgment. Supervision of students or teachers, for example, is not usually discretionary so immunity does not apply. School districts may be liable for the officials' acts under the theory of respondeat superior, which holds principals, such as schools and school districts, liable for the acts of agents, including teachers, when the agents are acting within their scope of authority. Schools will also frequently be responsible for their agents' intentional torts, such as battery or false imprisonment, if carried out within the scope of employment.

§ 9:16 Damages

If a court rules that a plaintiff has been damaged, it may award the plaintiff compensatory or punitive damages. If individual officials are liable, the school district will normally indemnify them and pay the damage awards. The award of compensatory damages depends somewhat on the cause of action. For example, in false imprisonment cases, courts may award compensatory damages for time lost while imprisoned, injury or illness resulting from confinement, and mental suffering and humiliation. *Id.* at 48. In cases of infliction of emotional distress, some jurisdictions require that the plaintiff show physical injury to recover damages but others allow recovery for the mental suffering alone. *Id.* at 55. *See also* Section 9:9.

Courts award punitive damages to punish the wrong-doer and deter future conduct. *See* Section 9:6. Whether an employer will indemnify an employee for punitive damages often depends on the terms of insurance contracts. Some insurance policies specifically exclude payment of punitive damages. *Id.*

§ 9:17   Attorney fees

Unlike actions under 42 U.S.C.A. Section 1983, in a tort case plaintiffs generally do not recover attorney fees if they prevail. The traditional rule in American litigation is that parties pay their own attorney fees and costs, but some states have recently passed statutes authorizing attorney fees in certain situations.

§ 9:18   Avoiding civil liability

(1)   All school officials should learn their school's search and seizure policy.

(2)   Policy-makers should make sure the search and seizure policy conforms to the law.

(3)   All officials should understand the "reasonable suspicion" standard.

(4)   Officials conducting searches should be careful not to touch a student's body or clothing without consent unless they are certain the search meets the "reasonable suspicion" standard.

Chapter 10

Standards Developed by the States

Research References

West's Key Number Digest
Schools ☞89, 172; Searches and Seizures ☞169.5

KeyCite®: Cases and other legal materials listed in KeyCite Scope can
be researched through West's KeyCite service on Westlaw®. Use
KeyCite to check citations for form, parallel references, prior and
later history, and comprehensive citator information, including citations to other decisions and secondary materials.

---

§ 10:1   How the states have answered the questions left unresolved by the U.S. supreme court in *New Jersey v. T.L.O.*

The U.S. Supreme Court in New Jersey v. T.L.O. left
several questions unanswered pertaining to school
searches and seizures. States have answered some of the
questions by statute or by court decisions. This section

reviews the questions left unresolved by T.L.O., and the standards developed in some states that have chosen to impose or maintain higher standards in school searches and seizures than those required by T.L.O. The list of states is not intended to be inclusive, but rather representative. Practitioners and school officials will want to check their appropriate state references.

§ 10:2　How the states have answered the questions left unresolved by the U.S. supreme court in *New Jersey v. T.L.O.*—Does the exclusionary rule apply?

The first question raised and left unanswered by the T.L.O. Court is whether the exclusionary rule is the appropriate remedy for illegal school searches and seizures. New Jersey v. T.L.O., 469 U.S. at 332 ns.2, 3. State courts that have answered this question affirmatively include Arizona (In re Pima County Juvenile Action, 733 P.2d 316, 318 (Ariz. App. 1987)); California (In re William G., 709 P.2d 1287 (Cal. 1985)); Florida (T.J. v. State, 538 So. 2d 1320, 1322 (Fla. App. 1989)); Illinois (People v. Pruitt, 662 N.E.2d 540 (Ill. App. 1996), appeal denied, 667 N.E.2d 1061 (Ill. 1996)); Louisiana (State v. Mora, 307 So. 2d 317, 317–18 (1975)); New York (People v. Scott D., 34 N.Y.2d 483, 315 N.E.2d 466, 469 (1974), although this position seems to have been reversed in the decision rendered in In the Matter of Juan C v. Cortines, 679 N.E.2d 1061 (N.Y. 1997), where the court ruled that the collateral estoppel rule did not prevent evidence excluded from criminal proceeding from being considered in school diciplinary proceedings); Oklahoma (State v. M.A.L., 765 P.2d 787 (Okla. Crim. App. 1988)); Oregon (State ex rel Juvenile Dep't of Lincoln County, 925 P.2d 913 (Or. App. 1996)); and Pennsylvania (In re Dumas, 515 A.2d 984 (Pa. Super. 1986)). Reaching a contrary decision is Thompson v. Carthage Sch. Dist., 87 F.3d 979 (8th Cir. 1996). For a more complete discussion of the applicability of the exclusion rule, *see* Chapter 7.

§ 10:3 How the states have answered the questions left unresolved by the U.S. supreme court in *New Jersey v. T.L.O.*—Do students have a privacy expectation in their lockers?

The second question raised and left dangling in T.L.O. is whether students have a privacy expectation in "lockers, desks, or other school property" used by students for storage. New Jersey v. T.L.O., 469 U.S. at 337 n.5. State courts that have decided students have a privacy expectation in lockers and other school property include California (In re Cody S., 121 Cal. App. 4th 86, 16 Cal. Rptr. 3d 653, 657, 190 Ed. Law Rep. 436 (4th Dist. 2004); In re William G., 40 Cal. 3d 550, 221 Cal. Rptr. 118, 709 P.2d 1287, 29 Ed. Law Rep. 394 (1985)); Iowa (State v. Jones, 666 N.W.2d 142, 178 Ed. Law Rep. 934 (Iowa 2003) (ruling that a student has "a measure of privacy in the contents of his locker," but nonetheless finding that an annual inspection of the lockers for health and safety purposes was permissible); Mississippi (In re S.C. v. State, 583 So. 2d 188, 191–92 (Miss. 1991) (albeit less of a privacy interest than the student would have at home or in an automobile); New Jersey (State v. Engerud, 94 N.J. 331, 463 A.2d 934 (1983)); New Mexico (State v. Michael G., 748 P.2d 17 (N.M. App. 1987)); Washington (State v. Brooks, 718 P.2d 837 (Wash. App. 1986)); and West Virginia (State v. Joseph T., 336 S.E.2d 728 (W. Va. 1985)). States that have statutory or regulatory recognition of a student expectation of privacy in individually assigned school property include Hawaii (Department of Education Regulations, Chapter 19, Subchapter 4, § 8-19-14 (1986)). A Wisconsin court ruled, in contrast, that students have only a "minimal expectation of privacy" in their jackets hanging in school cloak rooms, and that an undifferentiated pat-down search of all jackets to search for a missing portable radio was constitutional. In re L.J., 468 N.W.2d 211 (Wis. App. 1991). Another Wisconsin decision held that students had no reasonable expectation of privacy in their lockers where the school system had a written policy retaining ownership and possessory control of school lockers and the students were put on notice of this policy. In re Isiah B. v. State, 500 N.W.2d 637 (Wis. 1993). The Pennsylvania Supreme Court has also ruled that public school students have only a minimal expectation of privacy in their lockers. Commonwealth v. Cass, 709 A.2d 350 (Pa. 1998).The Maryland Court of Appeals ruled that under the rules promulgated by the Maryland State Board of Education, lockers are not the personal property of the student, but rather are school property, and can be searched at will, without any probable cause or reasonable suspicion whatsoever. In re Patrick Y., 746 A.2d 405 (Md. 2000). *See generally* Chapter 13 *and see also* Rebecca N. Cordero, No Expectation of Privacy: Should School Officials Be Able to Search Students' Lockers Without Any Suspicion of Wrong Doing? A Study of In Re Patrick Y and Its Effect on Maryand Public School Students, 31 U. BALT. L. REV. 305 (2002).

§ 10:4   How the states have answered the questions left unresolved by the U.S. supreme court in *New Jersey v. T.L.O.*—What standards apply when the police are involved in a search?

The third question is whether the reasonable suspicion standard articulated in T.L.O. is the appropriate standard for school searches and seizures conducted in conjunction with police or whether the more stringent requirement of probable cause should apply. New Jersey v. T.L.O., 469 U.S. at 341 n.7. The answer to this question depends in part on whether the police initiated the search or were called in by school officials to help their investigation. *See* In re D.D., 146 N.C. App. 309, 554 S.E.2d 346, 352–53, 158 Ed. Law Rep. 855 (2001), appeal dismissed, review denied, 354 N.C. 572, 558 S.E.2d 867 (2001), In Interest of Angelia D.B., 211 Wis. 2d 140, 564 N.W.2d 682, 687, 118 Ed. Law Rep. 1191 (1997); People v. Dilworth, 169 Ill. 2d 195, 214 Ill. Dec. 456, 661 N.E.2d 310, 317, 107 Ed. Law Rep. 226 (1996). State courts that require probable cause when police are involved include New Mexico (State v. Tywayne H., 933 P.2d 251 (N.M. App. 1997), cert. denied, 934 P.2d 277 (N.M. 1997)) and Oklahoma (State v. M.A.L., 765 P.2d 787 (Okla. Crim. App. 1988)). *See also* Jennings v. Joshua Indep. Sch. Dist., 877 F.2d 313 (5th Cir. 1989) (summoned police officer conducted own investigation and obtained warrant prior to search); Patman v. State, 537 S.E.2d 1118 (Ga.App. 2000) (ruling that a member of the police department working a special detail at the high school and conducting a search of a student identified by a school official as smelling of marijuana, "[u]nlike a school official, . . . must have probable cause to search a suspect"). Tennessee requires probable cause by statute (School Security Act, Tenn. Code. Ann. § 49-6-4209) and caselaw (State v. Russell, 1997 WL 84661 (Tenn. Crim. App. 1997)). Hawaii regulations prohibit school officials from joint searches or searches requested by police when results would be used in criminal investigation (Department of Education Regulations, Chapter 19, Subchapter 4, § 8-19-18 (1986)). In the case of In the Matter of Dengg, 1999 Ohio App. LEXIS 851 (Ohio App. 1999), the court seems to indicate that the "reasonable suspicion" standard applies to any search conducted on school property, in a case involving a dog-sniff search conducted by the local police department, but the opinion also contains alternative grounds for its conclusions.

Several cases involve security officials or "school police officers" employed by the school or the school districts, and these decisions allow the security officials to operate under the same reduced "reasonable suspicion" standard that a vice principal or other school official can use. *See, e.g.,* In re S.F., 607 A.2d 793 (Pa. Super. 1992) (a plainclothes police officer for the Philadelphia School District was authorized to conduct a search based on the reasonable suspicion standard); In re Alexander B., 270 Cal. Rptr. 342 (Cal. App. 1990) (an officer of the Los Angeles Unified School District was warranted in acting pursuant to the dean's instructions in conducting a search that met the reasonable suspicion standard of T.L.O.); In re Frederick B., 237 Cal. Rptr. 338, 344 (Cal. App. 1987) (allowing a search where the school police officer had "reasonable if minimally grounded suspicion" that the student was engaged in criminal activity); In re Devon T., 585 A.2d 1287 (Md. Ct. Spec. App. 1991); Arizona v. Serna, 860 P.2d 1320 (Ariz. App. 1993) (public high school security guards were agents of the high school principal and thus subject to the reasonableness standard); S.A. v. State, 654 N.E.2d 791 (Ind. App. 1995)(ruling explicitly that the conduct of a trained police officer acting as school security officer on school premises is governed by the "reasonable suspicion" standard rather than the "probable cause" standard); People v. Dilworth, 169 Ill. 2d 195, 661 N.E.2d 310 (1996), cert. denied, 517 U.S. 1197 (1996)(ruling that the "reasonable suspicion" standard applies to the activities of a police liaison officer); People v. Pruitt, 662 N.E.2d 540 (Ill. App. 1996), appeal denied, 667 N.E.2d 1061 (Ill. 1996)(same); In the Interest of Angelia D.B., 564 N.W.2d 682 (Wis. 1997) (same, emphasizing that the search was initiated by school officials who then sought the assistance of the police liaison officer); Commonwealth v. J.B., 719 A.2d 1058 (Pa. Super. 1998)(applying the "reasonable suspicion" standard to a search undertaken by a school police officer); In the Matter of Murray, 525 S.E.2d 496, 498 (N.C.App. 2000) (ruling that the reasonable suspicion standard applied to a search conducted by a school official assisted by the school's "Resource Officer" who had been summoned to provide "greater strength" and who had handcuffed the student); Russell v. State, 74 S.W.3d 887, 165 Ed. Law Rep. 829 (Tex. App. Waco 2002) (ruling that the "reasonable suspicion" standard applied to a school police officer assisting a principal in conducting a search); Cason v. Cook, 810 F.2d 188, 193, 37 Ed. Law Rep. 473 (8th Cir. 1987), and Shade v. City of Farmington, Minnesota, 309 F.3d 1054, 170 Ed. Law Rep. 529 (8th Cir. 2002) (both ruling that the reasonable suspicion standard applies when school liaison officers conduct a search with school officials); In re William V., 111 Cal. App. 4th 1464, 4 Cal. Rptr. 3d 695, 180 Ed. Law Rep. 840 (1st Dist. 2003), review denied, (Dec. 23, 2003) and cert. denied, 124 S. Ct. 2182, 158 L. Ed. 2d 747 (U.S. 2004) (ruling that an officer in the Hayward Police Department assigned to the Hayward High School as "school resource officer" for a two-year term can engage in searches and seizures utilizing the "reasonable suspicion" standard of *T.L.O.*).

A decision that allows police officers to participate with school officials to conduct searches under the reduced "reasonable suspicion" standard is Commonwealth v. Carey, 554 N.E.2d 1199 (Mass. 1990) (a detective from the Woburn police department was at the school when the housemaster searched the student's locker and delivered the incriminating contents of it to the detective). Florida's decisions clearly allow school security personnel to conduct searches under the reasonable suspicion standard (S.D. v. State, 650 So. 2d 198 (Fla. App. 1995); State v. D.S., 685 So. 2d 41 (Fla. App. 1996)), but they appeared to require the probable cause standard for searches by actual police officers (F.P. v. State, 528 So. 2d 1253, 1255 (Fla. App. 1988); A.J.M. v. State, 617 So. 2d 1137 (Fla. App. 1993)) until 1997 when an appellate court permitted an assistant principal to summon a deputy sheriff to conduct a pat-down search for weapons based solely on the reasonable-suspicion standard (J.A.R. v. State, 689 So. 2d 1242 (Fla. App. 1997)). *See also* State v. D.S., 685 So. 2d 41 (Fla. App. 1996), where the rule that the reasonable suspicion standard applied when an assistant principal ordered a student to empty his pockets on a table, even though a police officer was sitting in the same office at the assistant principal's desk doing paperwork. A federal court in Alabama has ruled that the reasonable suspicion standard applied to a situation where school officials asked law enforcement personnel to come to the school to conduct a search. Rudolph ex rel. Williams v. Lowndes County Bd. of Educ., 242 F. Supp. 2d 1107, 1114 (M.D. Ala. 2003).

The Pennsylvania Supreme Court, however, reached an apparently contrary conclusion, in In re R.H., 568 Pa. 1, 791 A.2d 331, 334, 162 Ed. Law Rep. 453 (2002), where the court, by a 4-2 vote, ruled that school police officers were obliged to advise students being questioned of their constitutional rights to remain silent and to the assistance of a lawyer under Miranda v. Arizona, 384 U.S. 436, 86 S. Ct. 1602, 16 L. Ed. 2d 694, 10 A.L.R.3d 974 (1966), because these school police officers, although "employees of the school district," were "judicially appointed and explicitly authorized to exercise the same powers as municipal police on school property."

§ 10:5   How the states have answered the questions left unresolved by the U.S. supreme court in *New Jersey v. T.L.O.*—Is "individualized suspicion" always required?

The fourth question left opened by T.L.O. is whether "individualized suspicion is an essential element" of the reasonable suspicion standard articulated in the case. New Jersey v. T.L.O., 469 U.S. at 342 n.8. Decisions requiring particularity have been reached in Hawaii (In re Doe, 887 P.2d 645 (Haw. 1994)); Arizona (In re Pima County Juvenile Action, 733 P.2d 316, 317–18 (Ariz. App. 1987)); Texas (Jones v. Latexo Ind. Sch. Dist., 499 F. Supp. 223 (E.D. Tex. 1989)); and Virginia (Burnham v. West, 681 F. Supp.

1160 (E.D. Va. 1987)). States that have statutory or regulatory requirements of particularity include Hawaii (Dep't of Education Regulations, Chapter 19, Subchapter 4, § 8-19-16 (1986)); and Tennessee (School Security Act, Tenn. Code Ann. § 49-6-4205). A decision implying that individual suspicion is not an essential element of the reasonable suspicion requirement is DesRoches v. Caprio, 156 F.3d 571 (4th Cir. 1998). *See* Chapters 12 and 13 for further discussion of this issue.

State courts and legislatures have tended generally to adopt more stringent requirements than those required by the Supreme Court's T.L.O. decision in areas such as the requirements under which searches and seizures are permissible, conditions to be met when questioning a student, and guidelines to use when conducting the search. But the recent cases allowing mandatory or random searches of students for weapons or drugs indicate a move away from requirement of "individualized suspicion" prior to a search. *See* Sections 3:5 and 9:6 and Chapter 12.

The Supreme Court noted in T.L.O. that a search is reasonable when school officials would find evidence of a violation of "either the law or the rules of the school." New Jersey v. T.L.O., 469 U.S. at 341–42. States that require more than "a violation of school rules" include Hawaii, which requires a "threat to health or safety" (Department of Education Regulations, Chapter 19, Subchapter 4, § 8-19-16); Oklahoma, which requires the search to be for a specific list of items (School Code, Okla. Stat. Ann. § 24-102); and Tennessee, which requires a "life or health threatening" situation (School Security Act, Tenn. Code Ann. § 49-6-4203). Hawaii's standards, as an example of a state requiring greater protections for students than those articulated in T.L.O., will be developed more fully below.

Oklahoma and Hawaii require fulfillment of certain conditions not called for in the T.L.O. decision. Oklahoma, for example, requires the presence of "parents, guardian, attorney or legal custodian" when a student is questioned. State v. M.A.L., 765 P.2d 787, 789 (Okla. Crim. App. 1988), citing 10 O.S. Supp. § 1109(a) (1986). Hawaii requires school officials to inform students of "the purpose of a search" and "give them an opportunity to voluntarily relinquish" the object of the search. Department of Education Regulations, Chapter 19, Subchapter 4, § 8-19-16.

Some states have promulgated guidelines for school officials to use when conducting a search. One example is the requirement that searches be conducted by a person of the same sex. Another example is the prohibition against strip searches. Hawaii Department of Education Regulations, Chapter 19, Subchapter 4, § 8-19-17; Oklahoma Stat. Ann. § 24-102.

§ 10:6 Standards adopted by Hawaii's board of education

Soon after the T.L.O. decision, the Board of Education of the State of Hawaii adopted Subchapter 4 (School Searches and Seizures) of Chapter 19 (Student Misconduct, Discipline, School Searches and Seizures, Reporting Offenses, Police Interviews and Arrests, and Restitution for Vandalism and Negligence) to address the issues raised by T.L.O. In these regulations, the Board reiterated its policy that students have legitimate expectations of privacy in school and during off-campus Department supervised activities. These expectations extend to their: (1) persons; (2) possessions; and (3) school property assigned for individual use. Subchapter 4 permits school officials to search only for items connected with infractions that threaten health or safety or which themselves threaten health or safety by nature or because of the way they are used. This requirement generally means that a student search is not allowed when neither the suspected infraction nor the object poses a threat to health or safety. Naturally, a search is also prohibited if there is no underlying infraction at all. The only exceptions to this rule are for plain view seizures, consent searches, and emergencies which are permitted even when no threat to health or safety is present.

§ 10:7 Standards adopted by Hawaii's board of education—When is there a threat to health or safety?

Subchapter 4 requires that if a student is reasonably suspected of violating the law or engaging in conduct prohibited by Chapter 19, a search for items related to that infraction may be conducted only if necessary to protect health and safety. The proper determination that a search is necessary to protect health or safety should be made after examining all of the relevant surrounding circumstances, especially:

(1) *The nature of the infraction.* Sometimes the suspected infraction is inherently threatening to health or safety. This criteria is obviously met for any actual or threatened physical violence against another person. In other cases, the commission of an infraction may endanger nearby innocent bystanders, cause a health hazard, or create a risk of harm or injury. It does not matter whether these consequences may be deliberate or inadvertent.

(2) *The nature of related items.* Some items inherently threaten health or safety by nature, such as weapons that are primarily intended to cause harm or injury. Unstable, flammable, caustic, or poisonous compounds are another category of examples. Some items may pose a risk of accidental injury.

It is also possible for otherwise innocent items to threaten health or safety because they are misused in some way. An example would be something used as a projectile or weapon (even if it was not designed or intended for such application). A toy doll might be transformed into a weapon if it is used to bludgeon another student. A threat could also arise from the misapplication of an item (e.g., marking large areas of skin with certain permanent markers might cause toxic effects). Items that do not normally present any obvious threat to health or safety cannot be seized unless they have been misused in ways that have created an actual threat.

§ 10:8 Standards adopted by Hawaii's board of education—Items inherently threatening to health or safety

As a general guide, the following items are inherently threatening to health or safety, and can be the object of valid searches as contraband or the fruits, instruments, or evidence of any student infraction. It does not matter whether the related infraction threatens health or safety because the items themselves pose such a threat.

This list is illustrative and is not intended to be exhaustive or used mechanically:

   (1)   Any harmful or dangerous items
   (2)   Any weapon, such as guns, knives, and arrows
   (3)   Fireworks
   (4)   Illegal drugs
   (5)   Alcohol and other intoxicants
   (6)   Lighters and matches
   (7)   Animals and pets (bites/sanitation)
   (8)   Slingshots
   (9)   Bats/clubs
  (10)   Flammable compounds
  (11)   Darts
  (12)   Homemade bombs
  (13)   Heavy chains
  (14)   Spray paint (fire hazard/inhalant)

§ 10:9 Standards adopted by Hawaii's board of education—Items that do not necessarily threaten health or safety

These items are often the subject of local school rules, usually as prohibited contraband. A school official in Hawaii cannot automatically search for these items as contraband, however, because they do not pose any obvious inherent threat to health or safety. (*But see* Section 6:9 for a discussion of the open public view seizure of contraband.)

A school official can search for these nonthreatening items only if: (a) they are the fruits, instruments, or evidence of infractions that threaten health or safety (e.g., using a heavy radio to batter another student); or (b) these otherwise innocent items are misused in a manner that threatens health or safety (e.g., chewing gum used to clog a fire sprinkler system).

§ 10:10 Standards adopted by Hawaii's board of education—Additional procedural requirements specific to Hawaii's Subchapter 4

Subchapter 4 specifies three preliminary procedural

requirements for conducting a search in addition to those discussed in Chapter 4.

(1) *Proper authority to conduct a search.* Searches may only be conducted by school officials who are responsible for supervising the student or school property searched. This category includes school administrators (e.g., principals and vice-principals) and classroom teachers. Hawaii's State Attorney General has also determined (in an opinion letter dated October 29, 1987) that School Security Attendants and other Noneducational School Personnel may conduct student searches.

(2) *Prior notification of principal or designee.* The principal or designee must be informed by all other school officials of their intention and purpose in conducting a student search before they take any such action. It is not necessary to notify the principal or designee in an emergency when immediate action is called for and time is of the essence.

(3) *Witness.* Subchapter 4 also requires that a witness accompany a school official when conducting a search, except in an emergency. The accompanying witness should not participate in conducting the search, to preserve impartiality.

(4) *Prohibition against force.* Subchapter 4 (Subsection 8-19-17(b)) prohibits the use of force against students unless there is an imminent threat to health or safety.

It is worth emphasizing that a primary purpose of student searches and seizures under Subchapter 4 is to protect health or safety. Consequently, there is no justification for applying any manner of force that might create an even greater threat to health or safety than the infraction being investigated. This could happen when the suspected infraction presents only a minimal threat to health or safety. It might also happen when the infraction is a serious threat but the student's strength or steadfast resistance requires the application of extreme or excessive force. In either case, the irrational application of any excessive force would be unwarranted.

§ 10:11   Standards adopted by Hawaii's board of education—Standards adopted in other states

Some state courts rely on their own state constitutional provisions in assessing searches and seizures of students. Several states now have constitutional provisions guaranteeing a safe school environment which must be considered when the constitutionality of searches and seizures is raised.

The California Constitution, for example, provides that: "All students and staff of public primary, elementary, junior high and senior high schools have the inalienable right to attend campuses which are safe, secure, and peaceful." Cal. Const. art. I, § 28(c). In In re Alexander B., 270 Cal. Rptr. 342 (App. 1990), two student gangs were about to clash, but were separated by a school official and a police officer. A member of one of the gangs told the school official that a member of a third group of students, observing the confrontation, had a gun. The California Court of Appeals ruled that—because of the "safe schools" provision in California's Constitution—the police officer's ensuing search of the accused student "and others in his group for dangerous weapons was not only reasonable, it was constitutionally compelled." Id. at 344. The California Supreme Court has stated that "the responsibility of school officials for each of their charges, the children, is heightened as compared to the responsibility of the police for the public in general." In re William G., 40 Cal. 3d 550, 563, 709 P.2d 1287, 1295 (1985). Another California appellate court has recognized that a "failure to ensure student safety can result in civil liability for educational authorities." In re Frederick B., 237 Cal. Rptr. 338, 342 (Cal. App. 1987).

A Pennsylvania appellate judge has similarly noted that "[s]chool officials have great responsibility to see that the vital process of education can take place in an environment conducive to learning." In re Dumas, 515 A.2d 984, 987 (Pa. Super. 1986) (Kelly, J., concurring), quoting Commonwealth v. Dingfelt, 323 A.2d 145, 147 (Pa. Super. 1974). This judge went on to say "in view of the state's compelling interest in educating its youth in an environment conducive to learning, schools may be expected to take reasonable measures to eliminate the disruptive influence of drugs and violence." In re Dumas, 515 A.2d at 988 (Kelly, J., concurring). The Pennsylvania courts have used the T.L.O. "reasonable suspicion" standard to evaluate school searches. In re S.G., 607 A.2d 793 (Pa. Super. 1992).

The New Hampshire Supreme Court also has held that "students are entitled to a safe and healthy educational environment." State v. Drake, 662 A.2d 265 (N.H. 1995). Public school administrators charged with fostering this environment have a responsibility "to protect school children from antisocial behavior on the part of irresponsible classmates." Id. at 266. Thus they should be "afforded greater flexibility than law enforcement officials when searching for contraband." Id. at 267. The New Hampshire Supreme Court then adopted T.L.O.'s "reasonable under all the circumstances" standard for school searches. Id. The court further noted that this reasonableness standard is a "totality test" and must "take into account the threat posed to the student body by the suspected illegality." Id. at 268.

The Washington State Constitution has a right-to-privacy provision that states that "[n]o person shall be disturbed in his private affairs, or his home invaded, without authority of law." Wash. Const., art. 1, § 7. The Washington Court of Appeals has ruled, however, that this provision does not require a higher standard than the T.L.O. "reasonable grounds" standard to search a child. State v. Brooks, 718 P.2d 837, 841 (Wash. App. 1986). See also State v. Sweeney, 782 P.2d 562 (Wash. App. 1989); State v. Slattery, 787 P.2d 932 (Wash. App. 1990). The Washington Supreme Court has articulated the factors for determining if reasonable grounds exist to justify a search, which include "the child's age, history, and school record, the prevalence and seriousness of the problem in the school to which the search was directed, the exigency to make the search without delay, and the probative value and reliability of the information used as a justification for the search." State v. McKinnon, 558 P.2d 781, 784 (Wash. 1977), quoted in Brooks, 718 P.2d at 840, and Slattery, 787 P.2d at 934.

The Hawaii Constitution has a similar right-to-privacy provision stating that "[t]he right of the people to be secure in their houses, papers and effects against unreasonable searches, seizures and invasions of privacy shall not be violated. . . . " Haw. Const., art. 1, sec. 7. The Hawaii Supreme Court has held that children in school have legitimate expectations of privacy protected by this provision and that public school officials must comply with it as well as the Fourth Amendment of the federal Constitution. In re Doe, 887 P.2d 645, 652 (Haw. 1994). The Hawaii court also explicitly recognized, however, that public schools are a "unique social environment . . . [where] . . . teachers and administrators . . . have a legitimate and substantial interest in maintaining discipline in the classroom and on school grounds to create an environment where learning can take place." *Id.* at 651. Because the warrant requirement is unsuited to the school environment, the court also held that public school officials do not need search warrants or probable cause to search or seize evidence from students under their authority. *Id.* at 652. Although free to give broader protection under the Hawaii Constitution than that given by the federal Constitution, the Hawaii Supreme Court explicitly adopted the T.L.O. "reasonable suspicion" standard for assessing searches in Hawaii public schools. *Id.*

The Texas Criminal Procedure Code contains provisions (articles 14.01 and 15.22) that govern the circumstances under which one person may place another person under arrest, and define when a person has actually been arrested. But the Texas Court of Appeals has ruled that these provisions do not "place a greater burden upon public school officials than the Fourth Amendment does." Coffman v. State, 782 S.W.2d 249, 251 (Tex. App. 1989). The Texas court in Coffman rejected the accused student's contention that he had been placed under arrest when an assistant principal, who was suspicious of the student because the student had gotten into trouble in the past and was in the hall without a hall pass, asked him to open his book bag. In other cases, the Texas courts have applied the T.L.O. standards (*see* Irby v. State, 751 S.W.2d 670 (Tex. App. 1988)); Minner v. State, 1994 WL 605761 (Tex. App. 1994)), but did in one case strike down a search as unduly intrusive. Coronado v. State, 835 S.W.2d 636 (Tex. Crim. App. 1992).

Chapter 11

Sample Forms

§ 11:1   Student search and seizure incident report form
§ 11:2   Item identification tag

> **KeyCite®:** Cases and other legal materials listed in KeyCite Scope can be researched through West's KeyCite service on Westlaw®. Use KeyCite to check citations for form, parallel references, prior and later history, and comprehensive citator information, including citations to other decisions and secondary materials.

§ 11:1   Student search and seizure incident report form

TABLE

Complete and file with principal

School _____ School Code _____
Reported by _____
Position _____ Date ____/____/____

1. STUDENT IDENTIFICATION
Name of Suspected Student
_____ Grade _____ Sex _____
Name of Student Searched (if different from suspect)
_____ Grade _____ Sex _____

2. REASONABLE SUSPICION
Suspected Infraction: _____
Why is the particular student suspected of this infraction?

_____

_____

☐   The infraction threatens health or safety; explain:

_____

_____

Item sought: _____
How is item connected with suspected infraction?

_____
_____

☐   The item threatens health or safety; explain:

_____
_____

Describe the place to be searched: _____
Why is the item sought suspected of being presently located in this place? _____

Indicate and/or name the sources of your information:

_____
_____
_____

3. THE SEARCH

Name of official conducting the search:
_____ Position _____
Witness _____ Position _____
Location _____ Date ___/___/___ Time
___:___

☐ school premises   ☐ off-campus activity
Type of Search/Intrusion:
☐ Student Search   ☐ Abandoned Property
☐ Open Public View   ☐ Investigative Stop
☐ Emergency Intrusion   ☐ Frisk for Weapons
☐ Consent Search

Explain these intrusions:

_____
_____
_____

Describe any search of the student's person:

_____
_____

Describe any use of force:

_____
_____

4. SEIZURE

Describe Item Seized	I. D. Number	TYPE OF SEIZURE		
		Student Search	Plain View; Explain	Open View; Explain
————	————	☐ ☐ ☐	————	————
————	————		————	————
————	————		————	————

———————————————————————————— Date
___/___/___

principal/designee

§11:2 Item identification tag

Use to label each seized item.

ITEM I.D.	RETURN RECEIPT (keep in file)	SEIZURE RECEIPT (to give student)
#: _____	#: _____	#: _____

Chapter 12

Searches for Drugs by Urinalysis

Research References

West's Key Number Digest

Drugs and Narcotics ⬥25; Narcotics and Dangerous Drugs ⬥182; Searches and Seizures ⬥25, 53

KeyCite®: Cases and other legal materials listed in KeyCite Scope can be researched through West's KeyCite service on Westlaw®. Use KeyCite to check citations for form, parallel references, prior and later history, and comprehensive citator information, including citations to other decisions and secondary materials.

---

§ 12:1   Supreme court approval of suspicionless drug testing

The U.S. Supreme Court gave school boards the green light to engage in wide-ranging urinalysis testing for drugs in the case of Board of Education of Independent School District No. 92 of Pottawatomie County v. Earls, 536 U.S. 822, 122 S. Ct. 2559, 153 L. Ed. 2d 735, 166 Ed. Law Rep. 79 (U.S. 2002), which, by a 5-4 vote, upheld the policy of the Tecumseh, Oklahoma School District to require all middle and high school students who engage in any extracurricular activity whatsoever to consent to have their urine analyzed for evidence of drug use. Each month a group of students in extracurricular activities was chosen, at random, to provide a urine sample. Those who tested positive were counseled, and, if they tested positively a second time, were suspended from their extracurricular activities. In an opinion written by Justice Clarence Thomas, joined by Justices Breyer, Kennedy, Scalia, and Chief Justice Rehnquist, the Court ruled that such testing was justified because it served the School District's important interest of protecting its students' health and safety.

This decision is significant not only because of its result, but also because of its reasoning. Searches in schools, the majority explained, must meet the Fourth Amendment's requirement that they be "reasonable," but they need not be based on a finding of "probable cause" or even "individualized suspicion," because such requirements would unduly interfere with maintenance of the swift and informal disciplinary procedures that are required by the schools' custodial and tutelary responsibility for the students. *122 S.Ct* at 2564–65.

The Pottawatomie County case built on the Court's earlier decision in Vernonia School Dist. 47J v. Acton, 515 U.S. 646, 115 S. Ct. 2386, 132 L. Ed. 2d 564, 101 Ed. Law Rep. 37 (1995), which, by a 6-3 vote, had upheld urine searches of students on the high school athletic teams. In both cases, the Court found that the students have only a limited expectation of privacy. The athletes have limited privacy rights because they are subject to regular physicals and communal undress as part of their athletic activities. Students in nonathletic extracurricular activities have similarly waived their expectation of privacy, apparently because, in the majority's understanding, "[s]ome of these clubs and activities require occasional off-campus travel and communal undress." *122 S.Ct* at 2566. The Court's majority viewed the urine test as a "negligible" intrusion into a student's privacy. Board of Education of Independent School District No. 92 of Pottawatomie County v. Earls, 536 U.S. 822, 122 S. Ct. 2559, 153 L. Ed. 2d 735, 166 Ed. Law Rep. 79 (U.S. 2002) (*citing* Vernonia, 515 U.S. at 658). The urine is put into a receptacle in a closed restroom stall while a faculty member listens outside the stall for the normal sounds of urination to guard against tampered specimens. The test results are kept confidential, are not turned over to law enforcement personnel, and do not lead to academic consequences other than limitations on the student's opportunity to participate in extracurricular activities. The majority balanced these intrusions against the School District's responsibility to protect the health and safety of the students, and ruled that a District would be justified in requiring the testing even if it could not produce evidence of a particularized or pervasive drug abuse problem. Board of Education of Independent School District No. 92 of Pottawatomie County v. Earls, 536 U.S. 822, 122 S. Ct. 2559, 2568, 153 L. Ed. 2d 735, 166 Ed. Law Rep. 79 (U.S. 2002). The need to prevent and deter the substantial harm of childhood drug use provides the necessary immediacy for a school testing policy.

Justice Stephen Breyer's vote was necessary to make the majority of five, and he wrote a separate concurring opinion stressing that "the drug problem in our Nation's schools is serious in terms of size, the kinds of drugs being used, and the consequences of that use both for our children and the rest of us." Board of Education of Independent School District No. 92 of Pottawatomie County v. Earls, 536 U.S. 822, 122 S. Ct. 2559, 2569, 153 L. Ed. 2d 735, 166 Ed. Law Rep. 79 (U.S. 2002). He explained that the schools have an *"in loco parentis"* responsibility to help prepare children for adulthood, and thereby must ensure "a school environment that is safe and encourages learning." Board of Education of Independent School District No. 92 of Pottawatomie County v. Earls, 536 U.S. 822, 122 S. Ct. 2559, 2570, 153 L. Ed. 2d 735, 166 Ed. Law Rep. 79 (U.S. 2002). The drug testing, he said, enabled a student to resist the peer pressure to use drugs by providing "a nonthreatening reason to decline his friend's drug-use invitations." Board of Education of Independent School District No. 92 of Pottawatomie County v. Earls, 536 U.S. 822, 122 S. Ct. 2559, 153 L. Ed. 2d 735, 166 Ed. Law Rep. 79 (U.S. 2002).

Justice Breyer acknowledged that "not everyone would agree with this Court's characterization of the privacy-related significance of urine sampling as 'negligible,'" and that some students will be "seriously embarrassed by the need to provide a urine sample with someone listening 'outside the closed restroom stall.'" Board of Education of Independent School District No. 92 of Pottawatomie County v. Earls, 536 U.S. 822, 122 S. Ct. 2559, 2570–71, 153 L. Ed. 2d 735, 166 Ed. Law Rep. 79 (U.S. 2002). Nonetheless, he was comfortable in supporting the School District's drug testing program, in part because it had been adopted after public meetings in which parents could exchange views and also because it allows objecting students to "refuse testing while paying a price (nonparticipation [in extracurricular activities]) that is serious, but less severe than expulsion from school." Board of Education of Independent School District No. 92 of Pottawatomie County v. Earls, 536 U.S. 822, 122 S. Ct. 2559, 2570, 153 L. Ed. 2d 735, 166 Ed. Law Rep. 79 (U.S. 2002). He also concluded that the alternative of requiring "individualized suspicion" prior to testing based on "court-approved factors" such as "tiredness, overactivity, quietness, boisterousness, sloppiness, excessive meticulousness, and tardiness" might lead to a watering-down of that standard and could "unfairly target members of unpopular groups . . . or leave those whose behavior is slightly abnormal stigmatized in the minds of others." Board of Education of Independent School District No. 92 of Pottawatomie County v. Earls, 536 U.S. 822, 122 S. Ct. 2559, 153 L. Ed. 2d 735, 166 Ed. Law Rep. 79 (U.S. 2002).

Justice Ruth Bader Ginsburg, who had joined the Court's majority in the 1995 Vernonia decision involving student athletes, wrote a strong dissent, joined by Justices O'Connor, Souter, and Stevens. The four dissenting judges questioned whether the balancing test used in Vernonia justified urine-testing of students seeking to participate in organizations such as the Academic Team, Future Farmers of America, Future Homemakers of America, the band, the choir, the pom pom team, and the cheerleading squad. Justice Ginsburg stressed that participation in extracurricular activities "is a key component of school life, essential in reality for students applying to college, and, for all participants, a significant contributor to the breadth and quality of the educational experience." Board of Education of Independent School District No. 92 of Pottawatomie County v. Earls, 536 U.S. 822, 122 S. Ct. 2559, 2573, 153 L. Ed. 2d 735, 166 Ed. Law Rep. 79 (U.S. 2002). She found no justification whatsoever for singling out those students who wanted to participate in such activities and subjecting them to urine-testing not required of other students, and explained that if students have a "reasonable subjective expectation of privacy in the personal items she brings to school [citing T.L.O.], surely she has a similar expectation regarding the chemical composition of her urine." Board of Education of Independent School

District No. 92 of Pottawatomie County v. Earls, 536 U.S. 822, 122 S. Ct. 2559, 153 L. Ed. 2d 735, 166 Ed. Law Rep. 79 (U.S. 2002). High school athletes have a different expectation of privacy, she explained, because they shower and change clothes together and are exposed "to physical risks that schools have a duty to mitigate," Board of Education of Independent School District No. 92 of Pottawatomie County v. Earls, 536 U.S. 822, 122 S. Ct. 2559, 153 L. Ed. 2d 735, 166 Ed. Law Rep. 79 (U.S. 2002), while many extracurricular activities involve nothing more than meeting in a classroom after school. Although those supporting the drug-testing program argued that members of the band who carry large instruments, future farmers who work with large animals, and future homemakers who work with sharp kitchen instruments have safety and health problems similar to those faced by student-athletes, Justice Ginsburg mocked this view by describing them as "nightmarish images of out-of-control flatware, livestock run amok, and colliding tubas disturbing the peace and quiet of Tecumseh." Board of Education of Independent School District No. 92 of Pottawatomie County v. Earls, 536 U.S. 822, 122 S. Ct. 2559, 2577, 153 L. Ed. 2d 735, 166 Ed. Law Rep. 79 (U.S. 2002). In her view, the School District's policy was perverse, because "[i]t invades the privacy of students who need deterrence least," because "students who participate in extracurricular activities are significantly less likely to develop substance abuse problems than are their less-involved peers." Board of Education of Independent School District No. 92 of Pottawatomie County v. Earls, 536 U.S. 822, 122 S. Ct. 2559, 153 L. Ed. 2d 735, 166 Ed. Law Rep. 79 (U.S. 2002). Those students "at greatest risk for substance abuse" may be discouraged from "extracurricular involvement that potentially may palliate drug problems." Board of Education of Independent School District No. 92 of Pottawatomie County v. Earls, 536 U.S. 822, 122 S. Ct. 2559, 153 L. Ed. 2d 735, 166 Ed. Law Rep. 79 (U.S. 2002). In closing, Board of Education of Independent School District No. 92 of Pottawatomie County v. Earls, 536 U.S. 822, 122 S. Ct. 2559, 2578, 153 L. Ed. 2d 735, 166 Ed. Law Rep. 79 (U.S. 2002), she quotes Justice Brandeis' famous statement from Olmstead v. U.S., 277 U.S. 438, 485, 48 S. Ct. 564, 72 L. Ed. 944, 66 A.L.R. 376 (1928), that: "Our Government is the potent, omnipresent teacher. For good or for ill, it teaches the whole people by its example." In her view, the School District does not provide the proper citizenship lesson for its youngsters by permitting these suspicionless searches of all students seeking to participate in extracurricular activities.

A year after the Court issued the Pottawatomie County decision, a New Jersey Supreme Court upheld a similar policy of random suspicionless drug testing of students engaged in extracurricular activities, ruling also that the New Jersey Constitution did not provide any greater protection for schoolchildren than does the U.S. Constitution with regard to drug testing in public schools. Joye v. Hunterdon Cent. Regional High School Bd. of Educ., 176 N.J. 568, 826 A.2d 624, 178 Ed. Law Rep. 349 (2003). *See also* Marble Falls Independent School Dist. v. Shell ex rel. Shell, 2003 WL 1730417 (Tex. App. Austin 2003) (upholding a mandatory extracurricular activity drug-testing program against charges that it violated the religious freedom of Jewish students who consume wine during religious services as well as arguments that it violated their rights to due process and privacy).

§ 12:2   Urinalysis is a "search" within the meaning of the Fourth Amendment

The Supreme Court had previously determined that state-compelled collection and testing of urine constitutes a "search" subject to the demands of the Fourth Amendment. Vernonia Sch. Dist. v. Acton, 515 U.S. 646, 652 (1995) (*citing* Skinner v. Railway Labor Executives' Ass'n, 489 U.S. 602, 617 (1989)); National Treasury Employees Union v. Von Raab, 489 U.S. 656, 665 (1989)). The Court recognized in Skinner that the collection of urine samples intrudes upon "an excretory function traditionally shielded by great privacy"; the degree of intrusion, however, depends upon the manner in which the collection of the sample is monitored. Skinner, 489 U.S. at 626; *see also* Vernonia Sch. Dist. v. Acton, 515 U.S. at 658. The testing of the sample is a search whether or not the actual act of urination is observed, because the analysis of urine is capable of disclosing facts about which an ordinary citizen has a reasonable expectation of privacy. National Treasury Employees Union v. Von Raab, 816 F.2d 170,

175–76 (5th Cir. 1987), aff'd, 489 U.S. 656 (1989)). The majority opinion in Pottawatomie County acknowledged that the collection of urine samples by public school officials "implicate Fourth Amendment interests" and that it must meet the Fourth Amendment requirements of "reasonableness."

§ 12:3   Legal standards for assessing the constitutionality of urinalysis search

For urinalysis testing in the public schools, reasonableness is measured by balancing the search's intrusion on the individual student's Fourth Amendment interests against its promotion of legitimate governmental interests. Vernonia School District, 545 U.S. at 652–53.

The Vernonia case involved a seventh-grader who signed up to play school-district-sponsored football and his parents refused to sign a consent form for drug and alcohol testing. They subsequently filed suit, claiming the policy violated the student's Fourth Amendment rights.

Under the terms of the drug testing program, all students who desired to participate in interscholastic sports and their parents were required to sign a consent form agreeing to random urinalysis testing. An athlete was tested at the beginning of the season and was subject to testing randomly throughout the season if chosen from a weekly pool of all student athletes. In the sample collection process, a student had to disclose any prescription medication that was being taken before providing a sample. A male remained fully clothed with his back to an adult monitor. A female produced her sample in an enclosed stall. In both cases, a monitor listened for signs of tampering.

The samples were sent to an independent laboratory that tested them for standard drugs like amphetamines, cocaine, and marijuana. The policy also incorporated strict procedures regarding chain of custody and access to test results. If a student tested positive, another test was administered soon thereafter. If the second test proved negative, the district took no further action. If the test proved positive again, the student's parents were notified and the student was given two options: (1) either participate in a six-week assistance program that includes weekly urinalysis; or, (2) be suspended from athletics both for the rest of the ongoing season and the next season.

In analyzing the school district's program, the Supreme Court first considered the nature of the privacy interest upon which urinalysis testing intrudes (noting that the Fourth Amendment protects only those expectations of privacy that society recognizes as legitimate). Vernonia School District, 515 U.S. at 654 (citing T.L.O., 469 U.S. at 338). Although the Court reiterated its belief that children do not "shed their constitutional rights . . . at the schoolhouse gate," id. at 655–56 (quoting Tinker v. Des Moines Indep. Community Sch. Dist., 393 U.S. 503, 506 (1969)), it also remarked that the "nature of those rights is what is appropriate for children in school." Id. The Court specifically stated that Fourth Amendment rights are different in public schools than elsewhere in light of the a school's "custodial and tutelary" responsibility for children. Id. at 656–57. Furthermore, because public school children routinely are required to undergo various physical examinations and to be vaccinated against various diseases, the Court concluded that "particularly with regard to medical examinations and procedures, . . . 'students within the school environment have a lesser expectation of privacy than members of the population generally.'" Vernonia School District, id. (quoting T.L.O., 469 U.S. at 345 (Powell, J., concurring)).

Student athletes, in particular, have a more reduced expectation of privacy. "[S]tudents who voluntarily participate in school athletics have reason to expect intrusions upon normal rights and privileges, including privacy." Vernonia School District, 515 U.S. at 657. According to the Court, the nature of interscholastic sports participation does not lend itself to privacy. For example, athletes must suit up and shower together in locker rooms that "are not notable for the privacy they afford." Id. at 657. Furthermore, by choosing to be on a sports team, athletes subject themselves to a higher degree of regulation than is required of the rest of the student body. Id.

The intrusion on the individual student's privacy interests (which have been weakened in the public school setting) is another factor to consider. The Court had recognized in Skinner that urine sample collection "intrudes upon 'an excretory function traditionally shielded by great privacy.'" Vernonia Sch. Dist. v. Acton, 515 U.S. 646, 658 (1995) (*citing* Skinner, 489 U.S. at 626). But "the degree of intrusion depends upon the manner in which the production of the urine sample is monitored." Vernonia Sch. Dist. v. Acton, 515 U.S. 646, 652 (1995). Hence, a school district considering a urinalysis testing program should attempt to ensure that its monitoring process does not significantly intrude upon or compromise a student's privacy interests. In Vernonia School District, males were fully clothed and were watched only from behind as they produced their samples at a urinal along the wall. Females produced their samples in an enclosed stall with a female monitor outside listening only for sounds of tampering. The Supreme Court concluded that the privacy interests compromised by this monitoring process was "negligible." Vernonia Sch. Dist. v. Acton, 515 U.S. 646, 652 (1995).

Another "privacy-invasive" aspect of urinalysis is the potentially revealing information it may disclose about the student subject's physical condition and any material the student may have ingested. In Vernonia School District, the Court found it "significant" that the testing screened only for standard drugs (marijuana, cocaine, amphetamines) and did not vary according to the student's identity. Vernonia Sch. Dist. v. Acton, 515 U.S. 646, 658 (1995). Furthermore, the results were limited only to school personnel who had a "need to know" (school superintendent, principal, vice-principal, and athletic directors) and were not turned over to law enforcement officials or used for internal disciplinary functions. Vernonia Sch. Dist. v. Acton, 515 U.S. 646, 652 (1995) (*citing* 796 F. Supp. at 1364; 23 F.3d at 1521).

The Court also addressed the issue of whether the school district may require students to disclose information of any prescription medication the student may be taking. Although the Court agreed that this issue "raise[s] some cause for concern," it appears that a prior disclosure policy would not necessarily be fatal. Vernonia Sch. Dist. v. Acton, 515 U.S. 646, 659 (1995). The Court stated that it had "never indicated that requiring advance disclosure of medications is per se unreasonable." Vernonia Sch. Dist. v. Acton, 515 U.S. 646, 652 (1995). Such advance notification, however, may have to be given confidentially and perhaps only to medical personnel associated with the testing. Vernonia Sch. Dist. v. Acton, 515 U.S. 646, 652 (1995).

The intrusiveness of urinalysis testing on a student's privacy rights must then be weighed against the governmental interests sought to be furthered by the testing. In order to assess the government's interest, one must examine three factors: (1) the nature of the concern, (2) the immediacy of the problem, and (3) the efficacy of the policy in addressing the problem.

The Supreme Court found that deterrence of drug use by schoolchildren is an important, even "compelling" state interest on par with the governmental concerns in Skinner and Von Raab where random drug testing programs were upheld as constitutional. Vernonia School District, 515 U.S. at 661; *see* Skinner, 489 U.S. 602 (1989) (deter drug use by railway engineers and trainmen); Von Raab, 489 U.S. at 656 (enhance drug importation law enforcement by customs officials). The Vernonia School District Court noted that the physical, psychological, and addictive effects of drugs are most severe during school years. Moreover, drug use in schools disrupts the entire educational process. And with regard to student athletes, drug use creates a high risk of physical harm to the student athlete drug user or those with whom he or she plays. Vernonia School District, 515 U.S. at 661–62.

In Vernonia School District, the Court did not even question the immediacy of the school district's concerns that were identified by the lower court. The district court had found that students were in a state of "rebellion," disciplinary actions were at "epidemic proportions," and drug use and misconceptions about the drug culture were fueling the situation. Vernonia Sch. Dist. v. Acton, 515 U.S. 646, 663 (1995) (*quoting* Acton v. Vernonia Sch. Dist., 796 F. Supp at 1357).

The Supreme Court indicated, however, that conditions may not necessarily have to be so dire and immediate for a drug testing policy to be valid. The Court noted that it had upheld similar drug testing programs in far less critical circumstances. In Skinner, for example, no evidence established that a drug problem existed at the railroad in question. Similarly, in Von Raab, no history of drug use by customs officials was documented. Vernonia Sch. Dist. v. Acton, 515 U.S. 646, 652 (1995).

The "efficacy" of the program is also a relevant consideration. In Vernonia School District, however, the Court had relatively little trouble finding that the random testing of athletes effectively addressed the problem of drug use by athletes and the "role model" they serve for the rest of the student population. Vernonia Sch. Dist. v. Acton, 515 U.S. 646, 652 (1995). The Court declared this conclusion to be "self-evident." Vernonia Sch. Dist. v. Acton, 515 U.S. 646, 652 (1995). Such a finding has strong implications for drug testing programs for other student subgroups or the student body as a whole.

Finally, despite concluding that the government's concern was perhaps "compelling," the Supreme Court left open the question whether the government's interest in random drug testing of student athletes must even reach this legal standard. Vernonia Sch. Dist. v. Acton, 515 U.S. 646, 661 (1995). Describing a "compelling" state interest as one "which appears important enough to justify the particular search at hand, in light of other factors which show the search to be relatively intrusive upon a genuine expectation of privacy," the Court found that in the Vernonia School District situation, "the relatively high degree of government concern . . . [was] met." Vernonia Sch. Dist. v. Acton, 515 U.S. 646, 652 (1995).

The Court specifically rejected the notion that only the "least intrusive" search practicable (i.e., testing only upon individualized suspicion) would be reasonable under the Fourth Amendment. Vernonia Sch. Dist. v. Acton, 515 U.S. 646, 652 (1995). In fact, the Court stated plainly that "testing based on 'suspicion' of drug use would not be better, but worse [than suspicionless testing]." Vernonia Sch. Dist. v. Acton, 515 U.S. 646, 664 (1995). The Court was concerned about the accusatory nature of a suspicion-based regime because it would transform the process into a "badge of shame" and increase the risk of school officials targeting "troublesome but not drug-likely" students for testing. Vernonia Sch. Dist. v. Acton, 515 U.S. 646, 663 (1995).

Concurring in the opinion, Justice Ruth Bader Ginsburg expressed concern over the scope of the Court's opinion.

Indicating that her concurrence was based on the fact that the school district's drug testing policy applied only to students who voluntarily choose to participate in interscholastic athletics, Ginsburg noted that the Court left open the question of whether mass, suspicionless drug testing of all students required to attend public school would be allowable on no more than the showing made in this decision. Vernonia Sch. Dist. v. Acton, 515 U.S. 646, 666 (1995) (Ginsburg, J., concurring).

In a strong dissent, Justice Sandra Day O'Connor, joined by Justices Stevens and Souter, criticized the Court for dispensing with the individualized suspicion requirement for Fourth Amendment searches on the policy grounds that the evenhandedness of the district's suspicionless drug program diluted the accusatory nature of the search and precluded possible arbitrariness in selecting whom to test. Vernonia Sch. Dist. v. Acton, 515 U.S. 646, 667 (1995) (O'Connor, J., dissenting).

In the dissent's view, mass, suspicionless searches are generally considered to be *per se* unreasonable. The Court's opinion failed to recognize that both "history and precedent establish that individualized suspicion is 'usually required' under the Fourth Amendment . . . and that, in the area of intrusive personal searches, the only recognized exception is for situations in which a suspicion-based scheme would be likely ineffectual." Vernonia Sch. Dist. v. Acton, 515 U.S. 646, 676 (1995). For the dissent, nowhere is it less clear that an individualized suspicion requirement would be ineffectual than in the school context where students constantly are under supervision by school officials. Vernonia Sch. Dist. v. Acton, 515 U.S. 646, 678 (1995).

Stating plainly that "[p]rotection of privacy, not evenhandedness, was . . . and is . . . the touchstone of the Fourth Amendment[,]" Vernonia Sch. Dist. v. Acton, 515 U.S. 646, 671 (1995), the dissent argued that a suspicion-based scheme requiring individualized suspicion would be far less intrusive of students' privacy because it would involve fewer searches and would give potential search targets substantial control over whether they will, in fact, be tested. The dissent recognized that a suspicion-based regime may not be as effective as a mass, suspicionless testing scheme, but then noted that there was "'nothing new in the realization' that Fourth Amendment protections come with a price." Vernonia Sch. Dist. v. Acton, 515 U.S. 646, 680 (1995).

A "far more reasonable" alternative in this case, according to the dissent, would have the testing focus on the particular class of students found to be responsible for disruption in class and around campus, "disruption that had a strong nexus to drug use. . . . " Vernonia Sch. Dist. v. Acton, 515 U.S. 646, 685 (1995). This approach would encompass the two virtues of a suspicion-based regime mentioned above and would also reduce concern over the accusatory nature of the search "because the Court's feared 'badge of shame' . . . would already exist. . . . " Vernonia Sch. Dist. v. Acton, 515 U.S. 646, 686 (1995).

In this case, the dissent agreed with the majority that the blanket nature of the school district's search diluted the accusatory nature of the program. The dissent argued, however, that from a student's perspective, the program could never be considered "wholly nonaccusatory." Vernonia Sch. Dist. v. Acton, 515 U.S. 646, 683 (1995). The testing searched for evidence of wrongdoing. Furthermore, students would construe the consequences of a positive test—in this case, suspension from the sports program—as punitive. Vernonia Sch. Dist. v. Acton, 515 U.S. 646, 652 (1995).

The dissent also responded to concerns about the adversarial nature of a suspicion-based regime, noting that schools already have adversarial, disciplinary schemes (not necessarily involving drug use) to investigate wrongdoing, determine whether wrongdoing occurred, and impose punishment. "To such a scheme, suspicion-based drug testing would be only a minor addition." Vernonia Sch. Dist. v. Acton, 515 U.S. 646, 677 (1995).

Furthermore, the fear that a suspicion-based regime might lead to testing of "troublesome but not drug-likely" students ignored the fact that the required level of suspicion in the school context is T.L.O.'s "objectively reasonable suspicion." Vernonia Sch. Dist. v. Acton, 515 U.S. 646, 676–77 (1995). In fact, the dissent found it a "great irony" that most of the evidence used to justify Vernonia's suspicionless-testing program consisted of first and second-hand stories about particular students acting in certain ways that "plainly gave rise to reasonable suspicion of drug use" and would have justified a drug-related search under T.L.O. Vernonia Sch. Dist. v. Acton, 515 U.S. 646, 679 (1995).

Finally, the dissent found unpersuasive the majority's reliance on the widespread practice of physical examinations and vaccinations (medical examinations and procedures). A suspicion requirement for vaccinations and physical examinations would be "nonsensical" because vaccinations and physical examinations are not searches for wrongful behavior leading to punishment. Vernonia Sch. Dist. v. Acton, 515 U.S. 646, 683 (1995).

Between Vernonia and Pottawatomie County, the lower appellate courts had reached divergent views on the implications of Vernonia to other school situations. Both the Seventh and Eighth Circuits went far beyond the student-athlete context, and ruled that random drug-testing of all students who engage in any extra-curricular activities whatsoever is constitutional. Todd v. Rush County Schools, 133 F.3d 984 (7th Cir. 1998), rehearing denied, 139 F.3d 171, cert. denied, 525 U.S. 824 (1998); Miller ex rel. Miller v. Wilkes, 172 F.3d 574 (8th Cir. 1999), judgment vacated, (June 15, 1999) and reh'g dismissed, (June 15, 1999). The Eighth Circuit allowed the school district in Cave City, Arkansas to impose its random urine-testing on the students seeking to participate in extracurricular activity even though "there is no record evidence of any drug or alcohol problem in the schools," 172 F.3d at 580, because the intrusion of random urine testing on privacy interests "is not significant" and the "School District has an important and immediate interest in discouraging drug and alcohol use by its students." Id. at 581.

The Sixth Circuit ruled that a urine test can constitutionally be required of all persons who apply for, transfer into, or are promoted to any public-school teaching positions, even though "there is little, if any, evidence of a pronounced drug or alcohol abuse problem among Knox County's teachers," because of "the influence they exert upon the children" and the need to ensure that they are capable of dealing with emergency situations that may arise at the school. Knox County Education Association v. Knox County Board of Education, 158 F.3d 361, 374, 375,

378 (6th Cir. 1998). The Fifth Circuit upheld the constitutionality of the Louisiana Drug Testing Act which required even a custodian who mowed the elementary school grass to provide his urine for drug testing, because he interacted regularly with students, operated potentially dangerous equipment, and thus might pose a threat or danger to the students. Aubrey v. School Board of Lafayette Parish, 148 F.3d 559, 565 (5th Cir. 1998).

The Colorado Supreme Court, on the other hand, reached the opposite result in Trinidad School District No. 1 v. Lopez, 963 P.2d 1095 (Colo. 1998), even though "the evidence shows a serious drug problem in the general student body," *id.* at 1104, because extracurricular activities are not truly voluntary (persons enrolled in band for credit also participate in the "extracurricular" marching band and must have their urine tested), *id.* at 1107, and because "involvement in a school's extracurricular offerings is a vital adjunct to the educational experience." *Id.* at 1109. (Earlier, in University of Colorado v. Derdeyn, 863 P.2d 929 (Colo. 1993), the Colorado Supreme Court had ruled that random urine testing of intercollegiate athletes at the University of Colorado was unconstitutional).

See also Linke v. Northwestern Sch. Corp., 763 N.E.2d 972 (Ind. 2002) (holding that the school's policy of conducing random drug testing on students participating in athletics and extracurricular and cocurricular activities and on students wishing to drive themselves to and from school did not violate the search and seizure clause); Theodore v. Del. Valley Sch. Dist., 761 A.2d 652, 661 (Pa.Commw.Ct. 2000) (holding unconstitutional under the Pennsylvania Constitution's version of the Fourth Amendment a suspicionless drug testing policy applicable to students participating in extracurricular activities and driving to school because the government had not articulated "a single reason why the specific group it chose required testing over that of the general school population"); Gardner v. Tulia Indep. Sch. Dist., No. 2:97-CV-020-J (N.D.Tex. Dec. 7, 2000) (holding unconstitutional the random suspicionless drug testing of all students participating in extracurricular activities); Tannahill v. Lockney Indep. Sch. Dist., 133 F.Supp.2d 919 (N.D.Tex.2001) (holding unconstitutional a drug testing policy applicable to all students in grades six through 12 because of the "near dearth of evidence demonstrating a need to be met by the search," the privacy rights of the students, and the lack of any relationship to safety-sensitive functions).

The Seventh Circuit also seems to have had some second thoughts about this issue, because, a few months after Todd, it struck down as unconstitutional a school policy that required a urine test of everyone who had been suspended for three or more days for fighting. Willis v. Anderson Community School Corporation, 158 F.3d 415 (7th Cir. 1998). In this case, the court emphasized the important privacy interests at stake, found that the School Corporation's interests could be adequately served by requiring urine testing when individually justified by a reasonable suspicion rather than pursuant to an across-the-board rule, and distinguished Todd by noting that Willis had not engaged in his fight "voluntarily" in any meaningful sense, unlike the students in Todd who chose to join an extracurricular program. *Id.* at 420–22.

Two years later, the Seventh Circuit expressed serious doubts about the validity of the reasoning that had produced the Todd decision, but nonetheless felt constrained to follow that decision because of the importance of *stare decisis* and precedent. Joy v. Penn-Harris-Madison School Corporation, 212 F.3d 1052 (7th Cir. 2000). The court determined that it was appropriate to demand urine samples of those who drive to school and park on school property, but said that "there has been an inadequate showing that such an intrusion [into the privacy of those engaging in extracurricular activities] is justified." Although upholding the school rule randomly testing those engaging in any extracurricular activity, based on its previous decision in Todd, the court cautioned "against reading the opinion in Todd too broadly," warned that randomly testing all students would not be constitutional, and struck down the testing of student-drivers to determine if they were utilizing nicotine.

An example of a court permitting urine (and blood) testing of a student suspected of being high on marijuana or alcohol is found in Hedges v. Musco, 204 F.3d 109 (3d Cir. 2000). *See also* Rinker v. Sipler, 264 F. Supp. 2d 181, 178 Ed. Law Rep. 730 (M.D. Pa. 2003) (allowing carefully-monitored urine testing to determine if a student had been using drugs).

§ 12:4   What should school districts do now?

After the Supreme Court's June 27, 2002 decision in Pottawatomie County, teachers, administrators, and parents began meeting in many locations around the country to determine whether they should adopt a drug testing policy. *See* Tamar Lewin, With Court Nod, Parents Debate School Drug Tests, N.Y. Times, Sept. 29, 2002, at 1, col. 1. Since the Vernonia decision, about 5 percent of the country's school districts had begun conducting drug tests of student athletes. In the months that followed the Pottawatomie County decision, most large urban districts have shown little interest in drug testing, but smaller districts, especially those in the South and Midwest, have shown a lot of interest. In August 2002, the White House Office of National Drug Control Policy began distributing a guide supporting school drug testing. *Id.*

Some schools have wanted to test all students, but have held back after being threatened with lawsuits. The community in Autauga County, Alabama, has adopted the unique approach of asking students to take drug tests voluntarily, and if they test negative they receive an identification card giving them discounts at local stores and restaurants. Tamar Lewin, With Court Nod, Parents Debate School Drug Tests, N.Y. Times, Sept. 29, 2002, at 1, col. 1. Many communities remain deeply divided on this issue.

Chapter 13

Random/Dragnet Searches in Public Schools

Research References

West's Key Number Digest
Schools ☞169.5; Searches and Seizures ☞22, 42, 67, 70

KeyCite®: Cases and other legal materials listed in KeyCite Scope can be researched through West's KeyCite service on Westlaw®. Use KeyCite to check citations for form, parallel references, prior and later history, and comprehensive citator information, including citations to other decisions and secondary materials.

---

§ 13:1 Introduction: Our traditional abhorrence of random/dragnet searches

As earlier chapters have explained, the Fourth Amendment to the U.S. Constitution provides that the Federal Government shall not violate "[t]he right of the people to be secure in their persons, houses, papers, and effects, against unreasonable searches and seizures, ..." "This restraint on government conduct generally bars officials from undertaking a search or seizure absent individualized suspicion." Chandler v. Miller, 520 U.S. 305, 308 (1997); City of Indianapolis v. Edmond, 531 U.S. 32, 121

S. Ct. 447, 148 L. Ed. 2d 333 (2000). The Fourteenth Amendment extends this guarantee to searches and seizures by state officers, including public school officials. New Jersey v. T.L.O., 469 U.S. 325, 336–37 (1985).

The ultimate measure of the constitutionality of a government search is "reasonableness." Vernonia School District 47J v. Acton, 515 U.S. 646, 652 (1995). "To be reasonable under the Fourth Amendment, a search ordinarily must be based on individualized suspicion of wrongdoing." Chandler, 520 U.S. at 313, and usually requires a judicial warrant based on a showing of probable cause.

Because of these basic perspectives on the legitimacy of searches, random or "dragnet" searches of students have traditionally been viewed with abhorrence. See, e.g., City of Indianapolis v. Edmond, 531 U.S. 32, 121 S. Ct. 447, 148 L. Ed. 2d 333 (2000) (ruling that vehicle checkpoints established to catch individuals with illegal drugs violated the Fourth Amendment, and confirming that searches or seizures without individualized suspicion of wrongdoing are unreasonable except in limited circumstances targeted at specific crimes such as drunk driving and transporting of illegal aliens near borders). Similarly, undifferentiated "sweep searches" of students have been rejected as impermissible and have subjected school officials to liability. In Bellnier v. Lund, 438 F. Supp. 47 (N.D.N.Y. 1977), school officials conducted a blanket strip search of an entire fifth-grade class after one student discovered that three dollars had been stolen from his jacket pocket. The court found the search to be illegal, particularly in light of the young age of the students, the intrusiveness of the search, and the insignificance of the infraction, and emphasized that officials are authorized to search only particular students whom they reasonably suspected may have stolen the money. A similar result was reached in Burnham v. West, 681 F. Supp. 1160 (E.D. Va. 1987), where a school principals was held to be civilly liable after he ordered three "sweep searches" without individualized reasonable suspicion. The first search occurred when the principal discovered defacement of school property and then directed teachers to search the book bags, pockets, and pocketbooks of all the students for magic markers. The second search of a larger group or students took place after a teacher informed the principal that she had seen students with portable radios. When a teacher reported that she had smelled marijuana in a hallway area, another search of all the students in the area was ordered. The principal was held to be liable under Section 1983, and the school officials were required to pay the students' attorney fees.

More recently, an appellate court in Ohio declared unconstitutional a statute authorizing school officials to search lockers at will, emphasizing the importance of protecting the privacy rights of students, particularly with regard to the personal possessions they keep on their person and in their lockers:

> Indeed, *one cannot envision any rule which minimizes the value of our Constitutional freedoms in the minds of our youth more dramatically than a statute which proclaims that juveniles have no right to privacy in their personal possessions.* The contents of a student's book bag in all likelihood represent the most personal of all student belongings. Included within this ever-present repository would be letters which are never meant to be sent; diaries which are not intended to be read by anyone; photographs of long lost friends or pets; and any other unmistakable evidence of the particularly unique stages of growing up. The government simply has no right to proclaim that, contrary to the right of privacy guaranteed by the United States Constitution, these personal articles will be subject to observation and dissemination by the adult community at will. *It is hypocritical for a teacher to lecture on the grandeur of the United States Constitution in the morning and violate its basic tenets in the afternoon.*

In re Adam, 697 N.E.2d 1100 (Ohio App. 1997)(emphasis added). *See also* Kennedy v. Dexter Consolidated Schools, 124 N.M. 764, 1998 -NMCA- 051, 955 P.2d 693, 125 Ed. Law Rep. 947 (Ct. App. 1998), cert. granted, (Apr. 2, 1998) and aff'd in part, rev'd in part on other grounds, 2000 -NMSC- 025, 129 N.M. 436, 10 P.3d 115, 148 Ed. Law Rep. 1047 (2000) (upholding a judgment by two searched students against the school board: "Although it was reasonable for school officials to believe that one of the ten other students in the classroom had taken Monica Fresquez's ring, that group is too large for each of its members to be considered individually suspect"); Watkins v. Millennium School, 290 F. Supp. 2d 890, 183 Ed. Law Rep. 454 (S.D. Ohio 2003) (ruling that an intrusive search of three students, without any individualized suspicion, after $10 was discovered to be missing was unjustified); *but see* In re A.D., 2004 PA Super 36, 844 A.2d 20, 27, 186 Ed. Law Rep. 857 (2004) (ruling that an assistant principal had reasonable suspicion to search seven students who were in a bleacher area near the location of a theft of $83, explaining that it "was not a large, random search of the general student population designed to effectuate a broad policy objective," but rather "was the type of immediate and flexible disciplinary procedure the United States Supreme Court condoned in recognition of the fact that school officials need to maintain an orderly educational school environment").

This perspective has been changing, however, as violence in schools has persuaded school systems to institute mandatory or random metal and canine searches, which have been upheld by the courts. In addition, school officials will occasionally encounter situations where it is valid to search all students for contraband merely because of their presence in a suspected place.

A warrant is not required to establish the reasonableness of all government searches; and when a warrant is not required, probable cause is not invariably required either. A search unsupported by probable cause can be constitutional "when special needs, beyond the normal need for law enforcement, make the warrant and probable cause requirement impracticable." Vernonia, 515 U.S. at 643 (emphasis added) (quoting Griffin v. Wisconsin, 483 U.S. 868, 873 (1987)). "[C]ourts must then undertake a context-specific inquiry, examining closely the competing private and public interests[.]" Chandler, 117 S. Ct. at 1301.

Courts determine whether a particular search meets the reasonableness standard by balancing two factors: the search's intrusion on the individual's Fourth Amendment privacy interests and its promotion of legitimate governmental interests. Vernonia, 515 U.S. at 653–54. Also important to consider is whether a more rigorous standard of suspicion is unworkable.

The first factor is the nature of the privacy interest upon which the search intrudes. The Fourth Amendment does not protect all subjective expectations of privacy, but only those that society recognizes as "legitimate." T.L.O., 469 U.S. at 338. The Supreme Court has stated that "[i]n limited circumstances, where the privacy interests implicated by the search are minimal, and where an important governmental interest furthered by the intrusion would be placed in jeopardy by a requirement of individualized suspicion, a search may be reasonable despite the absence of such suspicion." Skinner v. Railway Labor Executives' Assn., 489 U.S. 602, 624 (1989).

The Supreme Court has determined that legitimate governmental interests justify suspicionless "administrative searches" for: border checkpoints to discover illegal aliens, United States v. Martinez-Fuerte, 428 U.S. 543, 545–50 (1976); sobriety checkpoints, Michigan Dept. of State Police v. Sitz, 496 U.S. 444, 447, 455 (1990); administrative inspections in "closely regulated" businesses, New York v. Burger, 482 U.S. 691, 703–704 (1987); and drug-testing programs for customs officers, National Treasury Employees Union v. Von Raab, 489 U.S. 656 (1989), railway employees, Skinner, supra, student athletes, Vernonia, supra and other students engaged in extracurricular activities. Board of Education of Independent School District No. 92 of Pottawatomie County v. Earls, 122 S. Ct. 2559, 153 L. Ed. 2d 735, 166 Ed. Law Rep. 79 (U.S. 2002). Lower federal courts and state courts have approved such searches in airports, United States v. Epperson, 454 F.2d 769 (4th Cir. 1972), and Commonwealth v. Veccione, 476 A.2d 403 (Pa. Super. 1984); courthouses, McMorris v. Alioto, 567 F.2d 897 (9th Cir. 1978); Downing v. Kuzig, 454 F.2d 1230 (6th Cir. 1972); schools, In re Latasha W., 70 Cal. Rptr. 2d 886 (Cal. App. 1998), People v. Pruitt, 662 N.E.2d 540 (Ill. App. 1996), appeal denied, 667 N.E.2d 1061 (Ill. 1996), State v. J.A., 679 So. 2d 316 (Fla. App. 1996), review denied, 689 So. 2d 1069 (Fla. 1997), cert. denied, 118 S. Ct. 98 (1997), In re S.S., 680 A.2d 1172 (Pa. Super. 1996), and People v. Dukes, 580 N.Y.S.2d 850 (1992); and a school board administrative building, Day v. Chicago Bd. of Ed., 1998 WL 60770 (N.D. Ill., Feb. 5, 1998).

§ 13:2 Suspicionless searches in schools

Courts have examined suspicionless searches in public schools in three contexts: the use of metal detectors (both walk-through and hand-held types) to discover dangerous weapons and illegal paraphernalia, the use of drug-sniffing dogs to discover illegal substances, and the use of urinalysis programs to detect drug use in certain segments of the school population (discussed in the previous chaper). In these areas, courts have focused on the "special needs" involved. A fourth type of generalized search concerns searches of students because they are located where an infraction is thought to have occurred.

The Supreme Court has ruled that public schools in general have "special needs" that justify modifying the normal law-enforcement procedures. T.L.O., 469 U.S. at 340. The courts have recognized that the need to provide a safe learning environment renders certain kinds of searches constitutional even though they might be unconstitutional in other circumstances. When issues of safety are involved, the courts are more likely to rule that a search is justified, even though it invades the students' privacy rights. For example, the Supreme Court found that the warrant requirement "would unduly interfere with the maintenance of the swift and informal disciplinary procedures [that are] needed," and "strict adherence to the requirement that searches be based upon probable cause" would undercut "the substantial need of teachers and administrators for freedom to maintain order in the schools." T.L.O., 469 U.S. at 340–41.

Perhaps the high water mark of permitting random searches is found in State ex rel Juvenile Dept. v. Stephens, 27 P.3d 170 (Ore.App. 2001), where the Oregon Court of Appeals upheld a program in Portland's "Turnaround School," whereby students and their parents must agree to permit regular searches of all the students' possessions as a condition of enrolling. The Turnaround School is an alternative public school designed for students who have been expelled from other schools for violence, weapons, drugs, or alcohol offenses. The students' lockers are searched on a daily basis, the students must pass through metal detectors, and must submit to pat-down searches. In the Stephens case, a school official found three individually-wrapped rocks of cocaine hidden the battery compartment of his pager as part of the daily locker search.

A similar program was sustained in In re O.E., 2003

WL 22669014 (Tex. App. Austin 2003), at the Austin Alternative Learning Center, which has been requiring all students to pass through a metal detector, be patted down, empty their pockets into a tray, and remove their shoes for inspection, which the court characterized as a legitimate "administrative inspection").

The U.S. Court of Appeals for the Eighth Circuit has recognized, however, that public school students have some remaining rights to privacy and has struck down the "highly intrusive" random searches that have been undertaken in Little Rock, Arkansas. Doe ex rel. Doe v. Little Rock School Dist., 380 F.3d 349 (8th Cir. 2004). The school district has had a practice of randomly selecting classrooms, ordering all students in the class to remove everything from their pockets and then put all their belongings, including their backpacks and purses, on their desks, while they leave the room. The court ruled that this practice "intrudes upon students' legitimate privacy interests" and, unlike Thompson v. Carthage School Dist., 87 F.3d 979, 110 Ed. Law Rep. 602 (8th Cir. 1996) (discussed in the section that follows), was not justified by any identified immediate governmental need. The court explained that these "[f]ull-scale searches that involve people rummaging through personal belongings concealed within a container are manifestly more intrusive than searches effected by metal detectors or dogs." The Little Rock searches were also different than those upheld by the Supreme Court in *Vernonia* and *Earls* (*see* Chapter 12 above), because the fruits of the search were regularly turned over to law enforcement agencies, thus indicating that they were not designed to promote students' welfare but rather to assist in prosecuting students. The court acknowledged that "the line separating reasonable and unreasonable school searches is sometimes indistinct," but nonetheless concluded that the Little Rock search practice is in the unreasonable side of the line.

§ 13:3 Suspicionless searches in schools—Metal detectors

Metal detectors were first introduced into American life in the early 1970s to protect airport security. Courts have ruled that requiring persons to pass through metal detectors constitutes a search for purposes of the Fourth

Amendment. United States v. Epperson, 454 F.2d 769 (4th Cir. 1972), cert. denied, 406 U.S. 947 (1972); *accord,* Wilkinson v. Frost, 832 F.2d 1330, 1340 (2d Cir. 1987), cert. denied, 485 U.S. 1034 (1988). But they have nonetheless upheld the use of metal detectors in airports, courthouses, public administrative buildings, and schools, where the search is limited to people seeking to enter these sensitive facilities "if the search is conducted as part of a general practice and is not associated with a criminal investigation to secure evidence." Day v. Chicago Bd. of Ed., 1998 WL 60770 at *5 (citing Klarfeld v. United States, 944 F.2d 583, 586 (9th Cir. 1991)).

In Epperson, one of the first reported cases to address the constitutional issues, the court stated "that []the very purpose and function of a magnetometer [metal detector] [is] to search for metal and disclose its presence in areas where there is a normal expectation of privacy." 454 F.2d at 770. The court took judicial notice that "air piracy and its threat to national air commerce is known to all," United States v. Epperson, 454 F.2d 769, 771 (4th Cir. 1972), cert. denied, 406 U.S. 947 (1972), and ruled that no warrant was necessary to use a metal detector because "[t]he threat is well known, the governmental interest is overwhelming, and the invasion of privacy so minimal, that the warrant requirement is excused by exigent national circumstances." United States v. Epperson, 454 F.2d 769 (4th Cir. 1972), cert. denied, 406 U.S. 947 (1972). Innocent passengers, the court stated, would find the use of a metal detector "not a resented intrusion on privacy, but, instead, a welcome reassurance of safety." United States v. Epperson, 454 F.2d 769, 772 (4th Cir. 1972), cert. denied, 406 U.S. 947 (1972). If the metal detector indicated the presence of metal that was not satisfactorily explained by the passenger, a subsequent physical frisk would be entirely justifiable and reasonable. United States v. Epperson, 454 F.2d 769 (4th Cir. 1972), cert. denied, 406 U.S. 947 (1972).

In finding use of metal detectors in a public building constitutional, one court stated: "Unfortunately, all public buildings today face the reality of being potential targets of disgruntled citizens, such that the use of metal detectors is both prudent and appropriate. . . . [T]he metal detector method of search, 'being unintrusive, is constitu-

tionally unproblematic where . . . there is some reason-
there needn't be much-to expect that armed and dangerous people might otherwise enter.'" Day, 1998 WL 60770
at *6 (quoting Justice v. Elrod, 832 F.2d 1048, 1050 (7th
Cir. 1987)). The court concluded that the use of a metal
detector at the entrance of a school board administrative
building was a minimal intrusion justified by the government's interest in safety. *Id.*

Courts have upheld the use of metal detectors in schools
to search students entering the building or grounds and to
search them after they have entered the school. The cases
involve searches conducted by school officials, or by police
and private security companies hired by the school district.

The first reported decision on the use of metal detectors
in a school involved scanning posts set up in the school
lobby. People v. Dukes, 580 N.Y.S.2d 850 (N.Y. Crim.
1992). A team of police officers conducted searches of
students and their belongings using hand-held metal
detectors. Students had been informed at the beginning of
the school year that such searches could occur at random.
Signs were also posted outside the school alerting students
that searching was imminent. Explicit guidelines for
conducting the searches limited the intrusiveness of the
searches and the discretion of officers conducting them.

Officers followed a random formula in choosing students
to search and were prohibited from singling out particular
students unless they had a reasonable suspicion to believe
that the student was carrying a weapon. If unexplainable
metal was found on a student or in his or her belongings,
the student was escorted to a private area for a more thorough search. After allowing the student the opportunity to
explain the presence of metal, an officer of the same sex
conducted a pat-down search. If a metal object was felt,
the student was asked to remove it before the officer did.
The search ended when no more unexplained metal set off
the detector.

In denying a student's motion to suppress the evidence
of a switchblade knife found in her bookbag, the court
relied on the "administrative search rationale" discussed
above. The court defined such a search as one where "the
intrusion involved in the search is no greater than necessary to satisfy the governmental interest underlying the

need for the search." 580 N.Y.S.2d at 851–52. The court balanced the degree of intrusion against the severity of the danger imposed to find the search reasonable. The court found the governmental interest here to be "equal to if not greater" than the interest justifying searches in airports and courthouses. People v. Dukes, 580 N.Y.S.2d 850, 853 (N.Y. Crim. 1992).

In People v. Pruitt, 662 N.E.2d 540 (Ill. App. 1996), the court reversed the trial court order suppressing evidence of a gun found through use of a metal detector search at the school entrance. The court found that the "purpose of the search was to protect and maintain a proper educational environment for all students, not to investigate and secure evidence of a crime." Id. at 547. "Because all students were required to walk through the detectors no official discretion or opportunity to harass was involved. The intrusion was minimal, not involving any physical touching until the metal detector reacted. . . . Once the metal detector reacted, the facts were sufficient to justify a frisk." Id. The search met the Fourth Amendment reasonableness test established by T.L.O.: "the action was justified at its inception by the reality of violence in the schools; the search as conducted was reasonably related in scope to the circumstances which justified the interference in the first place." Id.

The Pennsylvania Supreme Court reached a similar result in In the Interest of F.B., 726 A.2d 361 (Pa. 1999), upholding metal-wand searches of students entering University High School in Philadelphia. The court's plurality opinion concluded that: "As we find that the search of the student population, as conducted herein, affected a limited privacy interest, was minimally intrusive, was preceded by adequate notice, was motivated by a significant policy concern, and was directed towards an immediate need, individualized reasonable suspicion was not a necessary pre-condition to the search." Id. at 363. One of the six judges on the court dissented, and two concurred in the result, one writing that he did not think the intrusion was minimal, but agreed nonetheless that it was justified by "the purposes for which it was conducted." Id. at 368 (Flaherty, C.J., concurring). See also Smith v. Norfolk City School Board, 46 Va. Cir. 238, 247 (1998)(upholding searches of students with metal-wands and dogs as reasonable, and also holding that a metal-wand scan is not even a "search" within the meaning of the Fourth Amendment because it "involves no physical invasion" and does not intrude into any "reasonable expectation of privacy"); In re O.E., 2003 WL 22669014 (Tex. App. Austin 2003) refusing to suppress the discovery of a marijuana cigarette in the shoe of a student found during daily morning ritual at the Austin Alternative Learning Center of requiring all students to pass through a metal detector, be patted down, empty their pockets into a tray, and remove their shoes for inspection, which the court characterized as an "administrative inspection").

The facts were somewhat different, but the result was the same, in In the Matter of Haseen N., 21 A.D.2d 505 (N.Y. App. 1998). The principal of an intermediate school instructed his staff to pat down the outer clothing of students as they arrived on Halloween morning in 1996 "with the aim of preventing a recurrence of the egg-throwing melees that had occurred on the three previous Halloweens." The pat down discovered that one 13-year-old was bringing a.22-caliber pistol. The court characterized the pat-downs as an unobtrusive and constitutionally legitimate administrative search.

The second type of search involves randomly searching students not at the entrance to the school, but based on some other criteria. An example of this is the system set up by the Dade County (Florida) School Board, which was upheld in State v. J.A., 679 So. 2d 316 (Fla. App. 1996), review denied, 689 So. 2d 1069 (Fla. 1997), cert. denied, 118 S. Ct. 98 (1997). An independent security firm hired by the board randomly selected a secondary school, selected a classroom by rolling dice, and then scanned each student in that classroom with a hand-held detection wand for metal objects. If contraband was discovered, then police were summoned to make an arrest. The court recognized that students have an expectation of privacy, but nonetheless found this practice to be constitutional because it involved only a "minimal intrusion into the students' privacy," it was justified by the School Board's responsibility to "promote a safe learning environment," and it was the "least intrusive" search practicable in light of "Dade County's open-campus high schools" which made it difficult to use fixed metal detectors at entrances. *Id.* at 320.

A California Court of Appeals held that a similar random metal detector weapons search of public high school students did not violate the Fourth Amendment. In re Latasha W., 70 Cal. Rptr. 2d 886 (Cal. App. 1998), review filed (Mar. 6, 1998). Students were searched using ostensibly "random" criteria, but in this case the school searched all students who entered the attendance office without hall passes and those who were late, using a hand-held metal detector. Relying on the cases discussed above, the court found the search to be minimally intrusive because students were chosen by random criteria, were not touched during the search, and were required to open pockets or jackets only if they triggered the metal detector. The court was convinced that no system of more suspicion-intense searches would have been workable. *Id.* at 887.

Another case that illustrates how far the courts have gone in accepting blanket searches without individualized suspicion is Thompson v. Carthage School District, 87 F.3d 979 (8th Cir. 1996). Because a school bus driver reported that the seats on the bus had been cut, all of the about 50 male students attending rural Carthage High School were obliged to come to the science room, remove their jackets, shoes, and socks, and empty their pockets. They were then checked with a metal detector by the science teacher and principal and all objects in their coat pockets were removed. The teacher removved a book of matches, a match box, and a cigarette package from a ninth grader's coat pocket and seized them as contraband. When they were opened, the cigarette package contained only cereal, but the match box contained a white substance, which upon testing proved to be crack cocaine. The district judge ruled that the student's Fourth Amendment rights were violated and awarded him $10,000, but the U.S. Court of Appeals for the Eight Circuit reversed, concluding that the search was "reasonable in all the circumstances" and only "minimally intrusive." *Id.* at 982–83. The Court of Appeals rejected the argument that because the search was aimed at weapons, the searchers should not have been permitted to remove items from pockets that were clearly not weapons, concluding that "in a school setting, Fourth Amendment reasonableness does not turn on 'hairsplitting argumentation.'" *Id.* at 983 (citing New Jersey v. T.L.O., 469 U.S. 325, 346 n.12 (1985)).

Although most metal detector programs in schools have been upheld as constitutional, courts have examined the procedures used to ensure that the searches are sufficiently random and are not targeted at specific individuals. An Indiana Court of Appeals rejected the state's argument that students impliedly consented to intrusive searches because of the school's policy of searching students with electronic wand metal detectors on entering the school. D.I.R. v. State, 683 N.E.2d 251 (Ind. App. 1997). Here a student arrived to school late, but the wand was locked up in the principal's office, so the security officer searched the student manually, and after reaching into the student's pocket, discovered marijuana cigarettes. The school argued that T.L.O. and its progeny were inapplicable because here the school official did not target this particular student for investigation. And because all students were routinely searched and impliedly consented to being searched, this particular search was justified even though it was conducted in a different manner.

The court rejected this argument, concluding that although the student was aware of the school's search procedures using metal wands, it does not follow that she impliedly consented to an intrusive physical search. "The improvisational nature of the search is precisely what renders it constitutionally infirm." D.I.R. v. State, 683 N.E.2d 251, 253 (Ind. App. 1997). "[T]he further intrusion of reaching into [the student's] pockets in light of her age, sex and nature of the search was not justified under the circumstances." D.I.R. v. State, 683 N.E.2d 251 (Ind. App. 1997).

Another example of a court recognizing the privacy rights of students is found in People v. Parker, 672 N.E.2d 813 (Ill. App. 1996), where a 16-year-old student was detained after he turned away from a metal detector at the entrance to his school. The police officer monitoring the metal detector would not let the student leave the area and told him to proceed through the metal detector. The student then revealed that he was carrying a semiautomatic pistol and was criminally charged with unlawful possession of a weapon. The appellate court agreed with the trial judge that the detention of the student "constituted an illegal seizure" because his freedom of movement was restrained (*id.* at 816) and that the student's turning away was not sufficient to provide a reasonable suspicion to justify a search. The appellate court agreed with the trial court's statement that the student "could have, even if there were no signs, if there was no metal detector, he could have just turned around and gone home for any number of reasons, being sick, forgot something, forgot his lunch, forgot his books, forgot his homework or what have you." *Id.* at 817.

§ 13:4 Suspicionless searches in schools— Canine-sniff searches: Overview

Suspicionless "sniff" searches by dogs have also usually been upheld by courts. Whether the use of dogs to sniff for drugs, alcohol, or other controlled substances is a "search" under the Fourth Amendment depends on the particular circumstances in each case. Courts are more likely to find a "search" where dogs are used to sniff individuals rather than possessions. When a court determines that a search has occurred, it must analyze whether the canine sniff meets constitutional requirements.

The first decisions examining canine-sniff searches concerned passenger luggage and lockers at airports and bus depots. In these cases, the courts usually required individualized suspicion. Once authorities have reason to believe that an individual may have illegal substances, they are justified in using dogs to sniff the individuals' possessions for such substances. The U.S. Supreme Court has held that, if a police officer reasonably believed that a passenger's luggage may contain narcotics, a canine-sniff search of the luggage at the airport did not constitute a search for Fourth Amendment purposes. United States v. Place, 462 U.S. 696 (1983). Lower appellate courts have found canine sniffing of a footlocker at a bus depot (United States v. Fulero, 498 F.2d 748 (D.C. App. 1974)), a storage locker (United States v. Venema, 563 F.2d 1003 (10th Cir. 1977)), and a semi-trailer (United States v. Solis, 536 F.2d 880 (9th Cir. 1976)), to be valid where authorities had individualized suspicion.

Most courts have similarly found searches of students' possessions or lockers to be valid with individualized suspicion, but they are divided on whether searches of students' possessions or persons conducted without any individualized suspicion constitutes a search for Fourth Amendment purposes. The decisions can be divided based on the object of the search: the student's person or immediate possessions, student lockers, and student automobiles.

§ 13:5 Suspicionless searches in schools— Canine-sniffs of a student's person or immediate possessions

One of the first dog-sniffing cases in schools involved having dogs walk up classroom aisles while the students remained seated; the court ruled that this procedure was not a "search" and therefore did not violate the students' constitutionally protected rights. Doe v. Renfrow, 475 F. Supp. 1012 (N.D. Ind. 1979), aff'd in part, 631 F.2d 91 (7th Cir. 1980), cert. denied, 451 U.S. 1022 (1981). The court found that use of the dogs aided school officials in their observation for drug abuse and constituted "a minimal intrusion at best and [was] not so serious as to invoke the protections of the Fourth Amendment." *Id.* at 1020. Furthermore, the court observed, public school students have diminished expectations of privacy because of their continuous supervision while at school. *Id.*

Because the use of the dogs was in furtherance of "the school's duty to provide a safe, ordered and healthy educational environment," the court held that school officials need only meet a "reasonable cause to believe" standard rather than "probable cause." Doe v. Renfrow, 475 F. Supp. 1012, 1021 (N.D. Ind. 1979), aff'd in part, 631 F.2d 91 (7th Cir. 1980), cert. denied, 451 U.S. 1022 (1981). Increased drug use threatened the health and safety of all students, Doe v. Renfrow, 475 F. Supp. 1012, 1022 (N.D. Ind. 1979), aff'd in part, 631 F.2d 91 (7th Cir. 1980), cert. denied, 451 U.S. 1022 (1981), and the court found no need for individualized suspicion at this stage of the process.

Once a dog alerted to the presence of marijuana, school officials had the necessary probable cause (individualized suspicion) to search the student's pockets. Doe v. Renfrow, 475 F. Supp. 1012, 1024 (N.D. Ind. 1979), aff'd in part, 631 F.2d 91 (7th Cir. 1980), cert. denied, 451 U.S. 1022 (1981). Requiring the student to remove the contents of her pockets was a search for Fourth Amendment purposes, but "school officials did not violate [her] right to be secure against unreasonable search and seizure." Doe v. Renfrow, 475 F. Supp. 1012 (N.D. Ind. 1979), aff'd in part, 631 F.2d 91 (7th Cir. 1980), cert. denied, 451 U.S. 1022 (1981). The court also held, however, that a nude search of the student based solely on the continued alert of the marijuana-sniffing dog after she emptied her pockets was unreasonable as "an intrusion into an individual's basic justifiable expectation of privacy." Doe v. Renfrow, 475 F. Supp. 1012 (N.D. Ind. 1979), aff'd in part, 631 F.2d 91 (7th Cir. 1980), cert. denied, 451 U.S. 1022 (1981). To justify such a search, school officials "must articulate some facts that provide a reasonable cause to believe the student possesses the contraband sought." Doe v. Renfrow, 475 F. Supp. 1012 (N.D. Ind. 1979), aff'd in part, 631 F.2d 91 (7th Cir. 1980), cert. denied, 451 U.S. 1022 (1981).

In adopting as their own the District Court's "lengthy, thoughtful opinion," the U.S. Court of Appeals for the Seventh Circuit held that the canine-sniff was not a search and was entirely lawful because of the school's responsibilities *in loco parentis* and the minimal intrusion involved. Doe v. Renfrow, 631 F.2d 91 (7th Cir. 1980). A judge dissenting from the denial of an *en banc* rehearing was "deeply troubled" by the finding that the "dragnet inspection" did not constitute a search under the Fourth Amendment, particularly when the dogs sniffed the students themselves rather than unattended objects. *Id.* at 93–94 (Swygert, J., dissenting). Similar concerns were echoed by Justice William Brennan in his dissent from the denial of certiorari. 451 U.S. 1022 (1981).

Doe has been widely criticized and later cases have ruled that indiscriminate canine-sniff searches of a student's person are unconstitutional for lack of individualized suspicion. In a 1980 case involving almost identical facts (dog walking up classroom aisles sniffing students required to remain seated), the court held that the indiscriminate search was unconstitutional because the school officials lacked any individualized suspicion that the students possessed illegal substances. Jones v. Latexo Independent School Dist., 499 F. Supp. 223 (E.D. Tex. 1980).

The Jones court set out a two-part test to decide whether the canine sniff procedure violated students' Fourth

Amendment rights. "First, it must be determined whether a search of constitutional dimension actually occurred. If it is found that a search occurred, the second issue is whether or not the search was reasonable." Jones v. Latexo Independent School Dist., 499 F. Supp. 223, 231 (E.D. Tex. 1980). The court ruled that the dog-sniff was a search because the dog "replaced, rather than enhanced, the perceptive abilities of school officials." Jones v. Latexo Independent School Dist., 499 F. Supp. 223, 232–33 (E.D. Tex. 1980). Analogizing the use of the dog to use of a portable x-ray machine by police to discern what citizens were carrying on the street, the court found that "[t]he dog's inspection was virtually equivalent to a physical entry into the student's pockets and personal possessions." Jones v. Latexo Independent School Dist., 499 F. Supp. 223, 233 (E.D. Tex. 1980).

The court's second step applied a balancing test to find out whether this search was constitutionally valid. The public need for the search was balanced against the individual's right to personal security. The court rejected the airport-search analogy because airport searches can be avoided by refraining from air travel, but students are required by law to attend school and "had no means of avoiding the impending searches, after they were announced, had they wished to do so." Jones v. Latexo Independent School Dist., 499 F. Supp. 223, 234 (E.D. Tex. 1980).

Explaining that the police could not lawfully search citizens indiscriminately by bringing a drug-sniffing dog into a restaurant, football stadium, or shopping center, the court stated that they likewise could not do so in a school "without any facts to raise a reasonable suspicion regarding specific individuals." Jones v. Latexo Independent School Dist., 499 F. Supp. 223, 235 (E.D. Tex. 1980).

The U.S. Court of Appeals for the Fifth Circuit has held similarly that the lack of individualized suspicion makes a "canine inspection of a student's person" unconstitutional. Horton v. Goose Creek Indep. School Dist., 690 F.2d 470 (5th Cir. 1982), cert. denied, 463 U.S. 1207 (1983). This court was particularly concerned that the dogs actually touched the students. Such "personal intrusiveness" would be considered offensive "whether the sniffer be canine or human," and therefore constituted a search for Fourth

Amendment purposes. *Id.* at 479. "[S]ociety recognizes the interest in the integrity of one's person, and the fourth amendment applies with its fullest vigor against any intrusion on the human body." *Id.* at 478.

The Fifth Circuit also ruled that the school officials were not acting only *in loco parentis* when carrying out the search, but also as agents of the government, and therefore that the Fourth Amendment applied to their actions. Horton v. Goose Creek Indep. School Dist., 690 F.2d 470, 480 (5th Cir. 1982), cert. denied, 463 U.S. 1207 (1983). Although school officials' have a duty to protect students "from dangers posed by anti-social activities-their own and those of other students-and to provide them with an environment in which education is possible," they must not disregard the students' Fourth Amendment rights. Horton v. Goose Creek Indep. School Dist., 690 F.2d 470, 480–81 (5th Cir. 1982), cert. denied, 463 U.S. 1207 (1983). The court ruled that school officials need only have "reasonable cause" rather than the stricter "probable cause" to validate a search, but also warned that "[a]lthough the standard is less stringent than that applicable to law enforcement officers, it requires more of the school official than good faith or minimal restraint. The Constitution does not permit good intentions to justify objectively outrageous intrusions on student privacy." Horton v. Goose Creek Indep. School Dist., 690 F.2d 470, 481 (5th Cir. 1982), cert. denied, 463 U.S. 1207 (1983). Through this analysis the court concluded that "the intrusion on dignity and personal security" involved with a canine inspection of a student's person was not "justified by the need to prevent abuse of drugs and alcohol when there is no individualized suspicion," and was therefore unconstitutional. Horton v. Goose Creek Indep. School Dist., 690 F.2d 470, 481–82 (5th Cir. 1982), cert. denied, 463 U.S. 1207 (1983).

Horton was followed by the Ninth Circuit, which concluded that a dog sniff of a student does constitute a search, because intensive smelling is indecent and demeaning, because dogs sometimes engender irrational fear, and because such searches can be distressing, particularly when they are unannounced. B.C. v. Plumas Unified School District, 192 F.3d 1260, 1266–68 (9th Cir. 1999). The Ninth Circuit noted that the record did not reveal "any drug crisis or even a drug problem at Quincy High in May 1996," and thus held that random and suspicionless searches of students there was "unreasonable in the circumstances." *Id.* at 1268.

A Louisiana court upheld an only partially random search in State v. Barrett, 683 So. 2d 331 (La. App. 1996), where a police officer with four dogs searched six high-school classrooms selected by the principal because these classrooms "were known to have some of the 'problem' students." *Id.* at 334. The students were required to empty their pockets and then leave the classroom. After a dog "alerted" on the wallet of an 18-year-old student, the principal searched the wallet and found no drugs, but did find $400 in cash. In response to the principal's query about the source of the drugs, the student said, "I sell drugs, ha, ha." The student's book bag was then searched. Again no drugs were found, but marijuana leaves were drawn on the bag and a beeper was found inside it. The police officer then asked about the student's car, and the student pointed it out to her and consented to a search of it. The officer found "some marijuana roach" in the ashtray, and a subsequent search of the student's locker found an issue of *High Times* magazine.

The appellate court rejected the student's argument that the initial search (requiring him to empty his pockets) was illegal because it was not supported by reasonable suspicion nor was it a random search conducted with a metal detector. The court concluded that a sniff by a dog is not a search, but that requiring students to empty their pockets was one. This search was "reasonable and hence constitutional" because of "the decreased expectation of privacy defendant had as a student, the relative unobtrusiveness of the search, and the severity of the need met by the search." State v. Barrett, 683 So. 2d 331, 338 (La. App. 1996). In fact, the court also concluded that, based on the dog's "having alerted on the wallet, the principal had probable cause to suspect the wallet contained drugs and was justified in searching the wallet without a warrant." State v. Barrett, 683 So. 2d 331, 339 (La. App. 1996).

§ 13:6 Suspicionless searches in schools—Canine sniffs of student lockers

In several cases involving random or blanket canine-sniff searches of student lockers, the courts have upheld the searches as valid either because they did not constitute searches under the Fourth Amendment or because they were reasonable and hence did not violate students' constitutional rights. In each of these cases, school officials had no individualized suspicion of drug use, but ordered the searches based on their general belief that drug use had become too prevalent among the student population and therefore that the searches were necessary to protect the students' health, safety and welfare. The facts of these cases are similar: trained dogs were brought into the school and walked through the hallways sniffing all student lockers. The dogs' action alerting their handlers to suspicious smells provided the necessary individualized suspicion to permit school officials to open and inspect the lockers.

In the earliest case, the court focused on the fact that the school had assumed "joint control" over student lockers and that the student handbook stated that the school reserved the right to inspect all lockers at any time. Zamora v. Pomeroy, 639 F.2d 662, 665 (10th Cir. 1981). The court did not discuss the use of the dogs in the search, nor whether the dog-sniffing constituted a search for Fourth Amendment purposes, but stated simply that "the search was legal once the probability existed that there was contraband inside the locker." *Id.* at 670.

The second case is Horton v. Goose Creek Indep. School Dist., 690 F.2d 470 (5th Cir. 1982), discussed in the preceding subsection. That opinion addressed the issue of personal searches in detail, but gave only passing treatment to searches of student lockers. This court concluded that dog sniffing of student lockers did not constitute a search. These dog sniffs were like the dogs' sniffing luggage at an airport-it involved inanimate objects left "unattended and positioned in public view." *Id.* at 477. Use of dogs to ferret out odors of illegal substances was no different than if the school principal had smelled the odors. *Id.* Because the court found no search, it did not inquire into the reasonableness of canine-sniffing of the lockers. *Id.*

The third case upheld a random canine-sniff search of 2,000 student lockers. Commonwealth v. Cass, 709 A.2d 350 (Pa. 1998). The court's plurality opinion assumed that a "search" had been conducted and focused on the balance between the students' privacy interests and the school's reasonableness in conducting the search. "[I]f the decision to search was motivated by an interest of the school district, the importance of which outweighed the intrusion into the privacy rights of the students suffered as a result of the search," the search would be deemed "reasonable" under the Fourth Amendment. *Id.* at 356.

The plurality opinion followed the three-part analysis established by the U.S. Supreme Court in Vernonia School Dist. 47J v. Acton, 515 U.S. 646 (1995): first, consider the nature of the privacy interest upon which the search arguably intrudes; second, examine the character of the intrusion; and third, balance the competing policy concerns in deciding whether "the nature and immediacy of the concern at issue justified the means utilized for meeting those concerns." Cass at 356–57.

As in Horton, students had been forewarned in their Code of Student Conduct that their lockers would be subject to search by school officials without prior warning if school officials had a reasonable suspicion that "the locker contains materials which pose a threat to the health, welfare and safety of students in the school." Commonwealth v. Cass, 709 A.2d 350 (Pa. 1998). Furthermore, the lockers were considered property of the school and could be repaired by the school without notice. For these reasons the court concluded that the students had only minimal privacy expectations in their lockers. Commonwealth v. Cass, 709 A.2d 350, 357 (Pa. 1998).

Relying on United States v. Place, 462 U.S. 696 (1983), the court found that the canine-sniffing did not constitute a search. The "search" began once a dog alerted to a locker and its contents were searched, 709 A.2d at 357. But because of the students' limited expectations of privacy, the court concluded that "a search of the lockers was a minimally intrusive invasion of the students' privacy interest." Commonwealth v. Cass, 709 A.2d 350 (Pa. 1998).

Turning to the third step of the Vernonia test, the court found that the search was necessitated by "a heightened awareness of drug activity permeating throughout the entire school population, which appeared to be escalating as the school year continued." Commonwealth v. Cass, 709 A.2d 350 (Pa. 1998). Concluding that "deterring drug use within the public schools is an important and even a compelling concern for school officials, parents, the public at large, and the students themselves," Commonwealth v. Cass, 709 A.2d 350 (Pa. 1998), the court held that "the decision to search the entire school would reasonably serve two purposes: to discover actual evidence of drugs within the schools, and to warn the entire student body that bringing and storing drugs within the school would not be tolerated." Commonwealth v. Cass, 709 A.2d 350, 358 (Pa. 1998). The use of dogs in this search was reasonable because "[b]y using these highly trained dogs, the principal was able to further minimize the nature of the intrusion," while meeting "the compelling necessity of addressing the serious dangers caused when drugs invade the public school environment." Commonwealth v. Cass, 709 A.2d 350 (Pa. 1998). One justice filed a vigorous dissent in which he maintained that the search violated both the Fourth Amendment of the U.S. Constitution and a similar provision of the Pennsylvania Constitution. Commonwealth v. Cass, 709 A.2d 350, 366–73 (Pa. 1998) (Zappala, J., dissenting). For other cases invloving locker searches, *See* Section 10:1.

§ 13:7 Suspicionless searches in schools—Canine sniffs of student automobiles

On December 12, 2002, after the Scott County (Indiana) School Board authorized the use of dogs to conduct sweeps for narcotics, the local police notified the school officials at Austin High School that they would be conducting a canine search that morning. The school officials locked the students in their classrooms, and the dogs proceeded to sniff the student lockers and vehicles. After two dogs alerted on a red Jeep Cherokee in the school parking lot, the student connected to the vehicle was summoned and asked to unlock the door, whereupon a loaded handgun was found under the driver's seat. The Indiana Court of Appeals upheld the warrantless search, explaining that "smell testing by a trained dog is not a search within the meaning of the Fourth Amendment," Myers v. State, 806 N.E.2d 350, 353 (Ind. Ct. App. 2004) (*quoting from* Kenner v. State, 703 N.E.2d 1122, 1125 (Ind. Ct. App. 1999)), and furthermore that "[i]t is well settled that a trained dog's alert to the scent of narcotics gives rise to probable cause to search a vehicle." Myers v. State, 806 N.E.2d 350, 353 (Ind. Ct. App. 2004) (*citing* Kenner v. State, 703 N.E.2d 1122, 1125 (Ind. Ct. App. 1999)).

Canine-sniff searches of student automobiles are examined in Horton, discussed previously, and in Jennings v. Joshua Indep. School Dist., 877 F.2d 313 (5th Cir. 1989). Horton discussed searches of automobiles together with searches of lockers, finding neither to be a search for Fourth Amendment purposes, as discussed in the previous subsection. Jennings involved the use of dogs as part of a program to educate students on the dangers of drugs and to deter students from bringing them to school. 877 F.2d at 314. A private "sniffer-dog" service was used to detect narcotics, marijuana, alcohol, firearms, ammunition, and pyrotechnics on campus. The dogs were walked through the parking lot and if they were alerted by an odor from a car, school officials contacted the student responsible for the car. If the student refused to consent to a search of the car, the student's parents were contacted. If a parent refused consent, law enforcement officials were contacted. *Id.* at 315.

Citing Horton, the court found that "[t]he use of trained dogs to sniff automobiles parked on public parking lots does not constitute a search within the meaning of the fourth amendment." Jennings v. Joshua Indep. School Dist., 877 F.2d 313, 316 (5th Cir. 1989). Once the parent refused consent for a search, the matter was turned over to law enforcement and school officials could not be held liable for any constitutional violation that followed. Jennings v. Joshua Indep. School Dist., 877 F.2d 313 (5th Cir. 1989). Other decisions upholding canine searches of student automobiles are In the Matter of Dengg, 724 N.E.2d 1255(Ohio App. 1999), and Bundick v. Bay City Ind. School Dist., 140 F.Supp.2d 735, 738 (S.D.Tex. 2001) (upholding a seizure of a machete from a toolbox after "a dog duly trained and certified in exploratory sniffing 'alerted' to Bundick's truck . . . . The dog was trained to detect certain common illegal narcotics, gunpowder, alcohol and medications . . . . The fact that a machete was found and seized instead of any suspected substance, is of no consequence [because] taking possession of the machete constituted a valid 'plain view seizure.'").

The Eleventh Circuit has ruled in Hearn v. Board of Public Educ., 191 F.3d 1329, 1333, 138 Ed. Law Rep. 662 (11th Cir. 1999), cert. denied, 529 U.S. 1109, 120 S. Ct. 1962, 146 L. Ed. 2d 794 (2000), that the "alerting of a drug-sniffing dog to a person's property supplies not only reasonable suspicion, but probable cause to search that property." Based on that decision, a federal district court in Alabama upheld a search of an automobile, after a drug-sniffing dog had "alerted" on the car in the high school parking lot, which produced an exacto blade and a large pocketknife in the pocket of a jacket. Marner ex rel. Marner v. Eufaula City School Bd., 204 F. Supp. 2d 1318, 166 Ed. Law Rep. 224 (M.D. Ala. 2002).

§ 13:8   Suspicionless searches in schools—Generalized searches based on locations

If school officials have grounds to believe an infraction occurred at a specific location, it will occasionally be reasonable for them to search all students who were present at that place when the infraction occurred. The requirements for this sort of blanket search are: (a) that the location or area is closed or relatively confined so that innocent students are not likely to be wandering through the area; and (b) the infraction is or was so overt, open, and illicit that innocent persons would not likely remain or be allowed to remain in close proximity. An example might be a group of students in a restroom where a distinct smell of marijuana can be discerned, or where a group is standing around while another student is being assaulted. In these circumstances, it is reasonable to conclude that any student present has also been involved in the infraction and that evidence may be found on their persons. In Smith v. McGlothlin, 119 F.3d 786 (9th Cir. 1997), the U.S. Court of Appeals for the Ninth Circuit upheld a two-hour search of about 20 students who were discovered on a cul-de-sac near school by the vice-principal, who observed a cloud of smoke over their heads and furtive gestures suggesting the students were discarding smoking materials. Citing Vernonia School District 47J v. Acton, 515 U.S. 646 (1995), the Ninth Circuit's per curiam decision stated that "it is fairly clear that [the students were] not in fact entitled to

individualized suspicion before [they] could be searched."
119 F.3d at 788. Similarly, in In re Johnny F., 2002 WL
397046 (Cal. App. 2d Dist. 2002), unpublished/noncitable,
(Mar. 14, 2002) and review denied, (June 12, 2002) (unpublished), the court upheld as reasonable a search for
markers of the backpacks and pockets of all students in a
high school class, based on the report of the teacher of the
class that taggings had occurred during that class. The
court explained that "[i]ndividualized suspicion . . . is not
an absolute prerequisite for a finding of reasonableness"
and described the search as "reasonable" and "not excessively intrusive," emphasizing that the school officials "did
not touch the students." Id. at *2.

A decision that emphasizes the importance of protecting
the safety of students is Brousseau v. Town of Westerly,
11 F. Supp. 2d 177 (D.R.I. 1998), where the court permitted pat-down searches of sixth-graders who were eating in
the school cafeteria when a cafeteria worker announced
that a 13 1/2-inch pizza-cutting knife was missing. The
court determined that a pat-down search conducted by a
person of the same gender, lasting only a few seconds, was
not unduly intrusive and was justified by the urgency of
finding the missing knife, which presented compelling
safety concerns. The knife was later found in an empty
pizza box in a dumpster behind the cafeteria.

The district judge in DesRoches v. Caprio, 974 F. Supp.
542 (E.D. Va. 1997), rev'd 156 F.3d 571 (4th Cir. 1998),
ruled that the search of the backpacks of 19 ninth-grade
art students after a pair of sneakers was reported missing
from their classroom violated the students' Fourth Amendment rights, because no individualized suspicion existed.
The judge distinguished this case from cases involving
searches for drugs or weapons which involve the important
"need to protect the safety and welfare of students." Id. at
548. The Fourth Circuit reversed this ruling, acknowledging that individual suspicion for the search did not exist
when the school officials began searching through the
backpacks of the students, but holding that it did exist
with regard to the final student "by the process of elimination" after 18 backpacks had been searched without finding the missing tennis shoes. 156 F.3d at 578. See also
Kennedy v. Dexter Consolidated Schools, 124 N.M. 764,
1998 -NMCA- 051, 955 P.2d 693, 125 Ed. Law Rep. 947

(Ct. App. 1998), cert. granted, (Apr. 2, 1998) and aff'd in part, rev'd in part on other grounds, 2000 -NMSC- 025, 129 N.M. 436, 10 P.3d 115, 148 Ed. Law Rep. 1047 (2000), where the court ruled that a strip search of two students "simply on the ground of their being among ten people present at the scene of an apparent crime [a diamond ring was missing], with nothing to make them more suspect than any of the other nonvictims present" could not be constitutionally justified.

§ 13:9   Suspicionless searches in schools— Generalized searches prior to field trips

Another example of a blanket search that was upheld as constitutional involved a school district's policy of searching all students' hand luggage prior to field trips, despite the absence of any individualized suspicion. Desilets v. Clearview Regional Bd. of Educ., 627 A.2d 667 (N.J. Super. App. Div. 1993). Clearview's policy was one of deterrence, based on a school's duty to provide discipline, supervision, and control in a field trip context. The school district gave clear notice of the search and applied it without discretion to all students participating in the excursion.

A contrary result was reached in Kuehn v. Renton School District No. 403, 694 P.2d 1078 (Wash. 1985). The school announced that student band members had to submit their luggage to a search prior to a trip to an out-of-town concert. A band-member who was not allowed to make the trip after he refused the search sued under 42 U.S.C.A. sec. 1983. The court held that the reasonable search standard was not met because "the Fourth Amendment . . . requires that the suspicion be particularized with respect to each individual searched . . . [and] the mere announcement that a constitutional right must be waived in order to participate in a school activity cannot make the search reasonable." Id. at 1081–82.

Chapter 14

The Duty to Provide a Safe School Environment

Research References

West's Key Number Digest
Schools ⊕⇒89, 169, 169.5, 170

KeyCite®: Cases and other legal materials listed in KeyCite Scope can be researched through West's KeyCite service on Westlaw®. Use KeyCite to check citations for form, parallel references, prior and later history, and comprehensive citator information, including citations to other decisions and secondary materials.

---

§ 14:1　Introduction

For years, in the wake of TLO and its reasonable-suspicion test, courts have been weighing the privacy rights of students against a school's duty to provide a safe environment as they try to determine whether a particular search was reasonable. The more dangerous the threat to student safety, the more likely that a court will find a search or seizure to have been reasonable, even if it infringes on a student's privacy rights. Although the importance of providing a safe school environment is often discussed in search and seizure cases, it remains unclear just how far that duty extends and whether a school can be held liable for violating it. Chapter 9 of this volume discusses the standards that apply to lawsuits brought by students and their parents for searches and seizures thought to be unduly intrusive in violation of the Fourth Amendment. The present chapter looks at the opposite side of this coin — i.e., the standards that apply to lawsuits filed by students and their parents against school officials who allegedly have not taken adequate security measures to ensure the safety of students in the school environment. *See generally* Joseph R. Grodin, Rediscovering the State Constitutional Right to Happiness and Safety, 25 Hastings Constitutional Law Quarterly 1-34 (1997).

The school shootings that accelerated at the end of the Nineties have focused attention on violence in public schools, and raised tough questions about the duty of schools to protect their students. A federal district court judge in Texas has stated that schools have "dramatically compelling interests in maintaining a safe place of learning," and dismissed a claim brought against a school by students who had been frisked, handcuffed, taken to police headquarters, and detained without any individualized suspicion of wrongdoing, because "it is simply not improper to overreact" "in the aftermath of the Columbine High School violence . . . a genuine national tragedy, which has been mimicked at other schools." Stockton v. City of Freeport, Texas, 147 F.Supp.2d 642 (S.D.Texas 2001); *see also* Milligan v. City of Slidell, 226 F.3d 652, 655 (5th Cir. 2000) (stating that the goals of protecting students and deterring possibly violent misconduct are "compelling governmental interests"); Butler v. Rio Rancho Public Schools Bd. of Educ., 341 F.3d 1197, 180 Ed. Law Rep. 110 (10th Cir. 2003) (emphasizing that "[t]here is no doubt the School has a legitimate interest in providing a safe environment for students and staff" and thereby concluding that it was reasonable for the school to suspend a student for one year after he brought a weapon onto school property); Demers ex rel. Demers v. Leominster School Dept., 263 F. Supp. 2d 195, 178 Ed. Law Rep. 130 (D. Mass. 2003) (ruling that school officials acted properly to protect a safe school environment by requiring an eighth grader who had drawn pictures of the school surrounded by explosives and a gun pointed at the head of the principal to undergo psychological testing and concluding that such testing would not be an invasion of his privacy);

Porter ex rel. LeBlanc v. Ascension Parish School Bd., 301 F. Supp. 2d 576, 580, 185 Ed. Law Rep. 585 (M.D. La. 2004) (concluding that a search of a 14-year-old student's book bag was "necessary, justified, and clearly permitted" in light of drawings the student had made of the school "soaked with gasoline surrounded by an individual with a torch and missile. . .and a student throwing a brick" at the school's principal); Williams ex rel. Allen v. Cambridge Bd. of Educ., 370 F.3d 630, 188 Ed. Law Rep. 131, 2004 FED App. 0169P (6th Cir. 2004) (finding sufficient probable cause to justify arrests of students who had talked of violence against a school and its officials). New legislation attempting to address this epidemic of fear has been passed in many states, and parents of the slain children have contacted their attorneys for advice. Article I, section 28(c) of California's Constitution ensures every school employee and student the "inalienable right to attend campuses which are safe, secure and peaceful."

What steps can state officials take to prevent violence on school grounds, and should they be liable for failing to take these steps? If so, how will the responsibility to provide a safe school environment affect the way that schools provide security, and will the actions taken to protect students infringe further on their privacy rights? This chapter will examine the theories under which school officials may be held liable for injuries to students.

§ 14:2 School tort liability

In a state court, injured parties may bring claims for common law negligence or for a breach of a statutory duty. In a federal court, students or their relatives can attempt to sue for a violation of constitutional or statutory rights under 42 U.S.C.A. § 1983, under the special-relationship or state-created-danger theory, or (in the case of a sexual harassment situation) for a violation of their rights under Title IX of the Education Amendments of 1972, 20 U.S.C.A. sec. 1681.

§ 14:3 School tort liability—State causes of action: Common law negligence

In Comuntzis v. Pinellas County, 508 So. 2d 750, 751 (Fla. App. 1987), "[t]he complaint alleged that Comuntzis was physically beaten during the school lunch hour just outside the school cafeteria. The complaint sufficiently alleges the negligent breach of the duty to supervise by asserting that no teacher was posted to keep order in the cafeteria and that the beating was near enough, loud enough and prolonged enough to alert a teacher if one had been so posted." The court ruled that this complaint stated a valid cause of action: "The allegation that the plaintiff was a student at a high school run and operated by the School Board is sufficient to demonstrate the relationship between the School Board and Comuntzis giving rise to a duty. A school board's duty to properly supervise students entrusted to its care is well recognized in this state." *Id.* The court emphasized that the duty arose in part because school attendance is mandatory: "Because parents are required to entrust their children to the care of the school personnel, parents have a right to expect that their children will be protected." *Id.* at 753. The court emphasized that school officials were not required to be everywhere all the time, and were not obliged, for instance, to accompany kindergarten children to the bathroom, *id.*, but were expected to provide a reasonable amount of general supervision. *See also* Brantly v. Dade County School Board, 493 So. 2d 471 (1986)(reversing the dismissal of a claim by a student against the School Board for injuries suffered by being struck in the face by another student while walking by a school bus, in a situation where the bus driver was put on notice of the potential danger by a prior similar incident involving the same bus and passenger).

Another important Florida case is Gutierrez v. Dade County School Board, 604 So. 2d 852 (Fla. App. 1992), where the court reversed the dismissal of a claim brought by a student paralyzed by a gun shot from a nonstudent while the student was driving out of the school parking lot after a football game at 11:15 p.m. The school normally hired security guards for such events, but the official in charge of security knew that the guard who had been hired would leave at 10:30 p.m. The student sought to report his fears regarding the gun-toting nonstudent, but no security guard could be found prior to the assault. The court indicated that the school had a duty to provide a safe environment, and that it was irrelevant that the student was a few feet outside the school border when the bullet struck him in the neck: "A landowner is under a duty to invitees to maintain his premises in a reasonably safe condition. That duty extends to the means which the landowner has expressly provided for use by the invitees for ingress and egress."

Reaching a similar result is Dailey v. Los Angeles Unified School District, 470 P.2d 360 (Cal. 1970), where the California Supreme Court reversed the dismissal of a claim brought on behalf of a student who died after hitting his head on the playground asphalt near the gymnasium, fracturing his skill, while participating in a "slap boxing" fight with another student during the lunch break. The testimony revealed that no school official had any specific responsibility to supervise this area of the school facility, and that the physical education teacher "on duty" during this period was playing bridge in the dressing room. The court described the duty of care as follows:

> While school districts and their employees have never been considered insurers of the physical safety of students, California law has long imposed on school authorities a duty to "supervise at all times the conduct of the children on the school grounds and to enforce those rules and regulations necessary to their protection . . . ." . . . . The standard of care imposed upon school personnel in carrying out this duty to supervise is identical to that required in the performance of their other duties. This uniform standard to which they are held is that degree of care "which a person of ordinary prudence, charged with [comparable] duties, would exercise under the same circumstances." Either a total lack of supervision . . . or ineffective supervision . . . may constitute a lack of ordinary care on the part of those responsible for student supervision.

Id. at 363 (citations omitted). Applying this test to the facts, the court concluded that evidence existed to support a finding of negligent supervision:

> There was evidence to the effect that Mr. Maggard, the responsible department head, had failed to develop a comprehensive schedule of supervising assignments and had neglected to instruct his subordinates as to what was expected of them while they were supervising . . . . Mr. Daligney, the instructor ostensibly on duty at the time of the accident, remained inside an office during the entire lunch period, even though the area of his supervisorial responsibility was large and even though all students were

outside the gymnasium . . . . Neither defendant Daligney nor defendant Maggard heard or saw a 10-minute slap boxing match which attracted a crowd of approximately 30 spectators, although this took place within a few feet of the gymnasium. From this evidence a jury could reasonably conclude that those employees of the defendant school district who were charged with the responsibility of providing supervision failed to exercise due care in the performance of this duty and that their negligence was the proximate cause of the tragedy which took Michael's life.

The fact that another student's misconduct was the immediate precipitating cause of the injury does not compel a conclusion that negligent supervision was not the proximate cause of Michael's death. Neither the mere involvement of a third party nor that party's wrongful conduct is sufficient in itself to absolve the defendants of liability, once a negligent failure to provide adequate supervision is shown . . . . Nor is this a case in which the intervening conduct of the other student is so bizarre or unpredictable as to warrant a limitation of liability through the expedience of concluding, as a matter of law, that a negligent failure to supervise was not the proximate cause of the injury. There was testimony in the instant case that "roughhousing" and "horseplay" are normal activities for high school boys and it is the function of adult supervision to control just such conduct. The events which occurred in the instant case are precisely what one would expect from unsupervised adolescents. Of course, it is not necessary that the exact injuries which occurred have been foreseeable; it is enough that "a reasonably prudent person would foresee that injuries of the same general type would be likely to occur in the absence of adequate safeguards . . . ."

Id. at 365–66 (citations and footnotes omitted). California has reinforced this common-law duty with a specific provision in its state constitution, Article I, Section 28(c), which says that "All students and staff of public primary, elementary, junior high and senior high schools have the inalienable right to attend campuses which are safe, secure and peaceful." *See also* People v. Butler, 725 N.Y.S.2d 534, 538 (N.Y.Sup. 2001) ("Schools have a duty to adequately supervise the students in their charge and may be held liable for foreseeable injuries proximately related to the absence of adequate supervision.").

In Mirand v. City of New York, 637 N.E.2d 263 (N.Y. 1994), the New York Court of Appeals described the duties of school officials to protect their students as follows:

Schools are under a duty to adequately supervise the students in their charge and they will be held liable for foreseeable injuries proximately related to the absence of adequate supervision . . . . Schools are not insurers of safety, however, for they cannot reasonably be expected to continuously supervise and control all movements and activities of students; therefore, schools are not to be held liable "for every thoughtless or careless act by which one pupil may injure another" . . . The nature of the duty owed was set forth in the seminal case of Hoose v. Drumm, 281 N.Y. 54, 57–58, 22 N.E.2d 233: "[A] teacher owes it to his [or her] charges to exercise such care of them as a parent of ordinary prudence would observe in comparable circumstances." The duty owed derives from the simple fact that a school, in assuming physical custody and control over its students, effectively takes the place of parents and guardians . . . .

A case illustrating a different approach is Clark v. Jesuit High School, 572 So. 2d 830 (La. App. 1990), which is relevant to this analysis even though it involves a private school. The plaintiff suffered an eye injury resulting from being hit by a BB shot from an automatic pistol held by another student in his book bag. The court dismissed the claim against the school officials saying:

For a school to be strictly liable for injuries caused by a dangerous or hazardous condition on its premises, the school authority must have had actual or constructive knowledge of the unreasonably hazardous condition . . . .

Constructive knowledge of such a condition exists if the condition is so inherently dangerous that the school authorities should have known of it . . . .

Plaintiff argues that the foreseeability of Rene's act is a question of fact precluding summary judgment. We disagree. Jesuit submitted affidavits to the effect that there had not been prior violent incidents at school. It was plaintiff's duty to contradict these affidavits by presenting countervailing evidence. No such evidence was submitted . . . .

Under a negligence theory, a school can be held liable for failing to adequately supervise students only if the plaintiff proves that the supervision was inadequate and that there was a causal connection between the lack of supervision and the injury . . . . Spontaneous or planned acts of violence by students on school grounds do not create liability if the grounds were otherwise well supervised . . . . In the instant case, one teacher, Father Partridge, stated in his affidavit that he was outside supervising the students at the time of dismissal. We do not consider this to be inadequate supervision for high school aged students. Even if the supervision were found to be inadequate, however, plaintiff could not have established a causal connection between that and his injury. Rene Pagan did not even remove the gun from his book bag before firing. A teacher standing next to Rene would not have noticed anything suspicious about a student reaching into his book bag. The two students involved were admittedly not arguing or fighting. Therefore, in view of the fact that no amount of supervision would have prevented this incident, the trial court did not err in holding that there was no genuine issue of fact regarding inadequate supervision.

Id. at 831–32.

A later Louisiana decision did, however, impose a duty on the Orleans Parish School Board with regard to a student who was shot by a nonstudent while outside the school grounds in the process of trying to drive away from the school. Peterson v. Doe, 647 So. 2d 1288 (La. App. 1994). The injured student had asked the security guard for assistance in getting to his car, but the security guard said she had no responsibility outside the school grounds. The court said that the hiring of the guard indicated a recognition of the duty to provide a safe school environment: "[T]his case involves a situation where the defendant has assumed a duty to protect students, as evidenced by the fact that it hired security counselors specifically for that purpose. Thus, we see this case as analogous to the cases analyzing a business owner's assumed duty to protect patrons from the criminal actions of third parties." *Id.* at 1291.

These illustrative cases demonstrate that many courts recognize common-law responsibilities to provide a safe school environment, and certainly expect school officials to provide proper supervision over students (and nonstudents) on (and near) school grounds. Less clear is whether more active security measures, such as using metal detectors, urine inspections, and canine searches will be expected as a part of the duty to provide a safe school environment.

§ 14:4 School tort liability—Federal causes of action—Section 1983

Section 1983 of Title 42 of the U.S. Code provides juris-

diction in federal courts for claims based on the deprivation of constitutional and statutory rights:

> Every person who, under color of any statute, ordinance,
> regulation, custom, or usage, of any State . . . subjects, or
> causes to be subjected, any citizen of the United States or
> other person within the jurisdiction thereof to the depriva-
> tion of any rights, privileges, or immunities secured by the
> Constitution and laws, shall be liable to the party injured
> . . . .

A number of plaintiffs injured by violence in school have
tried to bring a cause of action against schools and school
officials under § 1983 for failing to protect them from being injured, arguing that bodily harm is a violation of
their Fourteenth Amendment Due Process rights, but such
claims usually fail. *See, e.g.*, D.R. and L.R. v. Middle Bucks
Area Vocational Technical School, 972 F.2d 1364 (3d Cir.
1993)(ruling that no special relationship based on physical
custody existed between a public school and two "exceptional" girls giving rise to a duty to protect them from being sexually assaulted by students, nor was the classroom
situation equal to a state-created danger); Lefall v. Dallas
Independent School District, 28 F.3d 521 (5th Cir.
1994)(rejecting a claim brought on behalf of a student
killed by random gunfire on a school parking lot after a
dance sponsored by the Parent-Teacher Association);
Mitchell v. Duvall County School Board, 107 F.3d 837
(11th Cir. 1997)(rejecting a claim brought by a student
killed by a nonstudent assailant while waiting for a ride
home from school in the evening, even though the student
was denied entry to the school's office to phone his father
and had to use an outside pay phone; the court ruled that
no custodial relationship existed between the school and
the student and that the killing did not result from a state-
created danger).

The U.S. Supreme Court has held that "nothing in the
language of the Due Process Clause itself requires the
State to protect the life, liberty, and property of its citizens
against invasion by private actors." Deshaney v. Win-
nebago County Department of Social Services, 489 U.S.
189, 195 (1989). Deshaney left the door slightly open for
students' § 1983 claims, by recognizing two exceptions to
the general rule, under which a student injured by a third
person at school might have a cause of action. The first

involves situations where a special custodial relationship exists, and the second is the "state-created danger" theory.

§ 14:5 School tort liability—Federal causes of action—Section 1983—§ 1983 "special relationship"

The DeShaney opinion says that the government has an affirmative duty to protect individuals from harm when it has restricted their freedom, thus creating a special custodial relationship and accepting responsibility for their safety. 489 U.S. at 199–200. Although a number of students have tried to recover under this theory, none have been successful so far because the school-student relationship is not recognized as sufficiently custodial, even in boarding school situations. *See, e.g.,* Walton v. Alexander, 44 F.3d 1297 (5th Cir. 1995) (finding no special custodial relationship between a multiple rape victim in a residential facility and the headmaster who allowed it to happen a second time).

§ 14:6 School tort liability—Federal causes of action—Section 1983—§ 1983 "state-created danger"

This theory of liability came from a suggestion in DeShaney that "while the State may have been aware of the dangers that [plaintiff] faced in the free world, it played no part in their creation, nor did it do anything to render him any more vulnerable to them." 489 U.S. at 201. Most of the plaintiffs who have tried to recover under this doctrine have been unsuccessful. *See, e.g.,* Graham v. Independent School District No. I-89, 22 F.3d 991 (10th Cir. 1994) (ruling, in a case where the school had warnings that shooting would occur, but failed to take steps to prevent the shooting, that failure to act is not a state-created danger); Leffall v. Dallas Independent School District, 28 F.3d 521 (5th Cir. 1994) (holding that a school's failure to protect a boy from students shooting into the air was not "deliberate indifference," which, under the state-created danger theory, requires abandoning the student in a dangerous situation or conspiring with the perpetrator to inflict injury); Mitchell v. Duval County School Board, 107 F.3d 837 (11th Cir. 1997) (concluding that the school was not responsible for a student's being shot off campus after leaving the school to use a pay phone, because it was his decision to leave the campus, and not school policy which forced him off of it). Under these rulings, mere negligence is not sufficient to create a cause of action. The school officials must actually facilitate the injury by putting the student in harm's way.

Although courts are rarely willing to find that an administrator has gone that far, one example of a student prevailing in a "state-created danger" case is Maxwell ex rel. Maxwell v. School Dist. of City of Philadelphia, 53 F. Supp. 2d 787, 137 Ed. Law Rep. 238 (E.D. Pa. 1999), involving a female special education student who was raped in the back of her classroom by two male students while the door to the classroom was locked and her substitute teacher, although aware of what was happening, failed to protect her. The court rejected the claim that a special custodial relationship existed, stating that: "Total and exclusive custody, not mere restraint, is at the heart of a due process claim relying upon a special relationship. Custody involves substantial curtailment over an individual's freedom, such that the state inhibits one's ability to meet his or her basic needs." *Id.* at 791. But the court ruled in her favor on the state-created danger theory. Applying a four-part test, the court found that the harm was foreseeable (the substitute teacher knew that the male students had attacked another student in the classroom earlier in the day and that they had hauled both the plaintiff and a portable blackboard to the back of the room), that the substitute teacher acted in willful disregard for the student's safety (in response to class disruption, she announced to the class: "I don't care what you do as long as you do not bother me," *id.* at 789, that a relationship between the state and the plaintiff, and that the school officials used their authority to create an opportunity that otherwise would not have existed for the crime by the male students to occur ("the state defendants locked the classroom door, isolating the victims with their attackers, and cutting the vulnerable students off from assistance," *id.* at 793). The court held the teacher's inaction rose to the level of a state-created danger under § 1983 and refused to dismiss the student's charges.

§ 14:7   School tort liability—Federal causes of action—Title IX

In Davis v. Monroe County Board of Education, 526 U.S. 629 (1999), a 5-4 majority held that under Title IX of the Education Amendments of 1972, 20 U.S.C.A. §§ 1681 et seq., a school board can be held liable for student-on-student sexual harassment, provided that plaintiffs establish that the school officials are deliberately indifferent to the harassment. This decision is presently limited to a statutory interpretation in the sexual harassment area, but it may indicate a later willingness to reexamine the strict rules in DeShaney, and to recognize that mandatory attendance at a public school does create a kind of "custodial" environment that can trigger responsibility on the part of school officials.

§ 14:8   School tort liability—Conclusion

Although holding schools and school officials liable for their failure to create a safe environment might increase their vigilance, and would ease the pain of students and families who suffer from school violence, it is important to ask whether the increased vigilance will further reduce students' privacy rights. Student rights may be infringed upon more often, as school policies change to prevent litigation and administrators become more zealous in their searches and seizures in order to avoid seeming negligent. Is the decrease in privacy in exchange for the increase in safety "reasonable" under the Fourth Amendment and acceptable according to our current values? Although this question must be faced by courts, ultimately it should be addressed and resolved by the students who must go to our schools and have their liberties threatened on one side and their lives threatened on the other.

Some of the measures now being utilized by school officials — such as metal detectors, canine searches, urine inspections, and random locker checks — are discussed in other parts of this volume, particularly Section 10:1 and Chapters 12 and 13. Whether the use of these procedures will be expanded in the desire to provide greater security for our schools, and whether they will in fact achieve that purpose, is one of the challenging issues for the coming years.

Table of Cases

References are to sections

C

Index